The Yellow Pad

The Yellow Pad

*Making Better Decisions
in an Uncertain World*

———— ◆ ————

ROBERT E. RUBIN

Penguin Press
New York
2023

PENGUIN PRESS
An imprint of Penguin Random House LLC
penguinrandomhouse.com

LIBRARY OF CONGRESS CATALOGING-IN-PUBLICATION DATA

Names: Rubin, Robert Edward, 1938– author.
Title: The yellow pad : making better decisions in an
uncertain world / Robert E. Rubin.
Description: New York : Penguin Press, 2023. | Includes index.
Identifiers: LCCN 2022035034 (print) |
LCCN 2022035035 (ebook) | ISBN 9780593491393 (hardcover) |
ISBN 9780593491409 (ebook)
Subjects: LCSH: Decision-making. | Crisis management. |
Social problems.
Classification: LCC HD30.23 .R825 2023 (print) |
LCC HD30.23 (ebook) | DDC 658.4/03—dc23/eng/20230126
LC record available at https://lccn.loc.gov/2022035034
LC ebook record available at https://lccn.loc.gov/2022035035

Printed in the United States of America
1 3 5 7 9 10 8 6 4 2

Designed by Amanda Dewey

To my grandchildren:
Eliza, Eleanor, Henry, and Millie

The only certainty is that nothing is certain.

—PLINY THE ELDER

———···━◆━···———

Doubt is not a pleasant condition.

But certainty is an absurd one.

—VOLTAIRE

CONTENTS

The Yellow Pad

INTRODUCTION

I have spent more than half a century in markets, business, government, and politics. Thanks to a variety of factors—luck very much included—I've gotten to know and work alongside many compelling, consequential figures of my era. I've participated in decisions that have affected millions, sometimes hundreds of millions, of lives.

Today, when people ask me what prepared me for the kind of life I've led, they usually expect me to reply with the name of a course in finance, economics, or political science.

Instead, the most formative college class I ever took was introductory philosophy.

The professor was named Raphael Demos. I still vividly remember him: a genial little man with white hair, standing on the lecture hall stage, using an overturned wastebasket as a lectern and speaking to a roomful of eager students.

I had arrived at Harvard the year before, in 1956, feeling overwhelmed academically. Unlike many of my classmates who had gone to rigorous private schools, I graduated from a Florida public school that in those days rarely sent kids to elite colleges in the North. But one upside of entering Harvard with less academic preparation than many of my classmates was that it forced me to think about matters I had never considered. And nothing forced me to challenge assumptions about the world more dramatically than my introduction to philosophy.

As Harvard's Alford Professor of Natural Religion, Moral Philosophy, and Civil Polity, Professor Demos was a scholar of classics. We read Plato and many other great philosophers. But gradually it dawned on me that, more than teaching students the contents of any book or treatise, Professor Demos was teaching us how to think about thinking. I came to believe that his underlying objective—the theme that tied the entire course together—was to demonstrate that nothing can be proven in an absolute sense. Approaching one proposition after another from the perspectives of great thinkers of the ages, he showed us that it is impossible to prove any of them with certainty.

This was a definition of "uncertainty" I had not really considered before. I knew, of course, what it felt like to be unsure of what to do. I knew geopolitical conditions and personal situations could be described as uncertain. But I had never truly thought about the possibility that *everything* is uncertain—that while there may be various degrees of probability assigned to predictions, outcomes, or assertions, that probability never reaches 100 percent. This, I discovered, was the ultimate point of Professor Demos' class.

You might think his view that nothing is absolutely provable would have made Professor Demos cynical or nihilistic. On the contrary, like the philosophers he studied, he relished the opportunity to try to figure things out. He showed us that by thinking critically, we could make our way in a challenging world while fully embracing its complexity.

At various points in my life, I have referenced Professor Demos in something I've written. But in 2018, fifty-eight years after graduating from college, I sat down to write an essay specifically about this course that had such a profound impact on my life. I imagined the piece would be short and, frankly, not very interesting to many people. After all, this wasn't dealing with public policy, finance, or other issues that I generally write about. When I decided to try to publish it, my first thought was to submit it to the *Harvard Crimson*, the student-run paper with offices not far from the lecture hall where I first took Professor Demos' class.

My friend Drew Faust, who was at the time the president of Harvard, encouraged me to try to reach a wider audience. But I was skeptical. I didn't think any newspaper would publish the piece, or that most people would care about it. So when *The New York Times* emailed to say they would run it, I was quite surprised.

What happened once the piece ran, however, was even more surprising. My essay became—by far—the most widely read op-ed I had ever written. I was told it remained the most popular article on the *Times* website for the whole day, not just in the opinion section, but in the entire newspaper. I received more email responses, by quite a large multiple, than I ever had to any previous piece of writing.

Admittedly, my typical topics—such as the economics of criminal justice reform, the importance of preserving the child tax credit, or fiscal and monetary policy—are not known for having mass appeal. But neither, I would have imagined, are memories of someone's favorite college lecture from back when Dwight D. Eisenhower was president.

In the days and weeks that followed, I was gratified by the response to my essay and pleased that so many readers seemed to find it helpful or relevant to their own lives. But I was also curious. Why had people who had never heard of Raphael Demos' class, much less taken it, responded the way they did?

The conclusion I eventually reached was this: while I had written about one course, with one professor, at one moment, I was also addressing a question that has been the focus of my entire life and career, whether in government or in the private sector. In a world of enormous complexity and uncertainty, how does one understand the issues at hand as deeply as possible and make the best decisions one can, especially when the stakes are high?

I've approached this question in a variety of ways, and over several decades. It's the reason my first book, written not long after I stepped down as secretary of the Treasury, was titled *In an Uncertain World*. But the truth is that compared with 2003, when that book was published, the world is far more uncertain today.

That's not to say we haven't made great progress over the past two decades in some important respects. Tens of millions around the globe have been lifted out of poverty; hugely consequential new technologies have reshaped how we live and work; medicine has made enormous strides against diseases from hepatitis to HIV/AIDS, and more recently developed vaccines against COVID-19 less than a year after the pandemic began. These are remarkable accomplishments.

We've also seen important cultural developments. During the bulk of my career, the so-called room where it happens left out many talented people who did not happen to be white and male.

We still have much to do to change this—and it is a complex challenge. But we have made real progress in recent decades toward giving more people the opportunity to make the most of their talents, regardless of their gender, sexuality, ethnicity, or race. That is important for our entire society, and for our economy as well.

Yet despite the real progress we've made, there is a widespread sense that the ground we stand on is shakier than ever. Political turmoil and dysfunction have been getting worse instead of better, despite some notable legislative accomplishments in recent years. In the twenty-first century we have been buffeted by a global recession more severe than any in my lifetime, a global pandemic that upended nearly every element of society, an attack on the Capitol building attempting to prevent the certification of the 2020 presidential election, and a land war in Europe that has threatened to fracture the post–World War II order.

Meanwhile, while globalization and technological development benefit consumers and producers in many ways, they also threaten jobs and wages. In the United States and around the world, incomes for many are lagging and income inequality is expanding. Democracy faces unprecedented threats at home and abroad. The impacts of climate change, already severe, are likely to become even worse in the short and medium term, and over the long term quite possibly threaten human life as we know it. Many of the conditions that allowed COVID-19 to spread worldwide could lead to a new global pandemic, even as we still feel the effects of the last one. The list goes on.

I have been part of teams engaging with many great challenges during my time at the White House, Goldman Sachs, Citi, the Treasury Department, and elsewhere. But I believe the threats facing my children's and grandchildren's generations will be significantly more complex—and more consequential—than those my generation encountered. At the same time, the national and transnational political systems to which those in my generation could turn to help address those threats have become far more dysfunctional. Our world, always uncertain, has become less certain than ever.

Perhaps most concerning, many of today's young people can't recall a time when peace and prosperity seemed anything other than tenuous. During the Clinton administration, the American economy gained more than 22.5 million jobs; the number of people living in poverty fell by 7 million; incomes grew for Americans across the economic spectrum, with those in the bottom 20 percent seeing the largest percentage gains; and the federal government achieved a year-end surplus instead of a deficit for the first time in twenty-nine years. All this was buttressed by a system of international institutions, led by the United States and other democracies, that seemed broadly capable of furthering stability around the world. In February 1999, a few months before I left office, 71 percent of Americans surveyed by Gallup were satisfied with the way things were going in the country—the highest number ever recorded, and one which is very hard to imagine today. (As of this writing, it stands at 21 percent.)

I know from experience that public officials get more credit than they deserve when things go well. But I also know that much of our shared success in the 1990s was due to sound decision-making. It worries me that at this moment of enormous global change, unrest, and danger, when we seem to be lurching from crisis to crisis, many Americans cannot recall a time marked by broad-based prosperity and general optimism about the country's future.

Given all that, it does not surprise me that arguments that once seemed permanently settled are springing back to life. Is democracy the best form of government, and will it endure? Can capitalism work, spurring both growth and widespread economic well-being? What is the role of business in society? How important is free expression and the open exchange of views? Does government debt matter? When I left the Treasury Department at the turn of the twenty-first century, it seemed that most leaders from around the globe and across the political spectrum believed they had answered these questions. Now, old debates are erupting once again.

Some members of my generation may see the resumption of once-settled arguments as a bad thing. I don't share that view. I have always believed that the best way to arrive at sound conclusions is through an unfettered exchange of views, and that when someone presents an idea you strongly disagree with, the best thing to do is to attempt to understand why they hold it.

Thanks to long conversations with people who disagree with me, my thinking has changed over the past twenty years in some significant ways. For example, I once believed that as long as all sectors of society were experiencing economic growth, income inequality was not in and of itself a threat. I now believe income inequality is counterproductive to our society even if it is accompanied by broad growth. Another example is climate change. While I recognized fairly early that it was a serious problem, I only later came to appreciate its existential urgency and magnitude. As my views changed, I became engaged on these and other issues in ways I could not have imagined two decades ago.

In other cases, however, my opinions remain unchanged. There is a rising enthusiasm for the idea that budget deficits don't matter. I think they do. And while much of the right focuses primarily on economic growth, and much of the left focuses primarily on broad-based economic well-being and reduced inequality, I still think these priorities are interdependent and that we won't have either without the other. Finally, while I am a Democrat and have been all my life, and I generally agree with my party's broad policy aims—everything from funding public programs by increasing taxation on wealthy individuals and corporations, to combating climate change, to expanding the social safety net—I don't always support the specific solutions proposed to achieve them.

But regardless of the conclusions one reaches, I think reengaging in old debates on crucial issues is good, especially as time passes and circumstances change. I've always believed in challenging assumptions and questioning positions—even when the positions being questioned are ones I've held for a very long time. That's especially true at a moment of tremendous disruption. Genuine open-mindedness, a seriousness of purpose, and intellectual integrity are necessary if we're going to engage in today's great clashes of ideas and meet the challenges we face.

Unfortunately, while today's debates are heated, they are often not particularly constructive. What's lacking, I believe, is twofold. First, we need an effective intellectual framework for thinking about thinking—an approach to the world that acknowledges complexity and uncertainty but can nonetheless help us make the best possible decisions. Second, although politics in democracies will always be messy and inefficient, and politicians will always take electoral considerations into account, we need elected officials—and leaders throughout society—who are committed to focusing on facts and analysis while engaging together across partisan, policy, and intellectual divides.

If we fail to meet these dual imperatives, our collective ability to make sound decisions will continue getting worse instead of better. Nor are leaders in business, politics, and government the only ones feeling the pressure of increasing complexity and uncertainty. This is perhaps best illustrated by COVID-19. Among its many other effects, the pandemic forced us all to become high-stakes decision-makers: calculating risks, considering broad arrays of consequences, and making choices with imperfect information. It's hardly surprising that so many felt so thoroughly overwhelmed.

But I worry that, faced with such unsettling uncertainty, too many people—and too many of our institutions—have responded by rushing toward absolutes and simplistic answers. We've seen the increasing prominence of leaders who promise easy solutions, rather than making genuine, nuanced, and serious assessments of the challenges we face. Us-or-them polarization, not just in Washington but across American life, has made us less able to meet consequential policy challenges, less able to engage in the give-and-take of compromise, and increasingly afraid or unwilling to discuss important issues with one another.

More and more, it seems as though each of us is caught between two bad options. We can become paralyzed by the complexity of the threats we face. Or we can ignore that complexity, turn toward absolutes and oversimplified approaches, and make poor choices.

Which brings me to the most important lesson I learned in Professor Demos' course: there's a better way. Looking back, I think I have always been temperamentally and psychologically suited to living with the complexity and uncertainty inherent in decision-making. But my introduction to philosophy—and the late-night, free-ranging intellectual discussions that followed at college, graduate study abroad, and then law school—created the underpinnings for a more fully thought-out approach to dealing with a complex world than I would have developed on my own.

What's more, I believe that whether or not you are by nature comfortable with uncertainty, you do not need to depend on simplistic positions or unrealistic ideas of absolute truth. As Raphael Demos demonstrated, anyone can engage thoughtfully with complex ideas, and everyone should.

Of course, no amount of critical thinking will guarantee that your choices will turn out the way you expect or hope. All of us inevitably make mistakes and errors in judgment, and often even a sound decision does not guarantee a positive outcome. But we can approach issues—even complex, difficult issues—in thoughtful, rigorous ways that make success more likely.

Put simply, we can navigate the world, even when stakes are high and outcomes uncertain. That's what I have spent a lifetime trying my best to do. There is no perfect approach to living with uncertainty. But this book presents my approach, which has served me well for many decades, and which I hope will be useful to others. This book also applies that approach to some of the major policy issues facing our country, to issues around investing and management, and to dealing with the inevitable pressures and ups and downs of life.

The foundation of my approach to understanding complex issues is "probabilistic thinking," and the essence of probabilistic thinking is this: if nothing is absolutely certain, then views can be expressed only in terms of probabilities. In life, in the markets, and in government, I never saw my goal as choosing the "right" path, in the sense of some absolute. Instead, I considered various possible outcomes, assessed the probabilities of each one occurring, weighed the cost-benefit trade-offs, and then made the choice I thought most likely to lead to the best result.

Probabilistic thinking, which was less widespread when I began employing it as a young man, is now more broadly recognized. You often hear people extol its virtues at conferences. There are plenty of online articles and guides for would-be probabilistic thinkers, as well as highly influential books (such as *Thinking, Fast and Slow* and *Thinking in Bets*) that help people more closely examine and refine the way they think. In a few cases—professional sports analytics, for example, or data-driven political reporting—discussions of probabilities have entered the mainstream.

Yet in my experience, the number of people who actually think probabilistically remains quite small. Some don't recognize that decisions are about probabilities. Others recognize the importance of probabilities, but fail to internalize it.

I suspect the reason for this is quite simple. Thinking probabilistically—approaching decisions with intellectual integrity and the knowledge that there are no perfect answers—is hard. Human nature makes acknowledging complexity and uncertainty discomforting.

Moreover, rigorously evaluating probabilities is a discipline. It requires time, commitment, a willingness to accept facts and conclusions at variance with your initial views, and a psychological ability to live with knowing that your decisions, no matter how well thought through, may not turn out as you hope. It takes no effort to be paralyzed by complexity. It takes little effort to ignore complexity and seek simple answers instead. But to think in a probabilistic way—to grapple with complexity, and then draw conclusions based on less-than-complete information—must be learned through conscious effort and through doing.

INTRODUCTION

For the first several decades of my career, I found that there was one indispensable tool for analyzing the world around me probabilistically: a yellow legal pad. I would write out, by hand, a list of possible outcomes in one column, and my estimated odds of each outcome occurring in the other. When I worked in the markets, the potential outcomes could generally be expressed in dollars, so I could multiply a selection of possible outcomes by the probabilities of each and add up the numbers to find what economists would call the "expected value" of each decision. Then I could choose the course of action that provided the highest total.

In some cases, expected value is much more difficult to quantify. The costs and benefits of policy outcomes, for example, cannot always be expressed in dollars and cents. Yet even in these instances, the yellow pad still works as a tool for comparing different courses of action and potential outcomes, because you can include nonquantifiable factors in your analysis. For this reason, the yellow pad is not just a calculation of dollars and cents. The weighing of "costs" and "benefits" can depend in large part on one's moral beliefs. Two people could make similar estimates of probabilities and outcomes and make very different decisions based on their different notions of right and wrong. But even then, the yellow pad will prove useful, because it gives people a way to balance different beliefs and priorities when they come into conflict, and a common framework for analyzing decisions with people whose beliefs differ from your own. The yellow pad, in other words, is more than just a means of calculation. The yellow pad is my way of expressing my own personal philosophy of decision-making— one that in many ways began in Professor Demos' class—and applying it to the real-world challenges I've faced.

In recent years, my yellow pad has frequently become an iPad.

Even more frequently, the yellow pad is more figurative than literal, because the more experience I've gained evaluating outcomes and probabilities, the more I can do in my head. But the method of thinking remains unchanged. And I still find that when I have the time, and if the issue is sufficiently consequential, writing out my thoughts and doing my best to express them in numbers leads to more rigorous and more exact thinking.

I have similarly found that encouraging others to think in terms of numbers helps clarify issues and improve the quality of decisions and debates. If someone tells me they think something is likely to happen (for example, that economic growth will be strong next year), I tend to ask them to attach numbers to their view. (What odds? What rate of growth?)

Part of the yellow pad's utility is its combination of simplicity and complexity. On one hand, an expected value table contains just two columns—the first for potential outcomes, the second for related probabilities—and requires nothing more than simple arithmetic. On the other hand, deciding how to construct those two columns forces you to consider extremely difficult questions. For example, how do you come up with a realistic list of possible outcomes? How do you make judgments about the probabilities? How do you consider trade-offs when priorities conflict? And how do you deal with potential scenarios that can't be expressed in numerical terms?

My answers to these questions—which is to say, my way of thinking about thinking, and the application of that approach to challenges large and small—is at the heart of this book.

At some points, I describe how I apply my approach to my day-to-day life—in particular to how I think about personal investing. While I've spent my life in and around the markets and making investment decisions, I've never claimed to be a personal-finance expert, and I don't want to give the impression that I have any secret strategy for success. There is none, in my view. But I will discuss my approach to investments, which I hope will provide an important, practical example of how my decision-making philosophy works in the real world and how it might be useful to others.

Throughout this book, I look back years or decades at the moments and experiences that helped me develop my yellow-pad approach. I describe some of my past decisions, both successes and failures, that helped me refine that approach. But I do all this for the purposes of looking forward, to give a sense of what it looks like to apply this approach to some of today's most pressing societal challenges.

As part of that discussion, I will set out my own views on a variety of subjects. But that is not because I believe the conclusions I have reached are certain to be correct. It's quite possible that you could approach the same issue, using the same process, and arrive at a different result. Rather than seeking to settle debates, my goal is to provide a framework for better debates—debates more likely to lead decision-makers to the best possible course of action.

It's strange, given Professor Demos' impact on my life and career, that I never actually spoke to him. As a student, I was just one of a hundred or so young faces in a lecture hall, taking in his every word, and I never sought him out during office hours or approached him after class. In 1968, a little more than a decade after I took his course, he suffered a heart attack onboard a ship taking him home to the United States after a year of teaching in Athens. He passed away at age seventy-six. I wish I had been able to thank him.

In some small way, then, this book is a measure of gratitude.

INTRODUCTION

I can think of no better way for me to remember Raphael Demos than to pass on, or at least try to articulate, the passion for thinking about thinking that he sought to instill in me and, I assume, in so many of his students. It is my view that his case for reason, and for reasonableness, is even stronger today than it was all those years ago. Sound judgment is more desperately needed than ever.

Whether it will be forthcoming, however, is far from certain.

Chapter 1

REACTING VERSUS RESPONDING

The invitation was written on lined, three-hole-punched paper. The handwriting was tidy, with every letter an identical height, signed by someone named Shadeed Wallace-Stepter.

"I know you're a very busy dude," it read. "But if you can ever find the time I want to formally invite you to San Quentin."

That's how I ended up giving a talk in a California state prison.

During my career, I've entered plenty of intimidating buildings, from the White House and the Capitol to Wall Street banks and corporate headquarters. Still, visiting San Quentin was different. A massive stone fortress overlooking San Francisco Bay, the prison has housed some of our country's most notorious figures over the years. More than any place except Alcatraz Island, San Quentin is synonymous with the American penitentiary. It was impossible not to feel the building's symbolic weight.

Before our arrival, my wife, Judy, and I were told which colors we could wear—different types of people were required to dress in different colors for easy identification. Upon arriving at the gate, we emptied our pockets and were checked for weapons by guards in green uniforms, who then took us to a large room filled with incarcerated men dressed in blue pants and blue shirts. After being introduced (and after Judy recovered my speech, which I had dropped on the floor while walking to the stage), I addressed a room filled with men who had been convicted of serious crimes: murder, drug dealing, and armed robbery, to name just a few.

Initially, I must admit, I had not been sure that agreeing to the invitation was a good idea.

I wasn't troubled, in a moral sense, about speaking to people who had committed crimes. It is my firm belief that we are all flawed. That view, coupled with my dislike for absolutes, means that while I have no problem thinking of individuals' actions as good or bad, I don't tend to sort people that way. Some people do serious and even terrible harm to others, and I believe that one of society's important functions is to protect people and appropriately punish those who violate our laws. But I also believe that the lawyer and activist Bryan Stevenson, who has advocated on behalf of dozens of people sentenced to death, put it well when he wrote, "Each of us is more than the worst thing we've ever done."

My concern in speaking at San Quentin was not with my audience, but with me. I worried that my story would simply not hold the attention of the people there. How could a debt crisis in Mexico or lessons learned at the risk arbitrage desk of an investment bank be of interest to men living behind bars? How could the challenges I'd faced on Wall Street or at the Treasury Department relate to the struggles they had gone through? I feared my experience might be alien to them—that they might find whatever

I had to say irrelevant or, even worse, off-putting, as though I were trying to say my experiences were identical to theirs.

What changed my perspective was a phone call I had a few weeks before my visit, which was set up by Delia Cohen, the organizer who planned the event. Shadeed, the letter writer who invited me (and who goes by "Sha"), was part of our discussion, along with several other incarcerated men.

Our conversation lasted an hour and twenty minutes. I took five pages of notes. As we talked, something dawned on me. I had spent time with many different kinds of people in my life. Yet I had rarely encountered a group as thoughtful and reflective, a group so willing to accept and engage with complexity, as the men I spoke with on that call.

Most impressive was how forthright these men were about the crimes they had committed, and how deeply they had considered the consequences of their actions. I was particularly struck by the way one man analyzed the decision-making that had led him to that point, describing what he had learned and how he hoped to behave differently in the future.

"We shouldn't react," he said. "We should respond."

To react, he elaborated, is to make a decision based on a split-second, emotionally charged impulse. Responding, on the other hand, involves thought and patience. It requires stepping back to consider the situation and the potential consequences of one's actions.

This man who had brought up reacting and responding—someone who was serving a long prison sentence for felony murder—understood something that eludes countless policy-makers, investors, and CEOs. If we want to make better choices regarding our lives, our economy, our country, and, ultimately, the criminal justice system itself, I can think of no better prescription than the one he offered on the phone.

We shouldn't react. We should respond.

In the Clinton White House, one of the speechwriters was a young man named Jonathan Prince. He was very bright, with a rare ability to think through problems and express the solutions. Among Jonathan's insights was a phrase he coined, "extreme disruption."

This was years before Silicon Valley made the word "disruption" its own and turned it into a cliché. What Jonathan meant was something closer to what most of us would call a crisis. But the importance of his language was that it captured the dynamic that underlies so many crises. In moments of extreme disruption, circumstances change dramatically in a relatively short period of time. In most situations, decision-makers can rely on experience to help them make the best possible choices. But in moments of extreme disruption, experience becomes far less helpful because so much has changed so quickly.

Moments of extreme disruption can be very different, depending on the circumstances. The people I spoke to in San Quentin described fights breaking out or robberies gone wrong. One incarcerated man I later spoke with told me that together, a group of twenty-eight incarcerated men had tried to quantify the personal cost of their decisions in such moments. In total, they concluded, crimes that had taken 4 minutes and 26 seconds to commit had resulted in prison terms that added up to 715 years. These men had reacted rather than responded, with permanent consequences for both the victims and perpetrators of their crimes.

REACTING VERSUS RESPONDING

Most of us, myself included, have little experience with such dramatic or violent moments of disruption. Yet everyone I know has experienced extreme disruption in their own lives.

Some of these moments are quite literally instants, when everything changes in a split second. On other occasions, the "moments" can take weeks, months, or years, but nonetheless are periods of rapid and intense change. As individuals, organizations, nations, and societies, we inevitably encounter occasions where the situation changes quickly, threats become more dangerous, and the way forward becomes unclear. Today, even younger people are familiar with such moments: they lived through 9/11, the Great Recession, a global pandemic, and the Russian invasion of Ukraine, all within roughly a two-decade span.

Unfortunately, these moments of extreme disruption are precisely the kinds of circumstances that often lead to bad decisions.

To use just one example, shortly after Donald Trump was elected president, a friend of mine, who generally has very sensible judgment, sold all of his stocks and mutual funds. In retrospect that may seem like an overreaction, but at the time his motivations were, broadly speaking, understandable. Like many people, myself included, he worried that an unstable president could precipitate a stock market crash.

But my friend nevertheless made a mistake in reacting to Trump's election, and exploring the nature of this mistake helps illustrate the usefulness of thinking probabilistically.

At a moment of extreme disruption, when circumstances were simultaneously more frightening and less stable, my friend made an emotional decision that didn't recognize the high levels of uncertainty associated with any big-picture prediction. The odds of a Trump-related crash were, of course, greater than zero and might have been significant—meaning that perhaps he should have sold off a percentage of his investments if he wanted to provide some financial security in case of a severe downturn. But something about the combination of sudden change and heightened stakes caused my friend to act as though the odds of a crash were 100 percent, which led him to an unwise choice: selling 100 percent of his portfolio.

This kind of thought process is common, perhaps surprisingly so. In every arena I've entered—finance, politics, business, personal investing, nonprofits—I've seen otherwise excellent leaders and thinkers abandon a sound approach to decision-making when extreme disruption strikes. When the future becomes harder to predict than ever, they paradoxically act as though they are completely certain as to what the future holds. In the short term, reacting in this way—instinctively, impulsively, and overconfidently—sometimes actually does lead to a positive result. After all, if I act as though a given outcome has a 100 percent chance of occurring, when in fact it has only a 10 percent chance of occurring, then 10 percent of the time things will work out the way I expected. But in the long run, this seemingly fortunate scenario will likely end poorly, because if I continue to double down on reacting instead of responding, eventually it's going to catch up to me. Lucky streaks have a tendency to end.

In other words, in almost all cases, an instinctual reaction to a moment of disruption leads either to bad outcomes in the short term, or to even worse outcomes over the long term.

The alternative, as many in San Quentin had come to understand, is to respond. At the moment of disruption, whether that moment is an instant or some longer period, a decision-maker must be able to overcome the pressure to act rashly and instead analyze costs and benefits, making the best possible choice given the circumstances and time available.

So what separates those who make thoughtful decisions in moments of disruption from those who do not? Why is it that some of us react, and others are able to respond?

The typical answer is temperament. I won't deny that temperament plays a role. For some, responding comes naturally. For others, reacting does. But I have seen plenty of otherwise thoughtful people default to absolutism in a highly charged moment, just as I have seen passionate people handle a crisis by carefully thinking things through.

In my experience, the key to sound decision-making is not to resist having strong feelings about an issue. It's human nature to have emotions. The question is: Do you get swallowed up by your emotions? Or do you have an emotional reaction, recognize it, and then manage to postpone your initial impulse long enough to make a considered choice? Responding takes discipline; reacting does not.

The best time—indeed, often the only time—to build that discipline is before a moment of disruption strikes. I have found that what distinguishes strong leaders and good decision-makers isn't that they have no emotional bias. It's that they understand their emotional biases and compensate for them.

For example, I know that as an investor, my instinct is to overweight risks—in other words, my risk aversion is a character trait rather than an investment strategy. But because I know this, I'm able to adjust my decision-making accordingly. At the very least, in the heat of the moment—or better yet, when building my expected value table on a yellow pad long before the moment arrives—I can question and evaluate my own instincts. Am I taking unnecessary precautions? Am I systematically overestimating the odds of negative outcomes occurring?

While I still might tend to err slightly on the side of caution, forcing myself to consider these possibilities helps me recognize where emotions may have affected my decision, and then readjust accordingly.

(Of course, other people might have to correct for the opposite emotional bias: if you're too comfortable with risk, you'll want to ask yourself whether you're systematically underweighting the chances of a negative result.)

Which brings me to another way in which decision-making can be improved during moments of disruption: instead of relying solely on one's individual judgment, decision-makers can harness the power of a group. This is difficult to do effectively. It requires leaders to be receptive to people who don't share their views and to seek out disagreement rather than gravitate toward easy consensus. But the benefits can be immense.

For example, during my time as the director of President Bill Clinton's National Economic Council, and later as secretary of the Treasury, I came to believe that one of the president's greatest strengths was that, if nobody disagreed with him, he would ask his team: "Okay, what's the other point of view?" He didn't just tolerate differing viewpoints. He embraced them as essential to understanding. And his psyche never seemed to feel threatened if someone who disagreed with him was better informed or seemed to be thinking differently about an issue than he was.

While those meetings with the president tended to have anywhere from half a dozen to about two dozen people, sometimes effective groups can be as small as just two or three. Early in 1995, when I was at the Treasury Department, Mexico was facing a sovereign debt crisis, and with it the prospect of a deep and prolonged economic downturn that would affect not just the Mexican economy but the American economy as well. We tried to support Mexico directly, by loaning their government money in the hopes of creating the conditions for a rebound, but at first, the markets didn't seem to be responding. At one point, I discussed the matter with Larry Summers, my deputy at Treasury and a renowned economist. We looked at the cost up to that point, which was several billion in taxpayer dollars, and concluded that the program simply wasn't working—the markets weren't reacting in a way that would support Mexico's financial sustainability—and thus wasn't worth continuing.

But when we went over to see Leon Panetta, who was then the White House chief of staff, and told him we were thinking about ending the program, he came at it from a different perspective. "My gosh, you can't do that," he said, urging us to reconsider. We replied, "That would be throwing good money after bad. There's no sense to that."

Leon was concerned about a political rather than a policy outcome—he wanted to avoid the embarrassment of publicly admitting an expensive intervention had failed. Yet precisely because his perspective was so different from ours, Larry and I agreed to take another look. When the two of us worked through it, we realized our initial analysis might have been wrong. While we'd run into a very difficult period and maybe our program ultimately wasn't going to work, it seemed that from a purely economic perspective, the expected value of continuing it was greater than the expected value of ending it. In the end, our intervention turned out to be a success. Mexico paid back its loans to American tax-payers in full plus interest, and the Mexican economy recovered and stabilized in relatively short order.

I'm not advocating making decisions by committee. What I am saying instead is that a decision-maker can be well served by having more people in the room, especially in moments when circumstances are changing rapidly. This was something we often did at Treasury. When facing a crisis, we'd gather people together to try to work our way through the problem. I'd try to make sure the group included people whose judgment and expertise I respected, and who also reflected a variety of viewpoints and emotional biases.

These groups were helpful for a variety of reasons. Intellectu-ally, having a number of people in the room helped us make sure we weren't ignoring any potential opportunities or challenges. We could put all the factors on the table. Emotionally, harnessing the power of a group helped me sort out my own reaction to whatever event was taking place. Seeing a variety of different instincts and biases helped me recognize—and correct for—my own. It also helped increase buy-in later on. Even if people didn't agree with the final course of action, they felt they had been included in the decision-making process.

Something I have come to appreciate, in a way I did not earlier in my career, is the extent to which both conscious and uncon-scious bias can affect decision-making. Fifty years ago, for example, when the vast majority of groups gathered before a high-stakes decision were entirely white and male, I can't recall anyone asking, "How is being Black in America different from being white in America? How might racial or gender dynamics exacerbate existing challenges and make them more difficult and complex? And how might important decisions therefore be improved if the decision-maker had access to a wider range of perspectives and personal experiences?" I suspect that if the opportunity to join those discussions had been open to more people, those questions would have been raised.

Finally, addressing moments of disruption as a group helps you realize not just what has changed, but what has remained the same. After the 1994 midterms, in which Republicans flipped control of the House of Representatives for the first time in decades, I was part of a meeting on political strategy with senior members of President Clinton's team. One official argued that the disastrous outcome proved that the old model of political persuasion no longer applied and that the president had to move further left to get reelected. Hillary Clinton disagreed. While the 1994 election results had been shocking, the First Lady argued, the underlying forces shaping our politics had not changed. Campaigns were still won by appealing to voters in the middle.

The debate about the politics of appealing to the center versus appealing to the base has been ongoing and vigorously argued for as long as I've been in Democratic politics. In this case it's impossible to know for certain which of President Clinton's advisers was right, because he could choose only one of the two options. But he chose the position Hillary was advocating, and it seems to me that he made the sound choice. In 1996, President Clinton won in a landslide, in part due to what exit polls found was a 24-point margin of victory among moderate voters. (In addition to moving President Clinton's policies more in line with the preferences of moderates, I believe Hillary's position was politically beneficial for another reason as well: by pursuing policies perceived as pro-growth, the president increased business confidence, which improved the economy, which in turn improved his reelection chances.)

Yet while groups are an essential tool to improve one's judgment, they cannot become a substitute for one's judgment. If you are responsible for a decision, getting input and advice from others is critically important—but you must ultimately choose the path that you think is best. When leaders abdicate this responsibility, using groups to avoid making tough calls rather than to make *better* calls, it rarely ends well. If you're the decision-maker, you've got to be willing to make the decision.

The decision-maker also must avoid the temptation to split the difference between what they think and what the group thinks. I've seen many people fall into this trap, particularly in business. Leaders say to themselves, "Well, after hearing all the different sides, I think X. But a lot of other people, presented with the same evidence, think Y. So let's do something between X and Y." It's one thing to conclude that your position is wrong and to change it, or to alter your decision around the margins in order to preserve morale. It's another thing entirely to believe, after careful consideration, that your position is the correct one, and to nonetheless take a substantially different position in order to mollify people.

My friend Tom Steyer, who has a long history of excellent, thoughtful decision-making, has spoken publicly about one particular decision he delegated to a group. Tom and I first met when I recruited him to work as an associate in the risk arbitrage department of Goldman Sachs in the 1980s. He was nearly twenty years my junior, but he immediately distinguished himself as an insightful analyst, with a balance of intensity and a good sense of humor. (It is perhaps surprising, given that he is today most widely known as a political donor and candidate, that I don't remember him talking about politics.) In 1985, Tom left Goldman and the next year started Farallon Capital, which he ran until 2012 and which became one of the world's most successful hedge funds, particularly when it came to generating consistent results over the long term.

In 2008, while running his fund, Tom examined the factors putting pressure on the economy and decided it would make sense to reduce his exposure to a potential downturn. But many of the people working at Farallon disagreed. Tom found their arguments unpersuasive, but ultimately agreed not to reduce his positions because he worried about damaging morale. Tom was able to weather the economic crisis that soon followed and the firm subsequently did very well again, but he (and his investors, myself included) lost far more than they would have had Tom chosen the course of action he felt was best.

When addressing moments of extreme disruption, what is true for individuals is also true for entire societies. When leaders channel and amplify our collective emotional reactions, instead of responding thoughtfully to the circumstances, they can create problems that ripple across countries and last decades.

Which brings me back to the stage at San Quentin, and the few hours I got to spend with some of the men inside. Because one instructive example of the dangers of a society-wide impulsive reaction is our criminal justice system itself.

My own views on the criminal justice system, and those who interact with it, are tied closely to my views on poverty. In 1982, I read *The Underclass*, by the journalist Ken Auletta. He followed a nonprofit organization called the Manpower Demonstration

Research Corporation, or MDRC, as it attempted to improve the lives of some of New York City's lowest-income residents. He profiled welfare recipients, former addicts, and other people at the margins of society.

I had no firsthand experience of poverty growing up, so Ken's book was eye-opening. His thesis was quite controversial, especially more than forty years ago. Ken argued that poverty is primarily the result of the circumstances an individual faces, not of his or her moral failings or character defects. The notion that Americans can simply "pull themselves up by their bootstraps"—an idea that had enormous influence at the start of the Reagan era—was an oversimplification and, in too many cases, a virtual impossibility.

The more I read and learned, the more I was persuaded Ken was right. Poverty is a vicious cycle, replicated over generations, that imposes tremendous costs on all of us. Out of self-interest if nothing else, every member of society ought to contribute to the effort to break that cycle. Antipoverty measures have been described as a "war," or even a "crusade." But ever since reading *The Underclass*, I have tended to think of fighting poverty in less dramatic terms, as a matter of economic common sense and shared self-interest.

I have also come to believe that crime is often both a cause and an effect of poverty's vicious cycle. Consider Sha, the young man who wrote the letter inviting me to San Quentin. Growing up in the Bay Area, he experienced a kind of adversity I could not have imagined during my own childhood, circumstances that profoundly shaped his life. Most of his earliest influences, including his own mother, were drug dealers. As a teenager he began to deal drugs himself, which led to other types of criminal activity. When he was a high school junior, he was arrested for attempted robbery and assault with a deadly weapon and sentenced to twenty-seven years to life.

In my view, Sha deserved to go to prison for his crime, because society has a clear interest in making sure that people do not become victims of crime, that those who break our laws are punished, and that those who might consider breaking our laws are deterred from doing so. But how best to accomplish these goals—while giving people growing up in circumstances such as Sha's the best possible chance to break the cycle of poverty and contribute fully to society—is a highly complicated question.

It is also a question asked with much more urgency today than when I was growing up. Between 1960, the year I graduated from college, and 1993, when I joined the Clinton administration, violent crime rates spiked. Quite rapidly by historical standards, crime had become a crisis.

As crime began to affect more Americans, emotions ran high. Willie Horton, a prisoner who had committed assault, armed robbery, and rape while on a state-supported furlough program, was made a central figure in Republican attack ads in the 1988 presidential election. During that campaign, I was an adviser to the Democratic candidate, Massachusetts governor Michael Dukakis. I liked Governor Dukakis a great deal. Yet I will never forget watching him struggle to answer one devastating question in an October debate with then–Vice President George H. W. Bush.

The moderator, Bernard Shaw of CNN, posed a graphic hypothetical: If Governor Dukakis' wife, Kitty, were raped and murdered, would he support the death penalty for the perpetrator? "I don't see any evidence that it's a deterrent," the candidate calmly replied. "I think there are better and more effective ways to deal with violent crime."

I happened to agree with the governor, and I appreciated that he was trying to give an intellectually sound answer to a highly charged question. But he failed to address the very understandable fear of violent crime that peaked during that period. By not expressing anger or a more visceral desire for punishment, he made a sound policy argument, but a catastrophic political mistake—one widely thought to have contributed to his defeat.

Four years later, when Bill Clinton won the White House, the crime rate had begun to dip slightly from its peak. Still, according to *The New York Times*, crime was voters' single highest priority as the 1994 midterm elections approached.

While I wasn't personally involved with the specifics of the '94 crime bill—criminal justice wasn't seen, at the time, as an economic issue—I do think it is fair to say that the bill was attempting to address a real, serious problem on which the voting public was demanding action. And I believe that some elements of that bill, including a ban on assault weapons, the Violence Against Women Act, and supporting community outreach initiatives such as Midnight Basketball to engage at-risk youth, were good policy.

The problem, however, is that many of the crime bill's most sweeping provisions—and those of the state-level laws that both preceded and followed it—addressed emotional reactions rather than effectively responding to the challenges at hand. For example, the final bill expanded the federal death penalty to sixty crimes. It also implemented a "three strikes" provision that imposed mandatory life sentences on repeat offenders, even if their crimes would ordinarily warrant far less prison time, and it ended nearly all educational programming for incarcerated people. Even back then, it was far from clear that these policies would make us safer. But in a way, their purpose was to do what Dukakis had failed to do during a debate six years earlier: satisfy a visceral desire, rather than put effective, well-considered policy in place.

Reacting rather than responding to the issue of crime has been immensely costly. In a rush to confront the very real costs of crime, many leading policy-makers—and much of the public— never fully considered the potential costs, or unintended consequences, of the changes new legislation made to the criminal justice system. As a result, the U.S. prison population dramatically increased even as violent crime rates fell. While the number of Americans in prison and jail has, as of this writing, begun to fall from its historic peak, the United States continues to incarcerate a higher percentage of its citizens than any other country.

Our collective emotional reaction to crime did not affect all groups within our society equally. Studies have consistently found racial disparities in many parts of the criminal justice system, including arrests, charging decisions, pretrial detention, and sentencing. This is complex and varies across types of crime, jurisdictions, and other factors. Yet while some groups of people feel the consequences of our misguided approach to criminal justice most acutely, we all pay a price for not responding more thoughtfully when we had the chance. Of course, it is crucial to protect public safety. And if crime is seen as being out of control, it is very difficult to summon the political will to enact necessary reforms. But many of the Americans in prison or jail either do not currently present a serious threat to public safety, or could be prepared for reentry into society with interventions that are far less expensive than incarceration. This drains enormous amounts of taxpayer money that could be otherwise invested in more important priorities. By removing so many people from the workforce, our current system of incarceration hurts businesses and the economy as a whole. This cost is compounded by policies that make it unreasonably difficult for people to find employment upon their release from prison.

As I mentioned, the reason I was not involved in the '94 crime bill was that crime was not seen as an economic issue. In retrospect, however, the approach that has shaped our criminal justice system in recent decades has been not just morally unfair but economically unwise. It is difficult to precisely quantify these costs. But in 2016, when one group of researchers from Washington University in St. Louis tried to do so, they found the aggregate financial burden of incarceration comes to one trillion dollars per year—a number equal to almost 6 percent of America's GDP at the time. If that number is anywhere near accurate, it suggests that we are making a very poor trade-off. The benefits of major aspects of our current approach to incarceration are far outweighed by the costs.

So what would a more responsive approach to the criminal justice system look like? I am not a specialist on this matter and don't claim to have the answers. But I have spent my career trying to make rational decisions in difficult circumstances. To get the greatest benefit to society at the lowest social and economic cost, we need a significantly improved criminal justice system. And to develop that system, we need to adopt a different decision-making process than the one that led to the system we currently have.

In other words, we need to fill in the yellow pad when it comes to criminal justice.

That should begin with recognizing our emotional biases. Crime is visceral. It is frightening. Stories of victims and their families quite rightly fill us with a sense of empathy and in some cases with a desire for retribution. But just because we feel these emotions does not mean we must be driven entirely by them. We should do our best to correct for our emotional biases in advance.

As part of that effort, we should include many additional voices and perspectives in the national conversation on criminal justice reform. We should continue to consider the impact of crime on victims and their families. But we should also consider, to a greater extent than we currently do, the impact of incarceration on the national economy, on local communities, on children and families of incarcerated people, and on incarcerated people themselves. While we've made some progress in this regard (including President Biden's recent decision to pardon all people convicted in federal court for marijuana possession), more needs to be done.

We should also more fully come to grips with the social and economic implications of our current criminal justice system. When we assess the full array of costs and benefits—when we examine crime and punishment using probabilistic thinking—it inevitably pushes us to go further, adding new items and points of emphasis to consider. To use just one example, we should re-form our sentencing laws for nonviolent offenders not just because long sentences for nonviolent crimes seem unduly harsh or cruel, but also because turning would-be taxpayers into people who must be cared for by the state while in prison reduces the funding available for other, more urgent public investments.

Similarly, we should recognize that the most cost-effective method of fighting crime is preventing crime. A growing body of evidence suggests that investing in pre-K education and other early interventions delivers large returns to taxpayers in the long run, partly because of reduced incarceration rates. Similarly, investing in education, mental health, substance abuse treatment, and job training, both for those in prison and those who have recently been released, will lead to better outcomes in reduced recidivism and greater productivity.

Another way to apply probabilistic thinking to criminal justice involves a deeper look at sentencing. Thus far, the national debate around sentencing reform has been focused almost exclusively on nonviolent crimes. But according to the Marshall Project, a nonprofit news organization that covers the criminal justice system, even though violent crime "careers" tend to drop off after one's early thirties, the number of incarcerated Americans aged fifty-six or older increased by 550 percent between 1990 and 2015.

In other words, keeping this many older people behind bars is hugely expensive and does little to deter or prevent crime. I therefore believe that a reasonable response to criminal justice could include releasing many older people convicted of violent crimes in their youth. It could also include rethinking extreme sentencing for certain violent offenders going forward, so that they do not remain in prison well into old age, when they are unlikely to be a threat to the community.

A yellow-pad approach to criminal justice also suggests that society should support people returning from prison after they've left the custody of the state—not just for moral reasons, but for practical ones. As one person said during the San Quentin event at which I spoke, "I don't understand why over the eighteen-year period of my incarceration, over $900,000 was paid to keep me in prison, but when I was paroled, I was given $200 and told 'good luck.'" He's right. That kind of approach makes little sense.

Still, I don't mean to suggest that implementing a better approach will be easy—especially since supporting public safety remains both an imperative and a very real challenge. Even as we deal with the consequences of the way we currently handle crime and punishment, we don't want to replace one careless approach with another. In the 1990s, America reacted rather than responded to the problems posed by crime. Today, it would be a mistake to react rather than respond to the problems that still plague our criminal justice system.

For example, since leaving government, I've been involved with the Hamilton Project, a nonpartisan organization devoted to evidence-based economic policy-making. Since 2008, we've examined the criminal justice system through an economic lens, helping to highlight the full costs of our current policies, and in 2019 we hosted a forum on pretrial detention and bail.

Nearly everyone at that forum agreed our current system of pretrial detention is unfair and counterproductive. In too many cases, what currently determines if someone charged with a crime remains free until trial is not whether they are likely to be a threat to their community, but whether they have the resources to make bail. But when it came to how to solve this problem, different advocates reached different conclusions. Many argued the best policy would be to eliminate cash bail entirely. But one participant, despite sharing a similar set of sympathies and priorities, urged caution. He warned that if you do away with bail, then a lot of judges, instead of releasing people, might simply hold people in jail because they're afraid they won't come back for trial. A well-intentioned policy choice might have profoundly negative effects down the road.

I'm not sure who is right. But I do know that good policy, even long overdue good policy, is never easy to make. We must balance our sense of urgency with a desire to get things right.

Achieving that kind of balance—making decisions throughout one's life in a careful way, especially when stakes are high—is something the people I met at San Quentin say they discuss frequently. And there is real hope that now, after so much time spent thinking about what they would do differently if allowed to reenter society, some of them may finally get that chance.

About a year after receiving the letter from Sha, I sat down to write a letter of my own to Jerry Brown, who was serving as governor of California. "From our brief time together," I wrote, "I observed a man who has spent a tremendous amount of time reflecting on and understanding his faults, while making a plan for his future." The letter was in support of Sha's application for a commutation of his sentence.

This was a risk, of course. As impressed as I was by Sha's thoughtfulness, I couldn't predict with any degree of certainty what he would do after release. Statistically, there will always be a chance that any incarcerated person whose sentence is commuted will go on to reoffend.

Still, I couldn't help but think about Willie Horton, not just in relation to how we treat crime, but to how we make choices more generally. When decisions affect thousands, or even millions, of people, there will always be outliers, extreme examples that rightly shock and upset people. No policy, no matter the topic, no matter how well-considered, will result in perfect outcomes. Individual instances and anecdotes, when blown out of proportion and examined without proper context, can cause people to react emotionally instead of thinking through matters statistically.

Based on everything I had heard and seen, I thought the risk was low, and I thought writing the letter in support of Sha's application was the right thing to do. So I did.

At thirty-six years old, nineteen years after his conviction, Sha Wallace-Stepter became a free man. Before his release, not even incorporating lost opportunity and productivity costs, taxpayers were spending approximately $75,000 a year on his incarceration. Today, Sha is a taxpayer himself. He is determined to be an entrepreneur and has been going to school while working on a documentary film.

Sha and I have seen each other only once since his release. But I often think about his experience. So many of us, no matter our circumstances, can relate to the feeling of living through a moment when everything seems to be changing. We know what it feels like to be tempted to react impulsively, and I suspect that at some point or another, most of us have succumbed to that temptation.

But hopefully, we can empathize with the second half of Sha's story, too. We can think critically about our own decisions—how we made our past choices, and how we can make better choices in the future. We can build the discipline to respond thoughtfully in high-stakes situations. We can recognize and correct for our emotional biases. And finally, by weighing options and considering probabilities, we can—not just as individuals but as societies—better handle moments of extreme disruption and give ourselves the best possible chance to achieve the outcomes we seek.

Chapter II

RISK AS A RANGE

W e can't afford to be wrong," said Vice President Al Gore.

I don't remember exactly when this conversation occurred, but it was some time while I was at Treasury. A few minutes earlier I had been in the Oval Office, meeting with President Clinton and several of his top aides. After what everyone considered the most urgent business had been covered, the subject of global warming came up. My reaction must not have been appropriately grave, because the moment we left the Oval, the vice president stopped me. "Walk with me to my office," he said.

Now I was sitting across from Al Gore as he warned me about what he saw as an existential global threat.

I had heard about global warming—or climate change, as it's now more commonly referred to—before that conversation. But it was rarely discussed with any urgency. That's what made the vice president's concerns so memorable. He was treating with utmost seriousness a subject that, at the time, almost none of the nation's most influential policy-makers viewed as a major cause for concern.

Back then, climate science was less definitive about the potential for catastrophic consequences than it is today, and the effects of climate change were not nearly as apparent. But Gore's argument went something like this: While we could not be absolutely certain global temperatures were rising as a result of human activity, a strong body of evidence suggested they were. If that evidence turned out to be correct, the effects would likely be disastrous over time, and because greenhouse gas emissions would remain in the atmosphere for centuries, they could not be reversed. In such a situation, adopting a wait-and-see attitude was highly dangerous. To avoid the real possibility of severe or even catastrophic outcomes, it was urgent that we act immediately.

The vice president's warning that "we can't afford to be wrong" was a very simple statement. But at the same time, he was addressing a broader question that goes beyond climate change and affects every part of our lives—from personal decisions and investments to managing businesses and even countries.

How should we approach risk?

More than two decades after that conversation with Vice President Gore, it seems increasingly clear that, at least when it comes to the risks posed by climate change, humanity has taken the wrong approach. There are a variety of complicated reasons for this. But the fact remains: if more leaders around the globe had thought about the issue the same way Al Gore did, the world would today be a different and much safer place.

Instead, back in the late twentieth century, most people either denied the evidence that climate change existed or failed to fully grapple with the implications. I fell into the latter category. In

2003, when I first wrote about my conversation in the vice president's office, I said that his warning had led me to believe that preventing the worst effects of global warming was "imperative." Yet at the time, I, too, hadn't internalized the risks. Instead, I viewed climate change as merely one of many potential great challenges that twenty-first-century society might someday face.

As is the case with many people, my view of the risks posed by climate change is very different today than it was twenty years ago. What began to change my mind was a series of conversations with Tom Steyer.

As I mentioned in the previous chapter, I met Tom several decades ago, and after I left the Treasury Department in 1999 we spoke from time to time, usually to discuss the markets. After a while I noticed a change in our conversations. We would start off talking about issues relating to Farallon's business, but before long, he would bring up the subject of climate change. "This is going to cause wars," Tom would say to me. "This is going to cause mass migration."

"Well, you know, you may well be right," I would reply. But I didn't know anything about the science, and the problems weren't immediate enough for me to focus on. I had no real interest in hearing about global warming. So I would let Tom talk a little bit and then I'd get him back to what I wanted to talk about, which was investing.

Not long ago, Tom reminded me of these conversations. "Ten years ago when I tried to tell you about climate change," he said, "you didn't want to pay attention."

But Tom was more persuasive than he himself might have realized. While I may have thought his predictions hyperbolic at first, the more he spoke about climate change, the more I began to think there might be something to what he was saying. I still didn't know anything about the science. But gradually I came to see that this was something I should learn more about. In the early 2010s, about a year after Tom started focusing so intensely on climate change, I sought out Steve Hyman, who was then serving as provost of Harvard University. Steve is a medical researcher, not a climatologist, but he is a highly and broadly knowledgeable scientist, and I asked him what he thought of Tom's concerns. He said they were grounded in scientific consensus.

"This is real," he told me. I began to take the issue much more seriously, and to seek out more expert opinions.

Around the same time, many other leaders in business and government were also beginning to express more concern about the potential danger of climate change. One of them was Hank Paulson, who served as President George W. Bush's Treasury secretary from 2006 to 2009 and who, like me, was a former chief executive of Goldman Sachs.

In 2016, Hank and I even went to see Mary Jo White, the chair of the Securities and Exchange Commission, and argued that the SEC should require financial institutions to publicly recognize the potential costs related to climate change. Under existing regulations, such institutions are required to fully disclose their "material risks," and we made the case that climate risk falls under that category.

Chair White told us that she agreed with us conceptually, and that the SEC was trying to grapple with the issue of climate-related risks, but that no mechanism or methodology existed for accurately calculating those risks or requiring companies to disclose them. I understood her point, and I think she shared our hope that such a methodology would soon be developed.

Still, I think our conversation illustrates a pitfall that is easy to fall into when approaching risk: ignoring risk until it can be quantified or fully understood in all of its aspects. In the case of the SEC, the agency may not have been equipped to mandate climate risk disclosures, but as a more general principle, it's dangerous to put off dealing with risks just because you don't yet know everything about them.

Another effort to highlight the potential economic impact of climate change was something called the Risky Business Project, on which I served as a senior adviser. It was spearheaded by Hank, Tom, and then–New York Mayor Mike Bloomberg. They each held different political and policy views, but they agreed on the importance of rigorously evaluating the long-term threat climate change posed to America's different regions and economic sectors. By taking the same approach to climate change that they had applied more broadly as investors and business leaders, they hoped to encourage more companies and executives to factor climate risk into their decisions.

It was several years ago, in conjunction with the Risky Business Project, that Hank and I found ourselves at a dinner in New York with a group of economists and climate scientists. They were discussing their findings and trying to help us understand the potential outcomes the world faced. I remember that night very clearly. The scientists focused primarily on the case that they considered most likely to occur if we continued along our current trajectory (what investors call the "base case").

In and of itself, such a scenario was alarming, with increased flooding due to storm surges; falling crop yields; lost productivity from extreme heat, especially in sectors like construction; and much else. The scientists also referred to a catastrophic worst-case scenario—for example, property loss from sea-level rise reaching more than $682 billion (in 2014 dollars) in Florida alone by the end of this century. But this was mentioned only briefly. For the great majority of the evening the scientists focused predominantly on the base case—the outcome they thought was most likely.

Neither Hank nor I have a science background, but we've spent our careers making decisions about matters where other people are experts and we are not. We've devoted great deals of time to evaluating information, parsing uncertainty, attempting to reach conclusions, and deciding what action to take as a result.

As part of that process, listening to the experts is essential. But in my experience, experts can sometimes be limited by their expertise. They are frequently uncomfortable going beyond what the available information can document or making statements they are unable to stand behind with a great degree of confidence.

This discomfort can distort your judgment, because all decisions are based on incomplete information. If you're the decision-maker, you must recognize that there's a lot you can't measure—but just because you can't measure something doesn't make it less real. You listen to the experts, and then you bring your life's experience to bear. Sitting at that dinner, both Hank and I felt strongly that although the scientists had done serious, important work, they weren't paying enough attention to the worst-case scenario they themselves had just described. It seemed to us that over the medium to long term there was far more uncertainty—and therefore a higher likelihood of a truly disastrous outcome materializing—than anyone cared to recognize.

"This could be catastrophic," Hank and I kept saying. "Let's really focus on that." But despite our efforts, we were unable to shift the group's focus from the base case. We both left the dinner deeply unsettled, with the sense that something just wasn't right. It's a feeling I'm familiar with: the sense that, in some important respect, decision-makers aren't thinking about risks in an effective way.

Everything in life—even matters which we don't typically think of as requiring serious decision-making—carries some measure of risk. For example, fly-fishing has been a passion of mine (sometimes bordering on an addiction) for the last forty years. One of my favorite pieces of water, a stretch of the Ruby River in Montana, is somewhat difficult to reach. The first part of the approach, wading across a shallow, slow-moving section of river, is no problem. But then the angler must walk along a narrow ledge right on the bank, with a drop-off of about five feet to rocks below covered by just a few inches of water.

If I ever lost my footing and fell, I could hurt myself pretty badly. Yet I never think through this decision or weigh the risks associated with it. I just assume I'll make it and start to cross.

On the Ruby River, my approach to risk has consequences for me, and me alone. However, at other times in my life I have found myself in situations in which a single person's choices could help—or hurt—thousands or even millions of people.

Yet all too often in business, politics, and policy-making, decisions are approached the same way I approach the decision to wade a stream. Decision-makers quickly identify what they think is most likely to happen and forge ahead without considering other possible outcomes.

Other common methods of approaching risk are more sophisticated, but not by much. Risk is sometimes seen as binary: "What will happen if this works out? What will happen if it doesn't?" Other times (such as at the dinner that Hank Paulson and I attended) risk is split into three possibilities: a best, middle, and worst case, with the middle case treated as the only one worth considering. Decision-makers acknowledge that less likely possibilities exist, but then put them to the side or ignore them altogether.

The many approaches to risk I've just described all have something in common. They reduce it from a complex array of possibilities and outcomes to something easy to digest and work with. For example, in the news, risk is often expressed as a single number: "If we continue on our current trajectory, global temperatures are set to rise 1.5 degrees Celsius by 2100." Banks have vast departments devoted to analyzing and quantifying outcomes—including risks—and producing careful forecasts, yet even they tend to express projections in single-point estimates.

In some ways this is understandable. A single number that quantifies risk is easy to comprehend and communicate. It sounds comfortingly precise.

But it is also quite dangerous. In virtually every case, risks cannot be expressed by a number. Risk is a range.

I am not proposing a method for quantifying the entire range of risk. That could be a book—and quite a long one—unto itself. Besides, for those not involved in the technical details of risk management, what matters is not the precise technique you use to measure risk, but the way in which you conceptually approach it. Individuals and societies who acknowledge the complex and changing nature of risk, and who internalize that understanding so that it informs their actions, will be better able to make sound decisions than those who do not.

A relatively easy way to improve one's approach to risk is to stop describing the most likely outcome of a given course of action using a single number, and to start using a narrow range of numbers instead. For example, rather than projecting that a country's GDP will grow by 2 percent, you might project an increase of 1.75–2.25 percent. Then, if you need a single number for calculations, you can take the midpoint. This may seem like an unimportant change, but using a small range of outcomes rather than a single number acknowledges uncertainty and complexity, and will be more accurate.

Even when the base-case projection is expressed as more than just a single number, however, to present it as the *only* possible case would still be wrong. The base case may materialize a majority of the time, but that means something else will occur some of the time.

This possibility is often dismissed, but it shouldn't be. Let's say the base case is 80 percent probable. One out of every five times, an "unlikely" outcome will still occur. Too often, decision-makers don't take that sort of thing into account. A tragic example is the Iraq war. Assuming for a second that the top officials in charge of our strategy were correct and the base case was a relatively painless occupation—a highly debatable assumption—there was still no adequate contingency plan to deal with the possibility that something other than a relatively painless occupation would occur.

Thus, the range that reflects the middle case, while preferable to a single point, is in fact only one part of a much larger range of possibilities. A better way to think about what risk looks like can be represented on a graph. (The technical term here is a histogram, but for our purposes graph works just as well.) For every decision, there is a set of possible outcomes, generally placed from worst to best along the horizontal axis, and the percentage likelihood associated with each of those outcomes, generally placed from lowest to highest along the vertical axis. In most cases you'll see something resembling a bell curve, with the likeliest outcomes in the middle and the more remote possibilities on either side.

Now, for example's sake, let's say you're graphing the potential returns on buying a stock over the next year, and you're anticipating a 10 percent return. Everything to the right of that point on the graph represents a better-than-expected outcome, from a reasonable chance the stock goes up 11 percent to the infinitesimal possibility that it doubles or triples in price. Everything to the left of your chosen point—the worse-than-expected outcomes and their probabilities—is your risk.

Generally speaking, the further left you go on something like a bell curve, the more remote the possibilities and the greater the magnitude of the potential negative outcome. For example, if you invest in a blue-chip stock like Procter & Gamble or Coca-Cola, the far left of your graph is where you would find the possibility that the company goes bankrupt. This type of risk, where the probabilities are lowest but the consequences most dire, is commonly referred to as "tail risk."

In my experience, most people overestimate the likelihood of the base case occurring, and underestimate the likelihood of rare scenarios occurring. Tail risks in particular are often difficult to quantify, both in terms of the probability of the event materializing and the magnitude of the impact if it does. And because the consequences of tail risks can be so large, they can be especially difficult to manage for. As a result, there is a strong temptation to disregard them in decision-making, and to operate under the assumption that there's zero risk of the extreme outcome, when in fact the risk is very low but not zero.

Moreover, precisely because the odds at the tail end of the graph are so low, something other than the worst outcomes usually happens. People then conclude—erroneously—that they were right to ignore tail risks. This leads them to repeat their error the next time around, only with more confidence, which leaves them even more exposed if the worst were to happen. The more time passes without the tail risk materializing, the more people disregard it, and the greater the potential consequences become.

For example, for many years before COVID-19 appeared, many experts and leading thinkers warned that a global pandemic might occur, and it didn't. I think it's likely that over time, people began to take their warnings less seriously. They should have recognized that even when warnings of a low-probability, high-magnitude risk are well-founded, the risk will still hardly ever materialize.

Even when we do recognize tail risks, it's hard to know what to do with them. If you act to protect yourself to some degree, you make a trade-off: you reduce the cost if things go poorly but also benefit less if all goes well. But if you don't act, and the worst happens, there's the chance of catastrophic damage.

It is also important to distinguish between a thin tail, which is an extremely low probability of a severe outcome, and a fat tail, which describes a probability still in the low range but greater. Though some allowance should be made for any realistically possible tail risk, it's clearly more important to adjust for the latter than for the former. When the potential consequences could be dire, the difference between a 1 percent chance and a 5 percent chance of a worst-case scenario matters a lot.

The problem is that when evaluating risk, it's very hard to know how fat a tail you face. How can we accurately determine if a potential event will occur once every hundred years or once every twenty?

All this leads to a common failure in decision-making. It is easy to examine the full range of risk, including the tail risks, become overwhelmed by the complexity, and then abandon the attempt to incorporate the full range of risk into one's decision-making. But that will never lead to sound, thoughtful choices. Instead, a decision-maker must estimate the probabilities of possible outcomes, estimate the magnitude of the effects, weigh the costs and benefits, and make the best judgment possible.

None of this is simple. Which is precisely why we need a tool that lets us acknowledge complexity and uncertainty in some readily usable way.

This is where the yellow pad comes in handy. Decision-makers can pick a few key potential outcomes—outcomes that reflect the full range of risk—and then use their judgment, based on facts and analysis, to attach a probability and magnitude to each.

These judgments are not guaranteed to be correct. But attempting to consider possible upsides and downsides, and the probabilities and magnitudes associated with them, drives rigor and organization in my thinking and leads to better choices, however imperfect they may be. The yellow pad produces more fully informed and better decisions, and the higher the stakes and greater the consequences, the more important that becomes.

Another critical point when evaluating risks involves the way that probabilities are estimated, which begins with asking the right questions. Too often, when examining a risk and trying to determine the likelihood of a negative outcome occurring, we don't think carefully about what the questions should be. Instead, we quickly decide the questions that are going to be asked, and then think about what the answers should be. If you don't start with the right questions, you may not be able to resolve whatever it is you're trying to decide on in a sound and sensible way.

Which brings me back to the yellow pad. When you do your best to calculate expected values, you are forced to consider crucial questions about risk that many people overlook. And regardless of whether those questions have good answers, or clear answers, grappling with them is important. Are the tails thin or fat? How much confidence do you have in your estimates—and would additional information give you more? Is the base case an overwhelmingly probable scenario, or merely the most likely one? What are the factors that are nonquantifiable but nonetheless real and significant? And, finally, when you put it all together, how do the risks—including the probabilities of various occurrences and of the magnitudes of their effects—compare with the potential rewards?

The number of leaders in the private and public sectors who view risk as a range, and who recognize the complexity and uncertainty in all decision-making, seems to me to be smaller than it should be. The number of leaders who truly internalize these views is smaller still. Whether in government, finance, or managing one's personal affairs, the real test is not whether you can describe a risk thoughtfully—that is important, but only the beginning.

The real test of whether you've internalized a risk is whether you are willing to pay an appropriate cost to manage it.

Sometime in the 1980s, when Steve Friedman and I were on the management committee of Goldman Sachs, we asked Hy Weinberg, our chief financial officer, to conduct a thorough analysis of the risks the firm faced, just so we could understand what would happen if something went severely wrong. (For example, if the markets completely came apart.) He went away, ran the numbers, and sometime later came back with sobering findings. If the extreme tail risks simultaneously materialized across a wide range of trading positions, principal investments, and other activities, we would be out of business.

Ultimately, there were limits to the usefulness of this study. The possibility of a worst-case scenario occurring was extremely remote, but there was no way to eliminate it entirely while still staying in business effectively. We had no choice but to accept some very tiny, but not quite zero, risk of catastrophe.

Yet this exercise did focus us on the broader question of tail risk. In light of Hy Weinberg's study, we strengthened a rule for everyone using Goldman Sachs' capital to make investments: even if you have extremely high confidence that you can't lose more than X amount on a given position, there's still a limit to the total size of the position you can take. That way if the loss turns out to be vastly greater than you've estimated, it will be painful, but bearable.

Even before these types of limits were put in place, I had learned how important they could be. When I was a young partner running risk arbitrage at Goldman Sachs, there was an announced acquisition of a copper company called Anaconda that was viewed across Wall Street as, for practical purposes, a sure thing to be completed. Someone in a similar role at a competitor of ours took a vast position on Anaconda, whose stock would be worth significantly more once the deal went through, and thought we were foolish for not doing the same. I, too, thought the odds were very high, and we took a large position, but with some constraint based on the view that the virtually zero percent chance that the deal would fail was still not zero.

Then the highly unexpected happened. The deal fell through, and to make matters worse, Anaconda's stock went down much more than had been expected in such an event. We lost money, but it was manageable. My competitor lost his job.

Putting guardrail-like position limits in place might seem like an obvious choice. But it comes at a cost. In order to greatly reduce the already low potential for an enormous loss, we limited our potential gains. I believe that was the right choice, since avoiding such a highly damaging loss was well worth the opportunity cost. Still, if Goldman Sachs had not internalized risk in a reasonably thoughtful way, we might not have made such a choice.

Unwillingness to pay an opportunity cost is not the only reason organizations fail to adequately protect themselves from risk. In 2011, for example, my former Goldman Sachs colleague Jon Corzine was running MF Global, a futures commission merchant and trading firm. In addition to serving as both a senator from and governor of New Jersey, Jon had a long history as a skilled, deeply experienced, and highly successful trading manager. After assessing the global picture, he concluded that the probability of the European Union and European Central Bank allowing a default on the sovereign debt of certain European countries was extremely low. Accordingly, he invested a massive sum—one his firm could not afford to lose.

Looking back, I think Jon was probably correct in his judgment of the odds. The chance of a worst-case scenario occurring was small. But it was not zero. European sovereign debt bonds fell far more dramatically than many expected, despite the initial efforts of Eurozone authorities.

The bonds eventually recovered, and would have been a good investment if MF Global had maintained the capital reserves to weather the storm. Instead, the fund went under in one of the biggest bankruptcies in U.S. history.

The firm's mistake, in my view, was not that it ignored questions of risk altogether. It was that it rounded risks with low probabilities down to zero. Making more rigorous judgments about outcomes, potential upside, and risks might have limited the firm's losses and allowed it to survive.

I similarly try to rigorously evaluate risks when considering my own personal investment portfolio. To begin with, I believe that virtually nobody—with the possible exception of a few professional traders—is very good at consistently predicting market behavior in the short term and that attempting to do so is a fool's game. (One thing that makes me furious is watching cut-rate brokerage firms advertise to consumers by suggesting they have analytic systems that can beat the market. Contrary to what one such advertisement claimed, there are no "Secrets of Wall Street." There's only knowledge and discipline. And if someone really did know such secrets, you can be fairly sure they wouldn't be sharing them with the public.)

When I evaluate potential personal investments—usually, in my case, commitments to a managed fund rather than individual stocks—I always try to make judgments about what will happen over years, not quarters. If I think the markets substantially underweight more immediate risks (for example, by not pricing in the possibility of a major geopolitical conflict or a spike in inflation), I might adjust my exposure to the market somewhat, but I don't engage in short-term market timing.

I also recognize that whatever my judgments about short-term or long-term risks, there is unavoidably a good deal of uncertainty around whether those judgments will turn out to be correct. The same holds true when I'm evaluating others' predictions. When people express a judgment to me about markets, I always ask them, "What level of uncertainty do you put around that judgment?"

There are many forms that uncertainty surrounding my expectations could take. First, I could misjudge the odds of adverse outcomes occurring. This is especially true if I mistakenly assume the future will inevitably look like the past, which investors tend to do, especially when conditions have been relatively stable or positive for a relatively long time. Eventually they realize that the world has in fact changed, perhaps because of a shift in economic conditions or because markets have simply gone too far. But by then, it's usually too late. The markets have come apart.

Second, I could be right about the odds of an event occurring, but wrong about the magnitude of the consequences.

Third, I could be right on both the odds and magnitude, but simply get unlucky when a lower-probability event occurs.

I can't eliminate these uncertainties. What I can do is take them into account. If I think there's a 10 percent chance of losing a large sum of money, and I average it all out and I get a favorable expected value, I might then say something like, "Yes, but you know something? There's a reasonable chance that I'm wrong, and not by a little bit, but by a lot." So I may moderate what I would otherwise do.

My views regarding uncertainty and risk affect the amount of estimated beta I'm willing to have in my overall portfolio. ("Beta" is the term for the correlation between the performance of the market and the performance of your portfolio. For example, let's say the market goes down one dollar. If your beta is 0.7, you'll lose 70 cents, if your beta is 0.6, you'll lose 60 cents, and so on.) Not only do I recognize that there's some probability that I'll lose money, but I also recognize that my judgment about that probability and the magnitude associated with it may not be correct.

Therefore, while I still aim for "alpha"—which is a measure of how much better your investments do than the market on a risk-adjusted basis—my beta is somewhat lower than that of many similar investors. It's not that I'm risk averse (although I am also that, to some extent). It's that I believe the uncertainty regarding outcomes is likely greater than most investors acknowledge, and while that uncertainty could cut both ways, I want to limit the effects on the negative side.

I also try to consider that every investment—whether a stock, a real estate purchase, a fund, or anything else—has not just downside risk, but a real tail risk as well. Some people might invest in a blue-chip company on the assumption that while the stock price may go down, there's no chance the company will deteriorate radically or go completely out of business. The odds of that happening are, in fairness, extremely small. But they are not zero. For example, many people invested in General Electric when it was considered one of America's absolutely premier companies, and then watched in more recent years as GE experienced a steady decline.

A commonly held view is that all risk, including tail risk, can be mitigated by diversifying. It's true that diversifying can help. If I make twenty investments and one of them performs poorly, that might not matter much. But if overall equity markets decline sharply and don't recover relatively quickly, that can overwhelm diversification. And diversification across asset classes can also falter. In really stressed markets, prices across seemingly unrelated asset classes—like stocks, bonds, commodities, and real estate—might correlate, with everyone heading for the exits at the same time.

Another commonly held view is that while investors must be conscious of tail risk during periods of strong market growth, buying during a significant downturn is almost always a great opportunity. This once came up at a meeting of an organization I was involved with, with respect to investing its funds. We were discussing how the organization might react to a severe drop-off in the market. "If the market does decline very substantially, then we're in a good position," said the person in charge, a highly capable and experienced asset manager. "We have cash to take advantage of that, so we should buy."

Most of the committee seemed comfortable with this approach, but I jumped in. I told the trustees about something one of my former partners, Bob Mnuchin, used to say: "People who sell at the bottom aren't stupid." What he meant was that no one can guess where the bottom will be, or how long a recovery will take. Serious market declines usually occur for real reasons. There's always the possibility that markets could get worse and stay down for a very long time.

It's true that during every market cycle in the post–World War II period, if you bought on serious declines, you always came out well because the market eventually recovered each time. So you could say that, since the organization in question is a long-run investor, that's what it should do. But there remains a risk that those who advocate this approach generally ignore. Just because a strategy has always worked in the past doesn't mean it will work again. Maybe the time will come when the market doesn't come back. Or maybe the market will rebound, but it will take far longer than before. At the end of 1989, the Japanese stock index, the Nikkei, was close to 39,000. Then it crashed, and more than thirty years later it is still far from fully recovered. There's no basis to completely rule out the possibility—however remote—that something similar will happen after the next severe market decline in the United States.

My point was not that this organization (or anyone else, for that matter) should or shouldn't buy during a downturn. My point was that the chance of an extremely long recovery, or no recovery at all, is more than zero. That information should inform how much additional exposure we want to take.

Recognizing Bob Mnuchin's point certainly informs the approach I've taken to my personal investments. If equities appear to be deeply discounted during a market downturn, I might invest cash where I thought the longer-run expected value was highly favorable. But I would do so much more cautiously and to a considerably lesser extent than most others in my financial position. In other words, I would give up some amount of potential upside in order to avoid a greater loss in the event—highly unlikely by historical standards—that the decline worsens and is long lasting.

This leads to what I suspect is another significant difference between my personal investment strategy and that of many of my peers. Even in good times, I am likely to have a somewhat greater percentage of my assets in cash, where there's no possibility of a significant gain if markets do well, but also no possibility of a significant loss if they don't. (Technically, when inflation is high enough for long enough, cash also loses significant value, but the loss will still not be as great as the one from the combination of inflation *plus* a large decline in the market.)

In other words, I am paying an opportunity cost to lose less in the possible circumstance, however remote, that severe adverse outcomes occur. Whether I'm better or worse off in the long run,

I don't know. But I feel more comfortable this way. For me, the benefits, in the form of reduced risk, outweigh the costs.

This does not mean my approach is the only correct one. There are many prominent people in business and finance—people whose judgment and experience I deeply respect—who would advocate increasing the market exposure of a portfolio like mine and suggest aggressively adding to that exposure in significant downturns. They would look at market patterns over the past century, concede that there was some non-zero chance, however remote, that those patterns might not be predictive, but decide that this is nonetheless a risk they are willing to take.

Neither strategy is objectively better than the other, and neither decision is objectively correct. We might have different levels of comfort with risk, or we might disagree about the extent of the risks or the level of uncertainty attached to our judgments. But that doesn't mean that one of us is right and the other wrong. In fact, we could both be making the best possible choice, even though we arrive at different conclusions, so long as we share a probabilistic understanding of risk and apply it rigorously and with discipline.

In other words, there can be more than one reasonable decision, so long as you take a reasonable approach to decision-making.

Failure to take a reasonable approach, on the other hand, will likely lead to poorer outcomes over time. Whether you are investing a small or large amount, and whether your investment is in stocks, bonds, or any other asset, internalizing risk as a range, and analyzing risks and rewards with rigor and discipline, maximizes the odds that you will make sound choices and do well over time.

What is true in personal investment is equally true for organizations and countries. Internalizing risk as a range is crucial not just for individuals, but for companies and policy-makers as well.

For example, when we at Treasury went to President Clinton to recommend support programs to deal with the deep financial crises Mexico experienced in 1995, Southeast Asia and South Korea experienced in 1997, and Russia experienced in 1998, we thought through our recommendations in probabilistic terms, even if we couldn't put precise numbers on all of the variables. The president, to his great credit in my view, thought through his responses and decisions with that same approach. He recognized that there was a risk that our proposals would not work, and he weighed that against the benefits of acting and the risks of not acting. I think he ultimately made the right decision to act in each case, even when we could not perfectly ascribe numbers to each possible outcome, and even though not all of the programs wound up working as we hoped.

What might such an approach to risk look like in response to today's policy challenges? Let's return to the subject I initially discussed in Vice President Gore's office more than two decades ago: climate change.

The future Gore once described to me if we didn't act is now materializing. Even more threatening, the worst-case scenario Hank Paulson and I heard a group of scientists allude to briefly at dinner was, in retrospect, likely a fat tail. Exactly as we worried, what was once seen as an extreme and unlikely scenario is becoming the new base case. Hurricanes are more damaging. Wildfire seasons are longer. Droughts are more severe. In parts of Miami Beach, not far from where I grew up, sea-level rise frequently combines with high tide to flood streets.

Meanwhile, as Tom Steyer predicted years ago during our phone calls, changes in weather patterns are creating water scarcity, disrupting agricultural production, rendering some areas less habitable, and beginning to create refugee crises for which we are unprepared. And all this has the potential—in fact, the high probability—of becoming far worse, with some analysts suggesting that these conditions could at some point lead to wars.

More people are becoming aware of the danger posed by climate change. Despite concerted and well-funded campaigns to downplay the risks, the cadre that continues to doubt both the science and the increasingly tangible effects of human-caused climate change around the world is shrinking.

Yet the way the United States addresses climate change suggests that our people and our political system have not yet internalized the risks we face. Just as in business and investing, the real test when it comes to climate change is not merely whether we can describe the worst potential outcomes. The real test is whether we are willing to pay an appropriate cost to protect ourselves from them.

This does not necessarily mean that taking action on climate will be a net cost to society, even in the short term. I spoke to Tom a few years ago and he told me that, having run all the numbers, he now believes preventing the worst consequences of climate change will grow our economy, both in the shorter run and in the long run, by developing new industries, encouraging investment, and creating jobs. Most analysts do not share this view, but if Tom's analysis is correct, that would make protecting ourselves from a warming planet an even more obvious policy choice.

Even if Tom is not correct, when it comes to our approach

toward addressing risk, the important question is not whether we *will* pay a cost. The important question is whether we are *willing* to pay a cost if need be. In panels and private conversations, I have heard a surprising number of people who recognize the importance of climate change, and yet remain unwilling to accept meaningful trade-offs to deal with it. Often this takes the form of postponement: somebody will say, "It's real, but the economy's soft . . . let's wait and do it in the future." Anyone expressing this argument has not begun to internalize the magnitude and the immediacy of the risks.

Among Americans more broadly, there has been some progress. According to a poll from October 2021, 52 percent of Americans would be willing to pay a $1 monthly fee to combat climate change. However, the number of Americans who would pay $10 per month drops to just 35 percent. For some Americans, an additional $120 per year is a significant expense, and there are ways to make mitigating climate change progressive, so that the highest burden falls on those most able to afford it. But the fact remains that if climate change continues unabated, the additional costs to taxpayers in the form of disaster relief alone will be vastly more than $10 per American per month. Most of us are not even close to fully considering the range of risk we face.

Moreover, while many costs of climate change can be quantified, or at least approximated, others cannot. Economists have a variety of ways to attempt to attach dollar values to human life, but really, how do you put a price on the lives saved by avoiding war, refugee crises, or famine? Even if evaluated nonquantitatively, these costs must be included in a probabilistic analysis in some fashion.

We can start with the best-case scenario—which seems extremely unlikely—that taking no further action on climate turns out to be far less harmful than we currently expect. There is a non-zero chance that something dramatic happens—a breakthrough technological development that makes carbon capture and removal from the atmosphere affordable at scale, for example— and the warming of the planet either remains flat or is reversed. If such an outcome transpires, any additional action we take to protect ourselves from the changing climate could create costs without any real benefits.

Compared with the other side of the expected value table, however, these unnecessary expenses would be tiny. If the tail risk we now face—which is highly likely to be quite fat— materializes, "catastrophe" does not begin to describe what could occur. The most remote risk, but one that nevertheless exists, is that climate change ends human life as we know it.

When we survey the full range of risk in a probabilistic way, the conclusion becomes fairly obvious: the cost of acting if we don't need to is much, much less than the cost of not acting if we do need to. This is exactly the point Al Gore was making so many years ago, when he told me that "We can't afford to be wrong."

In a world full of enormous and growing threats—not just climate change, but issues such as nuclear proliferation, pandemics, mass economic disruption as a result of technological innovation and globalization, and more—we cannot afford an ineffective approach to risk. For this reason, a yellow-pad approach to risk is not just helpful. I believe it's the only way to adequately handle the uncertainty of a changing and complex world.

It might seem unsettling to replace a one-dimensional, single-point view of risk with one that recognizes the full range of outcomes and probabilities. But while recognizing uncertainty can be uncomfortable, it is absolutely essential.

In fact, the future of life on earth may depend on it.

Chapter III

MRS. COLLINS' QUESTION

Not long after the start of President Clinton's first term, and my own appointment as director of his National Economic Council, I was sitting in my West Wing office when I received a letter from Florida. I immediately recognized the letter writer's name: Mrs. Dorothy Collins.

"Are you the same Robbie Rubin," she wrote, "who was in my fourth grade class at North Beach Elementary School?"

On one level, Mrs. Collins' question had a very straightforward answer: yes, I was. I remembered her well, because she was an exceptional teacher. I said as much in my reply, and I kept up an occasional correspondence with her until she passed away a year or so later.

On another level, however, Mrs. Collins' question was far deeper than a simple yes or no. In 1947, when I sat in her fourth grade classroom, my life could have gone in any number of different directions. That it went the way it did was, to say the least, highly improbable.

As I think about my life—the experiences I've had, the people

I've worked with, and the various positions I've held—I find my-self contemplating a different version of the question Mrs. Collins asked me. Of all the ways a fourth grader's life could unfold, why did mine unfold the way it did?

Or to put it slightly differently, how did I become whatever I became?

At various points in my life I've been asked versions of this question, and I understand why: I've had a variety of experiences I never could have anticipated when I was growing up, and the probability that I would spend my life in the way I have, or take on the various roles I did, was exceedingly small. People are curious about how it happened.

Yet I'm inherently wary of any how-to guide that claims to be a blueprint for success. In fact, I'm wary of the idea of "success" in any objective, universal sense. When I think about people I've met who would typically be considered successful, I prefer to describe them as "successful by external metrics." It may seem like a small distinction, but it's one I think is important.

I don't claim to know exactly how or why I succeeded (in many respects, at least) by external metrics. I certainly don't claim to know how others did. One thing I can say, however, is that the people I have known who achieved a great deal of success, how-ever one defines it, have for the most part tended to possess some common characteristics.

One of the most successful-by-external-metrics people I have known was Vernon Jordan, a trailblazing lawyer, civil rights leader, political adviser, and, later in life, prominent figure in busi-ness. A few years before he passed away in 2021, the two of us were having lunch in the partners' dining room at the American headquarters of Lazard, the investment bank where Vernon served as a kind of elder statesman.

The dining room is located at the very top of 30 Rockefeller Plaza in New York City, not far from the former offices of the Rockefeller family itself. It is a space designed to make you feel as though you have reached the top, and looking out over Manhattan sprawled below, I remarked to Vernon, "You know, when I was a kid in Miami Beach, I never would have imagined being in a place like this."

To which Vernon replied, "I always thought I'd be here."

To Vernon, the answer to Mrs. Collins' question—how he became what he became—was something along the lines of "destiny." Vernon grew up in the segregated South, faced tremendous adversity in his early career, and even survived an assassination attempt by a white supremacist in 1980. Yet despite all this, I think that in many ways, he always felt he was destined for greatness.

I don't really identify with that feeling. It's not that I feel the universe is out to get me. I've simply never felt that the universe takes a rooting interest in me one way or the other. Nor, looking back on my earliest years, do I see much evidence I was destined to live the life I have led. I was a slow learner for the first few years of elementary school, and prone to anxiety whenever my parents weren't around. I never got in fights, but I was a difficult child. Doctors made house calls back then, and one time when I was very young and pretending to be sick because I didn't want to go to school and a doctor arrived to try to figure out what was wrong with me, I threw potatoes at him. At the end of third grade, when our family moved from New York to Miami, I was already quite behind academically.

In fourth and fifth grade, thanks in no small part to Mrs. Collins, I caught up with the other kids my age—my potato-throwing days were behind me. Still, I wasn't a notably exceptional child. In high school I got good grades, but I wasn't at the very top of my class. I was friendly with members of the popular crowd, but I was never quite one of them.

Even when I was admitted to Harvard, I don't think anyone would have expected that I would end up in the various places I eventually did. I arrived on campus feeling totally unprepared for Harvard's academic challenge, and frankly surprised my application had been accepted. Many decades later, as a member of the university's governing body, I recalled my feeling of surprise to my friend Bill Fitzsimmons, Harvard's director of admissions. Bill looked through the old files, found my application, and, after reading through it, said, "Well, you've got a point." (I made him promise not to retroactively revoke my acceptance.)

I think I've led a life full of fascinating experiences. But nothing in my first twenty years would necessarily have augured it.

Nor did I have any sweeping, long-term ambitions that stemmed from childhood. This is probably another difference between me and someone like Vernon. When I was in fourth grade, my goal was to get to fifth grade. When I was in college, my goal was to do well in my classes and graduate.

Even when I thought about what to do after college, I didn't have much of a career path in mind. I applied to Harvard Law School because it seemed like the sensible thing to do. But when I was admitted, and returned to campus as a law student, people were focused in a way I wasn't, buying books and talking about law. They seemed laden with stress and I didn't want any part of it. So after just three days, I called my parents and said, "I'm dropping out to take a year off." To my surprise, they were supportive, and I went to the London School of Economics for a nondegree program.

While I was in London, I decided to reenroll in law school the following year (although for various reasons, despite being readmitted at Harvard, I decided to go to Yale). Still, I suspect a different kind of person, one with their sights set on the positions I ended up serving in, would have never left Harvard Law just to take time off to figure things out. That was especially true in the early 1960s. In fact, leaving school was so atypical that before I left, the Harvard Law School dean of admissions said he would only consider allowing me to return if I went to see a psychiatrist so I could explain my thinking to him. (To the psychiatrist's credit, he reassured me that what I was doing was perfectly normal, and that if anything it was the dean of admissions who should be speaking with him.)

I don't think there's anything wrong with imagining one's life the way Vernon told me he did. I suspect that way of thinking helps many people achieve their goals. But when it comes to my own life, something other than a sense of destiny or a set of personal goals has been at play.

One element that shaped my career is easy to identify: good luck. In my experience, many people are reluctant to recognize the role that fortune, good or bad, plays in life. I suspect that if I gave you a list of fifty people who'd been very successful by external metrics, and you asked them, "How important do you think luck has been in your life?" the vast majority would underestimate it.

I would never argue that those people "just got lucky." I would, however, argue that the trajectories of their lives could not be explained by merit alone.

To begin with, anyone deemed highly successful must have, by definition, avoided many of the worst types of bad luck. At my age, I've known plenty of exceedingly capable people whose careers, and sometimes even lives, were cut short by illness or accident. In other cases, highly qualified individuals suffered from less extreme, but still damaging, misfortunes beyond their control—for example, an economic downturn or a change in the political climate.

There is another, broader type of luck that is important to note: whether or not one is subject to the most pernicious forms of societal inequality and discrimination. I was born into relatively favorable circumstances, in that both of my parents were college educated and my family was well off. I was white and male, which meant I was not the target of racism or sexism. While I am also Jewish, and antisemitism was and remains a reality in society, it did not affect my professional life in the way it probably would have had I been born just a few decades earlier. (When my father graduated law school, most of the major law firms wouldn't hire anyone who was Jewish. By the time I graduated law school, that was no longer the case.)

There are other ways in which I benefited from good luck. I was fortunate to enter investment banking at a moment when it was growing rapidly in scope and importance, and I was fortunate that Goldman Sachs' arbitrage department needed someone just as I was seeking to enter finance. Arbitrage was an important profit center for the firm, yet it employed a small number of people, so when the person ahead of me left for a job with a nonprofit just a few years after I arrived, I became the most senior nonpartner in the department. That never would have happened if I'd gone into a different department.

I think some people are uncomfortable acknowledging the importance of serendipity because they feel it diminishes the role their talents and work ethic played in their success. I disagree with that. I don't think being honest about the role of luck takes anything away from anybody. I think it helps ground people with a sense of appreciation and, perhaps even more important, humility. John L. Weinberg, the late senior partner of Goldman Sachs, used to say that "some people grow and some people swell." Recognizing your own good fortune helps you grow instead of swell.

At the same time, luck can explain only part of one's life trajectory. There are many other factors at play. I don't have a precise way of describing these elements, but the word I often find myself using is "wiring." When asked why I did or didn't do something in a certain way, I'll sometimes reply, "That's just the way I'm wired."

Throughout my career, I've seen people who are wired in a way that makes it much more difficult for them to accomplish whatever it is they set out to accomplish. For whatever reason, their psyches undermine them. People get in their own way, or don't relate well to others, or act too aggressively, or can't handle pressure, and their careers stall or just peter out. I've also encountered people who are wired in a way that helps them handle a wide variety of challenges and sets them up for success.

There's also a type of wiring that is not necessarily positive or negative but that nevertheless helps determine one's journey through life. For example, if I were wired differently, I would not have reacted the way I did when I found myself standing waist deep in a swimming pool while dressed in a suit and tie at the Democratic National Convention.

This took place in Charlotte, North Carolina, in 2012. On my flight from New York, it seemed that every other passenger was traveling to the convention as well. One of the people I bumped into was my friend Jane Hartley, a businesswoman who later became the ambassador to France and then the United Kingdom.

"We're having a party tonight at the Ritz-Carlton pool room," she said. "You should come."

I arrived at the party not long after landing in Charlotte. I was surprised to find that everyone was crowded around the edges of the room, and that no one occupied the shiny blue floor in the center. In the middle of a conversation, hoping to get a little space, I stepped casually onto the blue floor—and discovered that, while I had been in other "pool rooms" with a fountain or other water feature, this pool room contained an actual swimming pool.

Some people might have felt embarrassed, but all I really thought was "Okay, that was wet." I got out of the pool and continued the conversation I'd been having. Fortunately, someone was kind enough to get me a change of clothing from my hotel, but for the better part of an hour I stood in my dripping-wet suit, had a glass of red wine, and talked with friends and acquaintances about economic policy and politics.

I have already mentioned Bob Mnuchin's admonition that people who sell at the bottom of the market aren't stupid. Another of Bob's sayings was that we are all three people: how others see us, how we see ourselves, and who we really are. As a result, I cannot objectively say why I continued to enjoy the party instead of leaving in embarrassment. And what is true of this one small experience is true of much larger and more significant ones as well. I cannot definitively answer why I became whatever it is I became. I can only offer my perspective.

Still, I've now spent many decades both living and thinking about life. I may not understand my own wiring perfectly, but I think I have insights into the traits—the factors other than luck—that have played a significant role, and that help answer the question prompted by Mrs. Collins' letter.

One of these traits is intensity. This doesn't mean having one's long-term objectives mapped out. As I said earlier, I have never been someone who thinks much, if at all, about exactly what I hope to accomplish five, ten, or twenty years from now. I had some broad professional aims for my life: I knew that I wanted to be financially successful; I knew I wanted to be involved in some way, if possible, in politics. But I never had specific career goals, such as wanting to become a senior partner at Goldman Sachs or secretary of the Treasury.

The intensity I refer to is not about climbing career ladders. Instead, it's about accomplishing whatever I'm engaged in. In my life, I've worked with many people who are highly accomplished, each in different ways—but this kind of intensity is a trait nearly all of them share. I once went on a fishing trip with Hank Paulson, and one night he informed me that he planned to be out on the water at six o'clock the next morning.

"Six?" I said. "I'm not even getting up until seven. Why are you going at six?"

"I want to be out on the water when the sun rises, so I'll have the greatest opportunity to catch fish," he replied simply.

Hank has a fairly laid-back affect, but if there's something he intends to do—in this case, maximize his fish-catching potential—he's extremely persistent. At Goldman Sachs, if there was a potential client who wasn't interested in engaging with Hank on something, he called them back until he either succeeded or had no possibility whatsoever of success. He would pursue his aims with total commitment.

On our fishing trip I set my alarm for seven, so on that day at least, I was less intense than Hank. But looking back on my life, I think that I, too, tend to treat my more immediate purposes with a great deal of intensity. When I started working at Goldman Sachs, I didn't think I would ever become a partner, but each day I had things to take care of, and I would do everything I could to take care of them. I also reached beyond my specific job—if I could be engaged in other areas by helping people outside my department, I would try to get involved. I might not succeed at every task, but I would almost never give up before exhausting all my options. Like Hank, I'd pursue my goals until I could get them done or I just couldn't do them (though in fairness, probably not with quite the same level of vigor as Hank).

Intensity is especially important in times of great stress or turmoil, because it can help people stay focused on what they can accomplish and keep them from being distracted by things they cannot. For many years, I've chaired the board of the Local Initiatives Support Corporation, a nonprofit that in 2021 alone delivered over $2.7 billion, derived from a mix of federal tax credits, government programs, major corporations, and foundations, to organizations that promote community development in low-income areas in the United States. In 2020, like countless nonprofit organizations, LISC was hit by twin crises—the COVID-19 pandemic and a long overdue racial reckoning in the aftermath of George Floyd's murder.

It would have been easy for LISC to become overwhelmed by the scope of the new challenges—either by failing to stretch the organization's goals to meet the moment, or by stretching too far beyond our existing capabilities. But our CEO at the time, Maurice Jones, did an outstanding job staying focused on our core mission while recognizing opportunities to find new partners and expand the scope of LISC's efforts. During an incredibly stressful time, his intense focus on LISC's mission allowed the organization to launch a variety of new programs, while still maintaining the core of its work.

Another trait nearly all people with exceptional careers whom I've known have in common is mental toughness. People who make decisions that have large consequences must be able to weather the ups and downs of life. This is not the same as being cool, calm, or collected. For example, Gus Levy, who was running Goldman Sachs when I started my career at the firm, was anything but calm. When pressure built, he would berate people and storm through the office. But one way or another, he managed to preserve his ability to make sound decisions, even in these moments of turmoil. He may not have been calm, but he kept his head.

To some extent, one builds mental toughness over time: you make a high-stakes decision, it goes however it goes, and the next high-stakes decision becomes a little easier to make. But repetition alone does not determine who can keep their head. I see a lower-stakes version of this problem all the time in fishing. In spin fishing, which I did as a boy, casting a lure is a very simple process. In fly-fishing, however, casting the line is an art form. It's very difficult to do well and impossible to do successfully every time. There are some people who, when they learn to cast, will practice over and over, until they look quite good. But then, when they see an actual fish, their nerves kick in and their form falls apart.

In that sense, practice doesn't really make perfect. Facing stress and pressure in the real world, you have to find a way to put your nerves aside.

For some people, the mechanism that allows them to maintain their decision-making abilities during stressful situations is self-confidence. Larry Summers and I were once discussing this in the context of basketball. (I'm a lifelong Knicks fan, which may be proof that I do not always practice what I preach when it comes to rational thought.) Larry was saying that professional basketball players need to have an irrational sense of optimism: if the last shot didn't go in, they still have to believe the next one will.

"That may be true," I countered, "but they have to combine that with judgment—otherwise, they would shoot every time they got the ball."

I think anyone in a role that requires high-stakes decisions must find a way to be confident without losing the ability to make sound judgments—to be optimistic the next shot will go in while having the wherewithal not to take bad shots.

One of my own techniques for keeping my head during difficult moments is to do my best to reach an optimal decision, while acknowledging the possibility things might not work out. In taking on a large position in the arbitrage department, recommending a course of action to the president, or expressing my opinion to a board or senior leadership team, my attitude could usually best be summarized as, "I think the odds are that this is the right decision, but there are no guarantees. I may have misjudged the odds, or, even if I have estimated the odds correctly, negative possibilities may materialize."

If I were to attempt to further reassure myself, or someone else, it would only be to say, "I've done this many times, and it's worked out, and while that doesn't necessarily mean it's going to work out the next time, it should increase our confidence that it will."

To acknowledge the distinct possibility of failure may not seem like much of a self-soothing mechanism, but for whatever reason, it's worked for me. I've always been able to recognize the fact that no decision I make, no matter how well made, is certain to have a successful outcome—while still maintaining a fundamental sense of confidence in my decision-making.

There is another way in which I think I am similar to professional basketball players, though unfortunately it has nothing to do with ball handling or three-point range: like most people I've known who were able to reach very high levels of responsibility in their fields, I tend not to dwell on things that go wrong. On the court, when one of my Knicks misses a shot, he'll simply clap his hands together and move on.

This ability is important for anyone, but it's especially important for people in leadership positions, because everyone else in the organization takes emotional cues from the leader. For example, President Clinton, who became widely known as the "Comeback Kid" for rallying after a disappointing start to his 1992 primary campaign, is someone I've always felt was particularly adept at not getting immobilized by setbacks. I think that set the tone for his entire administration and made it easier for him to accomplish his goals.

Being able to keep moving forward has been quite helpful in my own life as well, beginning in the Goldman Sachs arbitrage department, where we made frequent, large decisions based on probabilities. It was unavoidable that some of those decisions would turn out poorly. When that happened, I would try to think about it carefully and critically: Should I have done something differently? Is there some way I could have avoided the outcome that occurred? But after that, I would just move on. I wouldn't dwell. The same was true of positive outcomes: I tended not to get carried away when things went well.

I think that type of personality is necessary to make decisions at high levels over time. You must be able to learn from mistakes, but you can't obsess over them. You have to clap your hands together and say, "Okay, that's the past. On we go." The same is true of successes—you can't let them create overconfidence, or lead you to rest on your laurels. Throughout my life, I've endeavored to make the best decisions I could. Some of them worked out the way I hoped, and others didn't. Regardless of the outcome, I tried to examine what went right or wrong so that I could learn for the future—but then I moved to the next challenge and the next decision.

Another element of mental toughness is the ability to weather criticism, particularly public criticism. A free press is vital to our democracy, and often when a public figure is being criticized in the media, the critics have a point. But I think the media also frequently sensationalizes and oversimplifies. Public criticism can undermine some people's ability to function, and probably almost everyone who experiences it is troubled by it.

But effective decision-makers don't let such criticism derail their efforts. For example, I always admired the way Tim Geithner, serving as Treasury secretary during the Great Recession, kept his head while pursuing an unpopular policy to support the financial system that was excoriated by both the right and the left. I'm sure the negative attention bothered Tim at times, but he didn't let it affect his judgment, and in the end his actions helped stabilize the markets, prevent the Great Recession from becoming even worse, and promote an economic recovery.

An additional common link I have noticed in people who are highly successful, albeit one that is hard to define, is the ability to get things done. That might sound amorphous—after all, all of us sometimes get things done and other times fail to. It may also sound redundant—accomplished people, by definition, have accomplished things. But having worked with many people who seem to possess this trait, I don't think it can be disregarded. Some people have a sense for the mechanisms and processes by which ideas become reality, and are able to effectively shepherd those ideas in ways others cannot.

One of the best examples I can recall of someone with the ability to get things done is my former chief of staff at Treasury, Sylvia Mathews. Regardless of the goal or proposal we had in mind, I could trust that Sylvia would understand the different avenues to take that would help us get there. She seemed to have a sixth sense about whom we should talk to, whose opinion might carry weight with whom, and in which order we should implement given decisions or ideas. And that innate understanding served her well not only when we worked together, but when she went on to other senior roles in the Clinton White House, and later became the director of the Office of Management and Budget and then secretary of health and human services under President Barack Obama.

Another trait I believe is partly responsible for my life taking the direction it has is what I call "energetic curiosity." Most people are curious to some degree or another, but when I say that someone has energetic curiosity, I'm describing something different.

One distinguishing feature of energetic curiosity is skepticism. Many people, in my experience, tend to take things at face value. I'm just not built that way. My instinct is to look under the hood. I took a legal accounting course in law school, and while the professor familiarized us with the basic principles of accounting, the most important thing I learned was to look underneath the numbers to see what was really going on. When Gus Levy was running Goldman Sachs, he built skepticism into the firm's culture, frequently reminding those around him, "Never assume anything."

Approaching subjects with constructive skepticism is not just a good way to handle oneself in business—it's a good way to go through life. Look into things. Figure out what questions should be asked. Probe to find out what is really happening. You reach better decisions and deepen your understanding of the world.

Energetic curiosity is active rather than passive. Lots of people have questions. But those with energetic curiosity *pursue* questions—if they can't figure out an answer, that only drives them to explore further. For example, during the pandemic I was talking with Drew Faust, the former president of Harvard, and for whatever reason we wandered onto the subject of national identity. Was the United States losing its sense of having a shared set of values, and a shared national unity and confidence, and if so, what did that mean for the country's future?

Our discussion of national identity could have ended when our conversation did. But instead, it led to a series of Zoom calls hosted by Drew, me, Tim Geithner, and the businesswoman and philanthropist Marie-Josée Kravis, and which brought together a small group of leading figures from academia, government, the military, business, and media. None of this was for any professional purpose—we just thought the subject was important, so we put together a thoughtful group to discuss it further. Unsurprisingly, we haven't arrived at any definitive answers to the questions Drew and I initially raised. But the exploration has nonetheless provided a broader understanding of the issues involved, and it's been both thought provoking and illuminating.

A final distinguishing feature of energetic curiosity is eclecticism. In my experience, many people have what I would describe as linear curiosity. They want to know about things that are directly relevant to them: their work, their professions, their families, and their hobbies. But energetically curious people are often interested in an enormous range of things, not just those most closely relevant to their lives. I think I could fairly describe my own curiosity as eclectic.

For example, I don't choose books because I think they'll be valuable in some way, and I seldom read ones about business, finance, public policy, or economics. Instead, I pick up whatever piques my interest as I wander through a bookstore, which generally means I'm reading several nonfiction books simultaneously, and often one novel as well. (As I write this, some of the books on my night table are a collection of short stories by Edith Wharton; a nonfiction book about the year 1215; a spy thriller; a historical reexamination of Henry Kissinger and those who shared his worldview; and, perhaps appropriately, the anthology *Reading for Pleasure*, compiled in 1957 by Bennett Cerf.)

To the extent that energetic curiosity can be fostered in others, I have tried to foster it. For example, at Centerview Partners, an independent investment banking firm where I serve as a senior counselor, young people will sometimes ask me for career advice, and I tell them what I used to tell young people at Goldman Sachs.

First, do your job and learn to do it well. But then get involved in activities outside of your business. You'll learn about other parts of the world in which you live, and you'll meet people from other walks of life.

It is true that expanding one's horizons in this way can sometimes be beneficial for one's career. Understanding the world outside of your business and gaining exposure to people with other interests and perspectives can help you in engaging with clients or making decisions. But that's not the reason I give young people this advice. I know some people who are very successful by external metrics who are broadly involved; I know others who are not. I just think a broad involvement with the world makes life much more interesting and fulfilling.

Another trait that I think bears a great deal of responsibility for my life's trajectory is a basic disposition to be true to myself. Being true to oneself can involve big, important issues—but it can also involve situations where the stakes appear to be quite low.

For example, shortly after I left the Treasury Department, I took on a role as a senior adviser at Citigroup. Citi had recently merged with Travelers Insurance Group, and in my new role I helped the two co-CEOs of the newly merged company work together. I also met with clients and potential clients, helped Citi form a management committee, and weighed in on broad strategic matters.

It's not unusual for firms to hire people for these kinds of advisory roles, but because I had until recently been serving as Treasury secretary, my hiring received extensive press coverage. The firm had arranged a press conference, and before it began, I was standing backstage with Sandy Weill, one of the co-CEOs of Citigroup, who was known for having an extremely forceful personality.

Right before we stepped out into the room packed with

reporters, Sandy handed me a small pin shaped like a red umbrella, the firm's logo at the time.

"Here," he said, "put this on."

The pin was not large or ostentatious. Sandy was extremely proud of his company. To put the pin on would not have inconvenienced me in any meaningful way, and he would have appreciated it.

But without having to think about it, I had a clear sense that I was not the kind of person who felt comfortable wearing a corporate logo. Furthermore—and this is the important part—I've never been the kind of person who does things the kind of person like me doesn't do. Put more simply, the umbrella pin just wasn't me. So I declined Sandy's offer and walked onstage pinless.

In theory, being true to yourself sounds straightforward. In practice, it can be quite complex. I've spent my life in and around organizations. I've seen how much excellent teams, whether small or large, can accomplish. I enjoy working with others. And I've served in many roles in which I was not the ultimate decision-maker and didn't always fully agree with the decisions that were made. I've had to figure out how to express my own views while still being helpful to the group, or at times, how to support a decision I didn't agree with without saying anything I didn't believe. Moreover, even when I have been the most senior person on an issue, it has sometimes been constructive to adjust my decision in ways I didn't totally agree with after taking others' views into account, because it was important to get buy-in or promote a sense of collegial engagement while remaining true to my views.

Here, then, is the real challenge of being true to oneself: how to maintain one's sense of self, intellectual integrity, and independence while still being part of something larger.

Faced with such a challenge, many people find it easier to (figuratively speaking) wear the umbrella pin, even when they have a strong sense that it's not something they would do. Others avoid this dilemma by never having strongly held views to begin with. I remember being in certain White House meetings where some officials seemed to me to be saying whatever they thought President Clinton wanted to hear, rather than expressing—or perhaps even forming—their own opinions. (Ironically, saying exactly what you thought the president wanted to hear was a good way to lose his respect.)

I can see why such a strategy might be convenient, particularly in the short term. But I think there is a tremendous professional danger in expressing views one does not hold. Whether in government or anywhere else, I've always felt that my responsibility was to contribute to reaching the best possible decision—and that meant giving my honest opinion. To do otherwise would be detrimental to the organization I was part of.

At the same time, being true to oneself does not preclude thinking carefully about how best to express one's views. When I worked in the White House and at Treasury, my team and I would give the president the best recommendation we could based on the available facts, whether or not we thought the president would like it. That's what he expected. But if we knew we were telling the president something he might find difficult to hear, or even not want to hear, we would think about how best to explain our points in ways that were diplomatic and that he would be most likely to relate to.

An old friend, the late Bill Lynch, once elaborated on this concept when he was serving as a deputy mayor of New York. "Sometimes you have to say one thing before you can say another thing," he told me. That advice has proven useful whether I was speaking to the president of the United States, colleagues in business, or friends in a social setting. I wouldn't deviate from what I thought, but there's a big difference between saying "You're wrong, and here's why," and saying "You know, you've got some good points and your view could be right. I happen to think on balance it's not right in this case, and here are my reasons."

When giving feedback to others, it is similarly important for tact and diplomacy to go hand in hand with being true to oneself. While I've frequently had to deliver criticism to someone who reports to me, I've tried to start by saying several positive things before saying the negative thing. This isn't disingenuous. I wouldn't say something positive that I didn't believe. But by thinking carefully about how my criticism was presented, I could deliver the necessary message while making it more likely that the other person would receive that message without getting unduly anxious, defensive, or antagonistic.

Of course, on some occasions, you may say whatever it is you believe, and the ultimate decision-maker nevertheless chooses a course of action with which you strongly disagree. This is another situation where being true to oneself presents a complicated challenge. Consider the debate over what was widely known as "welfare reform" that occurred during the Clinton administration. I was opposed to the plan because I thought it could lead to people falling through the cracks of the country's social safety net programs. I also doubted that the plan's requirements for welfare recipients to seek jobs would lead to meaningful increases in employment. I expressed my objections in a meeting of senior administration officials in the Cabinet Room. But President Clinton ultimately decided to pursue the legislation, and in 1996 he signed the Personal

Responsibility and Work Opportunity Reconciliation Act, answering his campaign promise to "end welfare as we know it."

The debate over the issue, and my role in that debate, illustrate a common problem. When your organization does something you disagree with, how can you help implement a decision you don't support while still remaining true to yourself?

One temptation is to avoid having to grapple with this question by changing your view to match the leader's. On occasion I've seen people say what they believe, and sometimes even clearly articulate the reasons for their beliefs, only to completely reverse their opinion when the ultimate decision-maker reaches the opposite view.

That kind of malleable thinking is by definition not probabilistic. One's estimate of probabilities and outcomes shouldn't change merely because the person in charge happens to judge them differently. That's another danger of failing to be true to oneself in these kinds of group settings: in an effort to be accommodating, and to avoid the emotional discomfort that comes from disagreeing with those around you, you can lose track of what you actually think, which impairs your ability to make sound decisions.

A better alternative is to separate one's actions as a member of the group from one's views as an individual. If a matter of fundamental principle is involved, that may not be possible. For example, if President Clinton had ordered me to fudge or misrepresent numbers (which he never would have done), I would have resigned. But in most cases when you disagree with an organization's decision, the challenge is to figure out how to support that decision, and sometimes even how to do so publicly, while remaining true to yourself.

After President Clinton signed the welfare reform bill, for example, I never would have said anything in public, whether to
reporters or in speeches, praising the new law in a way that didn't
reflect my true beliefs. At the same time, I also wouldn't have
publicly said, "I disagree with the president," because that's not
really an option while serving in a public position. Instead, I
would have talked through the various problems with the social
safety net, and the administration's overall goals, in ways that were
broadly supportive without expressing any views that weren't
mine. In the short term this would have been more difficult than
pretending to hold the president's view, or retroactively adopting
it just so that I was not out of sync with the ultimate decision-
maker. But it would have been worth the effort. (Fortunately, as
far as I can remember, no one ever did ask me about the topic, so
I never had to walk that particular tightrope.)

Being true to oneself may not be easy, but in my experience
it carries many benefits. For one thing, people generally—though
not always—tend to respect honesty, as long as it's presented in
a tactful way. Not every leader is as open as President Clinton was
to unfettered debate, but if you have the misfortune of working for someone who reacts badly to your saying what you really think, that is probably going to be an untenable situation
over time.

Another benefit of being true to yourself is that you don't have
to remember what you've said before; all you have to know is what
you think. You don't have to strategize about the views you express, because, again, you know where you stand, and everything
you say and do flows from that. That doesn't mean one's views
can't change over time or as you take in new information, rather
than digging in for emotional or tactical reasons. But by being

true to yourself, you can be clearer and more consistent in expressing your thinking, even as you leave room for it to evolve.

Being true to oneself is particularly important for those in leadership positions, because people tend to remember exactly what leaders say, long after the leaders themselves forget. If you say only things that reflect what you think, it's much easier to lead people in the same direction.

Another aspect of being true to oneself is acting with professional integrity. My father used to tell me that he always paid his taxes the way they were supposed to be paid—never cutting corners or exploiting legal gray areas. He cared about doing the right thing. He also didn't want to have to go through life worrying about whether someone would uncover an impropriety or misdeed.

Whether because of nature or nurture, I've taken a similar approach. I suspect that, like my father, I'm driven by a mix of motivations: Primarily, I hold the normative view that cheating financially is intrinsically wrong, and I would therefore feel uncomfortable doing it. But also, as a matter of self-interest, I wouldn't want to go through life constantly worrying about getting caught.

I have, at times, encountered people who don't share these concerns. Once, when I was just starting my career at Goldman Sachs, we were trying to do a piece of business jointly with another investment bank, and I went to see a senior partner there. I mentioned some problem or concern that had come up that might cause the client not to proceed with the transaction we were working on, and this person said, "Well, we'll just tell the client X, Y, and Z." Then he made up some story that would be quite reassuring to the client and lucrative for us, but was not true.

As it happened, this senior partner I had gone to see was a

difficult man—and he was also quite friendly with the head of our firm, Gus Levy. But I just didn't feel right going along with his suggestion. "We can't tell them that," I said. "I don't think it's true." He got really angry with me. I left his office, and by the time I got back to Goldman Sachs, he had called Gus and told him I should be fired because I was unwilling to do something that would have gotten us business.

Fortunately, while Gus could sometimes be hard to work for, he had a strong sense of professional integrity, and he dismissed his friend's suggestion to fire me with a laugh. I was lucky to be working with someone who cared about making money, but who was not willing to do so at the cost of dishonesty. If Gus Levy had been a different kind of person, my career might have taken a very different turn at that moment.

Which brings me back to Mrs. Collins' question. For the most part, my motivations for exploring how I became what I became are personal. I think I've led an interesting life, and I find examining that life interesting in its own right. But I also think that, in considering the role of both luck and personal wiring in the more than seven decades since I sat in Mrs. Collins' classroom, two implications become clear—one in the realm of policy, and another involving individual behavior.

The policy implication has to do with the relative importance of luck, as weighed against other factors, in determining a person's well-being and impact in society. Earlier, I mentioned my work with the Local Initiatives Support Corporation. I've seen the way that organization makes a difference in the lives of people in lower-income communities around the country—by financing supermarkets in "food deserts" that lack places to buy fresh groceries, turning derelict industrial buildings into spaces for small businesses and entrepreneurs, renovating large blocks of housing, and much more.

My work with LISC has also helped me understand in a more concrete way what I have long believed on an intellectual or theoretical level: far too many Americans have the misfortune to be trapped in a vicious cycle of poverty and, with too few exceptions, are unable to break out of that cycle for themselves and their families, no matter how talented they are or how hard they are willing to work.

Our society has made real, historic progress during my lifetime—when I sat in Mrs. Collins' classroom, it was part of a still-segregated school system in the South. At the same time, we still have a tremendous amount of work to do. In some respects, due to multiple factors—including globalization and automation, which have eliminated many good jobs in manufacturing, and the lack of policies to effectively address these dynamics—the cycle that keeps far too many families trapped in poverty for generations has become worse in recent decades. According to an analysis conducted by the lab of Harvard economics professor Raj Chetty, the odds of a child from a low-income family earning more than their parents at age thirty have decreased since I was a boy. Children born in America today remain subject to what is sometimes termed the "zip code lottery," in which the neighborhood and circumstances of one's birth—which are clearly beyond anyone's control—have an enormous amount of influence over one's future prospects.

There are obvious reasons for those who have already been successful to want to believe we are living in a pure meritocracy. But while personal abilities and work ethic do matter a great deal in determining one's success within our economy, luck continues to play an outsize role. And this has enormous negative implications for our society, because there is a huge cost to not doing all that is practical to equip all our people to succeed in the mainstream economy, and there is a huge benefit to be realized by doing so.

It's unlikely we'll ever fully realize how much has been lost because so many of us have been left behind. We will also never completely remove luck from the equation. But it seems to me that an important goal of economic policy should be to reduce the role of luck and to increase the role of talent, personal qualities, and hard work in determining one's odds of success.

Just as considering the role of luck has implications for policymakers, considering the role of people's wiring has implications for individuals. I would never suggest that I have a complete understanding of why my life has played out as it has, or that the qualities I identify are necessary for success. But I do think that the attributes I've identified as particularly important in my own journey—intensity, the ability to keep one's head, energetic curiosity, being true to oneself, and professional integrity—are qualities that anyone would find useful to adopt, regardless of where they are in their career.

Of course, this leads to the question of whether such characteristics can be acquired, or whether they're innate. I think the answer is complicated. Throughout my life, I've seen many people change—and I myself have changed in meaningful ways. At the same time, I have come to believe that at a basic level, people tend to be who they are. In most cases, the way someone has behaved is a good predictor of how they will behave.

I'm particularly skeptical of the idea that people can change quickly. There's a tendency to expect that a new location, a new job, or a new hobby can transform you into a different person. I've seen firsthand how a break in familiar routines and habits can improve one's mood and provide temporary relief from stress. But while you may be able to escape your circumstances, you can't escape yourself.

I remember making a version of this point at Treasury to Sylvia Mathews. Late one week, she came to me and said, "I'm exhausted." This was understandable—the job she held was relentless, and she worked tremendously hard. She told me she planned to go to Paris for the weekend to get away. I encouraged her to go (not that she needed my help deciding that spending forty-eight hours in Paris was a good idea).

But for whatever reason, I felt the need to augment my encouragement with a prediction: "I think what you're going to find when you go to Paris for the weekend is that you take Sylvia with you." If you're wired a certain way, there's no fundamental getting away from it.

Having said that, I don't believe that one's wiring or psyche determines the entire course of one's life. I've seen some people who did make significant positive changes in their behavior, with notable results. In some cases, they worked hard and examined themselves over long periods of time in ways that allowed them to draw out their most effective traits and suppress whatever might have been holding them back. In other cases, something has seemed to spark a dormant quality or set of qualities, a latent internal capacity.

That's why I believe Mrs. Collins' question is relevant not just to those looking back on decades of experiences, but to anybody, at any point in their life or career. We become what we become in part because of the way we're wired. But within that context, we also become what we become because of our choices: the way we meet challenges, the traits we cultivate, and the qualities we amplify throughout our lives.

Chapter IV

EMBRACING HUMAN
COMPLEXITY

In the 1980s, Larry Bossidy, who at the time was the second in command at General Electric, came to Goldman Sachs to deliver a presentation about management to the firm's partners. GE was a big deal in those days, and Larry was an important and respected figure in American business, so we were very interested in hearing from him.

Gathered in the partners' meeting room, we listened as Larry described the lessons about managing people he had learned in his role. I don't recall many of the specifics, but I do recall being struck with an overriding reaction: "Almost none of this relates to us."

That may have been an overstatement, but in essence it was right. My reaction to Larry's presentation was not a critique of his success or his own skill at leading organizations. His principles worked well for him, and perhaps they would work well for people with similar personalities at similar companies. But it seemed unlikely that a list of specific management lessons learned at

GE—at that time a giant command-and-control corporation—could translate equally well to all other organizations, regardless of size or culture.

My skepticism of specific rules and highly detailed lists of dos and don'ts is one reason I tend not to read books on management. Nor have I generally reacted well to the limited amount of executive coaching I've been exposed to (with the exception of one very helpful, not-by-the-book consultant we retained at Goldman Sachs, whom I related to because he made practical suggestions rather than providing management dogma and because he was a good fly-fisherman). I'm not suggesting that such books and coaching don't work for some people, perhaps for many people. But in the previous chapter I brought up the idea of "wiring," and I don't think I'm wired in such a way as to find them personally helpful.

Despite this, I have spent an enormous amount of time thinking about how best to effectively manage others, not just in the private sector, but in the public and nonprofit sectors as well. People I've been responsible for managing have, in turn, gone on to manage major organizations, from large businesses to cabinet departments and universities.

In other words, while I'm skeptical of the idea that there are universally applicable management rules, I believe strongly that managing well requires a great deal of thought and that good managers are key in any organization. An effective approach to management is therefore extremely valuable, even if a long list of dos and don'ts is generally not. The heart of the broad approach I've chosen to adopt involves embracing human complexity: recognizing and engaging with the inherent strengths, weaknesses, and motivations of individuals, and then working to give them the best chance to succeed.

I would never say my approach to managing people is the only successful one, or even that it's objectively the best. But the way I've thought about management has been very helpful to me throughout my career, and I believe it could be helpful to other individuals and organizations, too.

My thinking about management can be traced back to an epiphany from early in my tenure at Goldman Sachs. In 1975, when I was the number two partner in the arbitrage department, I worked for someone I greatly respected, a man named L. Jay Tenenbaum. One day, L. Jay told me that he was going to retire, even though he was relatively young. Soon after, another senior partner, Ray Young, came to see me.

"You're going to run the arbitrage department," he said. "But the real question is: What do you want to do with your life? If you want, you can continue to run the arbitrage department for a long time. It makes a lot of money, and you'll do very well financially and do very well in the firm. But it's a limited activity.

"Or," he continued, "you can start to relate to other people, recognize that they have all their own problems and try to help them succeed, become part of management in a much broader sense, and start to play a much broader role in the life of the firm."

To understand what Ray was telling me, it's important to note that fifty years ago, the culture of Wall Street trading floors was very different—and much less civil—than it is today. I vividly remember a time when one partner was furious at another partner who had sold a position of his without his knowledge. The first partner approached the second while he was sitting in his seat at the trading desk, wrapped his hands around the man's neck, and started to choke him on the trading floor. The two men were quickly separated by Gus Levy, who was still running the firm at the time. He said something to the effect of "come on, boys," and then the workday went on as if nothing had happened.

This was a one-time event, not a regular occurrence. Even so, it epitomized the way trading floors functioned at the time. And while I myself never strangled anyone, I wasn't exactly sensitive to others' feelings or perspectives. On one occasion, someone from the corporate finance department came to see me while I was sitting at my desk in the trading room. The firm was trying to structure a security, and the team this person led was trying to figure out how the markets might react. This individual was very bright, but in this case I felt the issues had been thought through sloppily, or perhaps not thought through at all.

"Look, I'm not going to do your homework for you," I snapped. "You go back and do your own homework. When you're ready, come back."

Could I have handled the situation better? At the time, I didn't even bother asking myself that question. I simply went back to work. This kind of blunt or even rude behavior never impeded my early success in the firm, but it was exactly the kind of thing Ray was saying I needed to change if I wanted to take on a larger role.

More broadly, by telling me that I'd have to think more about how I related to people if I wanted to manage them, Ray was making two very important points. The first is that success at a job does not necessarily translate into success at managing others. This point is often overlooked in organizations. People are promoted to management positions based on how effective they are at their operating role, rather than how effective they are, or are likely to be, at management.

Goldman Sachs was not immune to this mistake. Those who were terrific investment bankers often thought they should be managers and put in charge of a unit, and not infrequently they were given that chance. But in my conversation with Ray, he rightly pointed out there is a big difference between getting the best performance out of oneself and getting the best performance out of others.

The second point Ray made was, I believe, equally important: effective management requires one to understand that every individual is unique.

The idea that understanding individuals is an essential element of management may seem obvious. Yet my impression is that many managers don't fully embrace human complexity in their decision-making, even when they claim to and perhaps genuinely believe they do. Rather than truly acknowledging each person's combination of skills, motivations, and personal characteristics, and then considering those traits when dealing with each individual, it seems to me that managers often fall back on a set of practices that treats all employees the same way.

Obviously, in a large company, the top leaders can engage deeply only with the limited number of people who report to them. But I think a people-centered approach can be brought to even the largest companies by insisting that managers at every level adopt it. And I'm confident that in my own life and career, embracing the complexity of individuals has improved my decision-making as a manager.

For example, when my co-COO at Goldman Sachs, Steve Friedman, and I oversaw the firm's debt-trading activities, one of our young traders, Jacob Goldfield, occasionally refused to wear shoes on the trading floor.

Jacob was an extraordinarily bright young man, with the kind of mind that could identify gaps in thinking that others would miss. But on occasion he would arrive at our office building at 85 Broad Street, take the elevator to the fixed income department, and—at a time when business attire was far more formal than it is today—do his job in socks. Nor was this an isolated idiosyncrasy. While he has, in the decades since, grown as a person and become far easier to get along with, at the time he could be derisively critical of others, including the partners, and just generally difficult to deal with.

Some senior people, perhaps not surprisingly, took umbrage at this. But Steve and I had a very different view. We said to our colleagues, "Look, yeah, there are a lot of quirks and personality characteristics, but he really is smart, and he really is making a contribution."

"In fact," I told them, "I predict someday you'll make a partner of this guy."

The firm did in fact make a partner out of Jacob Goldfield, but I don't bring up my prediction simply because things happened to work out as I predicted. Instead, I believe it's a useful encapsulation of the way I think one should approach a task every manager faces: deciding who does—and who doesn't—belong on a team, and who gets advanced and who does not.

At many organizations, someone like Jacob might have had serious career problems, and perhaps even been demoted or dismissed. The traditional, strict, command-and-control theory of management may be out of vogue, but managers remain responsible for giving direction and their reports remain responsible for following that direction. With his penchant for challenging senior leadership and making life more difficult for those he reported to, Jacob's behavior might have been considered unacceptable.

Also, someone like Jacob might have bothered people on a personal level. It's natural to make management decisions based on feelings toward individual employees, and to want to reward those you enjoy being around and not those you don't.

So long as there are no ethical or legal issues at play, my view is that the criterion that should guide all personnel decisions is whether the person in question is helping or hurting the organization's long-term success and, in the former case, by how much. In Jacob's case, I felt strongly that he brought a great deal of value to Goldman Sachs.

What makes this question of long-term value complex, and what might make some people uncomfortable, is that any answer is at least partly subjective. When Jacob was difficult with people, I could say, with 100 percent certainty, that his behavior was counter to the culture we worked to maintain. But could I say with similar certainty that Jacob's insights and skill greatly outweighed the costs of his difficult behavior? I could not. I could only make a judgment.

Some might feel that my attitude allows certain people to get away with difficult behavior just because they're talented. As it happens, I was never personally bothered by Jacob's behavior. In fact, I got along well with him. As with many other people I've enjoyed working with and highly valued throughout my career, he was very bright, thought outside the box, and tempered his idiosyncratic personality with a well-honed sense of humor, including about himself. But other people found him disrespectful and hard to deal with. Is it fair that off-putting behavior should be accepted if someone is particularly talented, but not accepted if they're less outstanding?

My answer would be yes. Organizations aim to further their goals. It's true that if an employee or team member is abrasive on occasion, their behavior makes it harder to achieve those goals. It's also true that some lines must be drawn—if a person is engaging in abusive or predatory behavior, no amount of impressive job performance can or should outweigh that. But if those lines are not crossed, the issue then becomes whether the positive qualities a person brings to the organization outweigh the negative ones. If Jacob had made it difficult for other people to do their jobs, rather than merely bothering them, I might well have felt differently about him. As it was, I felt the benefits of putting up with his eccentricities far outweighed the costs.

I remember making a similar judgment regarding a colleague at the Treasury Department—she could at times be harsh with people, but she was highly effective. When people complained, I would say, "Okay, so you don't like something about her. But look at how effective she is and how much she contributes. Why worry about it?"

Organizations I have been involved with have benefited greatly when there has been a willingness to have difficult personalities in important positions, including at the very top. However, it is crucially important to take steps to help minimize the likelihood that conscious or unconscious biases are affecting who is considered "difficult" and who is not.

Just as managers should be willing to tolerate somewhat off-putting behavior from people who otherwise contribute a great deal to the organization, managers should be willing to make difficult decisions—regarding compensation, responsibilities, and sometimes even employment—about people whom they like personally but whose contribution to the organization is inadequate. I remember someone at Goldman Sachs who was extremely well liked and was up for partnership, but his work was relatively pedestrian and far from the level we expected from partners. It was an uncomfortable decision, but we didn't make him a partner, even though everyone enjoyed working with him. In such circumstances, it's critically important to put aside one's personal feelings, because carrying people who are not sufficiently effective in their jobs is a detriment both to the functioning of the organization and, ultimately, to the morale of those within it.

Such an attitude may sound too hard-nosed, but I think determining compensation, promotions, demotions, and the like on the basis of each individual's overall contribution is fundamental both to organizational success and to best providing opportunity and work satisfaction for the greatest number of individuals on a team.

Yet even as managers must approach their work in a fairly unsentimental way, they must also recognize that we are all fallible. In my experience, it's important for managers to be supportive when someone they are managing makes a mistake, especially if that person is feeling anxiety about having made it. The same pragmatic approach that requires managers to be brutally honest in their evaluations about people requires them to be understanding when things go wrong. That said, it is important to determine if there are underlying problems with the individual's decision-making that need to be addressed.

One way I've often described management to others is, "You work for the people who work for you." No matter what happens, it's the manager's job to keep people feeling good about what they are doing inside the organization. When problems arise, it's the manager's job to think, "What can I do about it?"

This is why a defining characteristic of any manager is how they distribute credit or blame. Some senior people in organizations take credit for successes and divert blame, either as a conscious tactic or because of their preexisting personal tendencies. The best managers do the opposite.

L. Jay Tenenbaum was a perfect example of this type of effective manager. When I worked for him in the risk arbitrage department, I noticed that when he had to tell other members of the firm about a big loss, which inevitably happened from time to time, he never blamed people who reported to him, even though we had done the work and were responsible for it. If things went well, he gave us the credit; if things went wrong, he took the blame. And if he had a critique to make, he did so constructively and privately, rather than in front of his colleagues.

I don't know if L. Jay's approach toward those working in his department was a product of his innate decency or a careful management strategy. I suspect it was a bit of both. But I'm quite confident that L. Jay's style of management served the business well, by creating a collegial and trusting environment in which we could openly examine situations that wound up badly in a postmortem analysis without worrying about accusations of fault when someone offered a useful criticism. On a personal level, L. Jay's approach contributed greatly to my career at Goldman Sachs, because when things went well he saw to it that other partners knew of my involvement, and when positions went badly he put it on himself.

I also learned a broader lesson about management from L. Jay, though I doubt if he himself was focused on it. In organizations, success accrues upward. If the group does well, it reflects well on the leader.

I have found that if leaders give credit to others, that also redounds to the leader's benefit over time. For example, when I served as the director of the National Economic Council, one of my two deputies was Gene Sperling, who was deeply knowledgeable about policy and politics, highly savvy politically, and totally trustworthy. When I left for the Treasury Department, he served as the NEC director for the remainder of President Clinton's presidency, and later he reprised that role for President Obama and served as a senior adviser to President Biden.

Still, back when he was serving as deputy director, I remember on more than one occasion coming upstairs to our offices, asking, "Where's Gene?" and hearing in reply, "Oh, Gene's briefing the president." What was happening was that the president was calling for Gene, and Gene was going straight downstairs to the Oval Office from our second-floor offices in the West Wing without informing me, which would have given me the chance to join him if I chose to.

I would guess that with some people, this kind of thing might have ruptured our relationship, or at least greatly strained it. But Gene is someone for whom I have always had a great deal of personal respect and trust. I could always be confident that he was focused on furthering the goals of the NEC and the administration, and that he was extremely well equipped to brief the president. I also recognized that the president's reliance on Gene was a good thing, both for the standing of the NEC within the administration and for my position as head of the NEC. I decided not to bring it up with Gene at the time, and I'm glad I didn't. The best managers, in my experience, seek to get the strongest people that they can find around them, rather than feeling threatened.

In calling Gene directly, President Clinton was demonstrating an aspect of his own approach to management: rather than follow the exact structure of an organizational chart, he relied on whichever individual he felt could be most helpful in a given moment. In my experience, this can be useful in getting the best results, but leaders must do it in ways that avoid creating organizational chaos or undermining the most senior members of their teams.

When I think about the value of looking past the organizational chart, I remember an instance from June 1970, when Goldman Sachs issued commercial paper—a form of short-term corporate debt—for a transportation company called Penn Central, and was sued after Penn Central went bankrupt. The suit was potentially serious, and it was seen by the partners as a real threat to the continued viability of the firm. They planned to use Sullivan & Cromwell, Goldman's long-standing, well-regarded, and highly capable law firm, to represent them. At the time, I was just a senior associate in the arbitrage department, and I had nothing to do with managing this litigation. Nevertheless, I went to Gus Levy and said I had views on the matter.

"There's just been a case where we had an arbitrage position, and Sullivan & Cromwell represented one of the companies involved, and I followed the litigation," I told him. "The judge in that case said that the partner at Sullivan, the same one who does Goldman's litigation work, was arrogant and unprofessional. I don't think you should use him."

In retrospect, this was a presumptuous thing to do. Gus, whose roughness and toughness were legendary, could easily have said

"Who the hell are you? Get the hell out of here. And don't bother me again." But instead, he listened to what I had to say. And on that basis, he went to see a friend of his who was a federal judge (one who, for the record, had nothing to do with the Penn Central case), and asked for his advice. The judge agreed that the Sullivan & Cromwell attorney in question was not right for this case, so Gus used a different lead litigating partner instead.

Sometimes, particularly in large organizations, relying on the organizational chart may be unavoidable. Organizations have to function in an orderly fashion. But there can be great value in doing, when possible, what Gus did when faced with a potentially fatal lawsuit and what President Clinton did when he called Gene: focus on the quality of the advice and ideas and not who offered them.

Disregarding the organizational chart can also be helpful when running meetings. Before I started at the National Economic Council, I asked people who knew President Clinton what he was like. I was told, "As long as you make sense and you're thoughtful, and you seem substantive and serious, he'll respect you when you disagree with him, even if he might ultimately decide you're wrong."

This turned out to be exactly correct. When President Clinton gathered advisers in the White House, he wanted to hear everyone's opinions and perspectives, including those of the less senior people. Just as important, when he made decisions he didn't take rank or title into account.

I tried to do the same thing when I was running the Treasury Department, and so did Larry Summers, who often ran meetings with me. I remember early in my tenure, during a meeting on our proposed Mexican support program, Larry stated his opinion, and other senior officials at the table either said nothing or agreed. Then, however, a more junior figure raised his hand, and explained why he thought Larry was wrong. I had the thought that the young dissident was about to have his head taken off. Instead, as I subsequently saw Larry do in many similar situations, Larry asked him to expand on his point.

Larry's reaction had three positive results. First, there was merit to the objections, and we made a better decision because of them. Second, it encouraged others to speak up when they had views at odds with more senior people. And third, I asked afterward who this young fellow was, and that became my first introduction to Tim Geithner.

Larry's willingness to listen to younger people gave us the opportunity to recognize that in Tim we had a major talent. Tim quickly became heavily involved in all of Treasury's international policy activity, and ultimately he became President Obama's Treasury secretary. Had Larry been more bureaucratic, we might have never discovered what Tim had to offer, which would have made our entire team less effective, and Tim might never have had the opportunity to play the major role that he wound up playing in U.S. policy-making in two administrations.

I understand why the natural impulse, when looking for input and contributions, is to simply rely on an organizational structure, implicitly assuming that the value of an idea is proportional to the rank of the person expressing it. In meetings of all kinds, the more junior people are generally expected to observe, not participate. But unless the highest-ranking people always have the best ideas, which in my experience is exceedingly unlikely, prioritizing the org chart above individuals means failing to get valuable contributions, and therefore making worse decisions.

One important caveat: I've never had much patience for people, regardless of rank or status, who speak up without knowing what they're talking about. But provided people are factually well informed, creating an environment where they feel they can express their views and ask for clarification, regardless of seniority, helps identify promising junior people. When I was at Treasury, I noticed that a relatively junior member of our team, Caroline Atkinson—who went on to serve as President Obama's deputy national security advisor for international economic affairs—would never let herself be steamrolled by her higher-ranking colleagues. If she had a question, she would raise it—and if the answer wasn't expressed in a way that made sense to her, she'd ask a follow-up. Or two follow-ups. Or three.

In some organizations, this kind of questioning might have been seen as inappropriate or intrusive, but I felt the opposite: her questions were very helpful, and the fact that she was willing to ask them gave me a great deal of confidence in her abilities and made our decision-making better.

At the same time, looking for the best idea regardless of where it comes from can be complicated. For example, around the time Steve Friedman and I began as co-COOs of Goldman Sachs, the firm was doing very well in its day-to-day operations. But we had learned from earlier senior partners, in particular John Whitehead, just how important it was to be strategic—to consider the long-term direction of the firm even as we dealt with the urgent challenges that arose. In this regard, we felt that Salomon Brothers and others were starting to outflank us, and that they were being more innovative than we were in certain respects, particularly in developing new financial products for corporate and investing clients. Steve was particularly worried about this. He said, "Look, you know, we're doing really well right now, but we won't continue doing well unless we become much more innovative and strategically dynamic."

The logical group to develop a new strategy would have been the management committee, which was made up of exceedingly capable people who headed the various segments of the firm. But for a variety of reasons, we felt they probably weren't the best suited to this particular strategic task. At the same time, we felt it would be a mistake to explicitly go around the management committee and to create a situation where they felt they were cut out of the process.

So we created a new committee, with a different name, co-chaired by Steve and me. We appointed partners who we thought would be particularly well suited to this effort, and that became our de facto strategic planning committee. And that committee then reported to the management committee. I think our willingness to seek out the best possible ideas for the task at hand was beneficial, even if it required some extra organizational effort and creativity.

I similarly believe that it is worth time and effort to foster the right kind of organizational culture. In my experience, culture is not something that just happens. Leaders need to sit down and figure out what it is they want their culture to be. Generally speaking, it flows from their own personal values and beliefs. People watch the leaders of the organization and take cues about all sorts of things: how to behave, how to treat people (including customers and colleagues), ethical standards, strategic focus, how to respond during a crisis or to someone making a mistake, and much else.

Different leaders have different ideas as to what type of culture they want to foster, and very different approaches can be successful. For example, former General Electric CEO Jack Welch, with his preference for a command-and-control structure, had a very different idea of what a culture should look like than someone like his friend John Weinberg, who ran Goldman Sachs during many of the same years Jack ran GE. But regardless of the specifics, strong cultures embrace what Steve Friedman calls "strategic dynamism," an environment in which tactics and long-term strategy shift and adapt, but core values and principles remain constant.

Without that kind of anchoring, organizations and the individuals who lead them can become unmoored and make decisions that are ultimately not true to themselves. In my experience, when leaders have inconsistency in adhering to values, people notice. As one friend puts it, "What you say today, people are going to be quoting back to you five years from now."

Even after leaders know what kind of culture they want an organization to have, it takes constant work to make that culture a reality. For example, not long after New York declared a lockdown to try to prevent the spread of COVID-19, I was talking with Blair Effron and Robert Pruzan, the co-CEOs of Centerview, the independent investment banking firm where I work as senior adviser. The firm had just moved its employees to remote work, and we were discussing what we needed to do to adapt. I remember that we focused not only on the technical and productivity challenges, but also on how to sustain our culture without everyone being in the same space. We were particularly concerned about incoming young people just starting their careers and lateral hires from other firms, who didn't know the people, the culture, and the ways of operating at our firm.

I didn't have an easy answer for this kind of dilemma, and

I don't think there is one. But I know it starts by consciously putting in effort to create and maintain culture, rather than hoping culture simply sustains itself. This is why, during the first few months of the pandemic, Centerview took various actions to try to instill its culture in new hires and reinforce it with everyone else. Blair and Robert would call key people just to check in and see how they were doing. Every other Wednesday we'd have a virtual town hall with an outside speaker to bring people together. It was impossible to fully replicate an office culture via videoconference, but what struck me was how much of an effort the firm made.

Culture is both a means to an end and an end in itself. For example, when Steve and I were leading Goldman Sachs, we wanted the workplace environment to be collegial and people to work together as much as possible. We wanted people to feel good about what they were doing, to feel appreciated, and to feel good about themselves. Above all, we wanted people to feel responsible for focusing on our clients and doing what was good for them in the long run. We believed that all of this led to a more successful firm. But it also reflected how we wanted to lead our professional lives, which had some intrinsic value because it made our work more satisfying.

Because we viewed culture as so important, it was a major consideration in our management decisions. For example, I always made sure to take culture into account in hiring. As I mentioned earlier, I was quite willing to work with people whom others sometimes found difficult. But if I felt that a person would deeply damage the culture of the group—if, for example, someone had a reputation for claiming credit for others' work or pushing people aside out of personal ambition—I wouldn't hire that person, even if he or she looked likely to be a strong performer. The likely costs outweighed the likely benefits.

I always felt the opposite principle was true as well: an employee who actively fostered culture was making a valuable contribution and deserved to be rewarded for it, even if that contribution was intangible. At Goldman Sachs, we used the term "culture carrier" for someone who embodied and promoted the kind of environment we hoped to create at the firm, someone who went out of their way to help others succeed even when it was not in their own immediate self-interest, and who could take their work seriously without being overly self-serious. Managers who had these characteristics could set the tone for people in the areas that reported to them.

"Culture carrier" wasn't an official designation, but positive effects on culture were a serious consideration when it came time to determine salary or yearly bonuses. In government, where culture carriers couldn't be rewarded with increased compensation, I nonetheless tried to reward them with recognition and, where it fit, increased responsibility. Sylvia Mathews, for example, was an important culture carrier when we were setting up the National Economic Council at the White House. She made people feel welcome, dealt with them graciously, and got the most out of them.

Along with recognizing and rewarding culture carriers, another way to foster a shared culture is to include younger people in meetings, even if their presence isn't strictly necessary. For example, the management committee at Goldman Sachs met once a week, and those meetings usually included a review of major transactions for clients. All we'd really need for these brief presentations was a partner and maybe one or two others.

But we sometimes went further. We would ask the partner

presenting to bring some younger people as well. Our reasoning was that we wanted people to feel part of a team and to feel part of the firm. This inclusion contributed to both. For the same reasons, we'd encourage partners to bring more junior people along on client meetings when appropriate. In those cases, we might not want lower-level employees to pitch in during the meeting in front of the client, because time is limited and having too many different people sharing opinions could be confusing. However, we saw their presence in the meeting as a valuable learning and morale-building opportunity, and we would encourage them to circle back and raise any thoughts later.

A final aspect of my approach to management is to ask questions rather than make statements. In the early 2000s, when I was starting my new role at Citigroup, there were regular meetings of a large group of the bank's leaders that I'd attend. Later I learned that Sandy Weill, the co-CEO, pulled aside Mike Froman, who had also come from Treasury to Citi, and asked, "Why does Bob ask so many questions all the time?" To which Mike replied, "That's just the way he is."

Mike knows me well. If I hear something, I start to wonder about it and to think about it. And when I think about something, I react largely with questions rather than opinions. My notes after meetings tend to include lots of question marks.

Most likely, my predilection for questions is simply part of my wiring. But it has been valuable to me as a manager. Most obviously, you learn a lot more that way. Also, genuine curiosity about people's work and thoughts tends to be appreciated and helps to build productive relationships. Even if people don't agree with the final decision, if they feel they've been heard, they're much more likely to buy into it, working to implement it even if it wasn't what they themselves would have chosen. Also, for leaders who are responsible for making the ultimate decisions, questions are often preferable to statements because they draw people out.

For example, I've noticed that in many meetings, the decision-maker tends to state their views first, and then let others follow. But I feel that running meetings by asking questions, letting others state their opinions, and only then stating my own opinions elicits more input from others and leads to a more productive discussion and better decisions.

Even when I want to make a point, including one I feel strongly about, I'll frequently phrase my view as a question. Instead of saying, "It seems to me China's economy has an awful lot of problems," I might just say, "Does China have more problems than most American investors think?" This way of engaging seems to draw people out to express their views and to stimulate further thinking. Sometimes their thoughts will differ from mine and I'll decide they're right and change my mind. Other times those views don't seem persuasive, which will make me more confident in my opinion.

A real-world example of this kind of question occurred at a conference a few years ago. (This was the kind of gathering where participants are permitted to disclose broad descriptions but not identify their fellow participants by name.) A prominent business executive who was at the time serving in the Trump administration was talking about what he had learned—or perhaps hadn't learned—going from the private to the public sector. His point was essentially that the transition was easy, and that all you needed to do to be successful was to treat government like a business.

I, too, had gone from the private sector to government, and to say that I had a strong opinion about this person's point of view would be an understatement. I think leadership and management in government and business do have some similarities—so that experience from one can be useful in the other—but there are many fundamental differences. I think that when private sector leaders go into government, recognizing and responding to these differences is necessary in order to be effective. And I thought the speaker was hugely arrogant.

But instead of stating my views, I phrased my argument as a question, which was genuine but also pointed: "Now that you've done both, what do you think the differences are?" While I don't remember his answer, I recall that its vacuousness made my point better than any statement from me could have.

For what it's worth, here's how I would have answered that question myself, based on my own experience. First, businesses generally have simpler missions and organizational structures than government does. Private-sector organizations may have different strategies and products, and may belong to different industries, but they generally share an overarching goal: strong profitability over time. In government, on the other hand, there are always competing and valid concerns, ideologies, interests, and objectives.

Second, although private-sector organizations frequently employ more inclusive and consultative management practices than they did several decades ago, decision-making power still tends to be centralized and hierarchical. Even in a private partnership, which is how Goldman Sachs was structured when I was there, the people in charge were still in charge. The person running things could say to somebody, "Okay, we're going to do it this way," and the organization would respond, at least in terms of overall direction. In government, there is rarely a single, final authority, not even the president. Different branches, politicians, cabinet agencies, and bureaucratic institutions each have power, and for the most part leaders need to find ways to get them to work in concert if they hope to get things done.

Third, decision-making in government is subject to far more intense examination by and commentary from the media than most decision-making in the private sector. In certain ways the gap may be narrowing: business-focused cable TV, social media, and the growing pressure on businesses to serve broader social purposes beyond profitability increase the odds that a decision made in business will be subject to public scrutiny. But even so, government is a function that directly affects the public, often in highly palpable ways. The "shareholders" of government are in effect all Americans. And much of what government does is seen by the public through coverage in the media.

Government's intense ongoing involvement with the media is so different in magnitude from that of private businesses as to be different in kind—a routine government decision can, if it leads to a negative outcome, become a major national story. Moreover, the executive branch is subject to aggressive oversight from lawmakers, who can play an important function, but who can also be partisan and hostile, looking for opportunities to criticize or demonize. During my time in the White House and the Treasury Department, we were highly focused on how to best deal with the public perceptions and the coverage of our decisions by the media in a way that would not have been necessary in the private sector. That can be a big and complicated adjustment for leaders who move from the private sector to the public sector, and it took me a lot of time and constructive criticism to become at least moderately competent at it.

A final difference between public- and private-sector organizations is compensation. Private-sector managers can use financial incentives to help foster culture, reward top performers, or accomplish whatever else it is they want to do. For the most part they can promote, demote, or dismiss people in ways they believe further their organizations' goals. In the federal government, on the other hand, compensation for career staff is generally based on a pay system known as the General Schedule. In the cases of certain political appointments, prestige and power are a substitute for income in many ways, but even so, salaries fall into ranges that are set across the government, and they generally are not comparable with similar roles in the private sector. When I was at Goldman Sachs, if the firm had a good year, everyone got a bonus. When I was at the Treasury Department, if the U.S. economy did well, no one did.

In cabinet departments such as Treasury, managerial discretion and control is further reduced because most of the staff are career officials with civil service protections against transfer or removal. I was fortunate that Treasury had a very strong career staff, but if that hadn't been the case, there was little I could have done about it. There are very good reasons for an independent civil service in government—it helps keep public servants free of undue political influence—but this necessary independence creates a management challenge that does not exist in the same way in private companies, and it removes a useful tool for accomplishing organizational goals.

In other words, as complicated as management can be in

business, management is far more complicated in government. Yet when I went into public service, even though the specific challenges I faced became quite different, my underlying approach to management did not change. If anything, the absence of a straightforward, profit-driven mission and compensation tied to performance made management that acknowledged the complexity of individuals even more useful. Employee buy-in became even more necessary. Culture became even more essential to success. Surrounding oneself with people who were committed to the mission and to helping the organization achieve its goals became even more important.

Nearly fifty years after Ray Young pulled me aside at Goldman Sachs, here is the closest thing I have developed to a universal truth of management: While every organization is different, and each will have its own goals and challenges, one similarity they all share is that the individuals within them are endlessly complicated.

Managers who embrace that complexity won't make the right decision every time, but they will give themselves a far greater chance of success than those who do not. Given the enormous challenges that organizations, nations, and societies face in the coming decades—and the consequences of failing to meet those challenges—it's hard to overstate how beneficial increasing our chances of success would be.

・ Chapter V ・

APPLIED EXISTENTIALISM

On February 12, 1987, I was sitting in my office at Goldman Sachs with Senator Tim Wirth, a Colorado Democrat who was widely believed to have ambitions of becoming president. I forget what we discussed in our meeting. Perhaps that's because I so vividly remember how it ended.

Norma, my assistant at the time, opened the door. "Bob Freeman needs to speak with you," she said.

Bob had taken over the Goldman Sachs arbitrage department after I left it to become involved with the firm more broadly. I had great regard for him. Still, I was meeting with a United States senator, and I was surprised Norma was interrupting me.

"Tell him I'm with Senator Wirth," I told Norma. "I'll get back to him as soon as I'm finished." But she was firm. "No, it's urgent." So I picked up the phone.

"I'm at my desk. I'm being arrested for insider trading," said the understandably panicked voice on the line.

I told him we'd get in contact with the firm's lawyers. Then I returned to the senator sitting in my office. "The craziest thing just happened," I said. "One of my partners is being arrested."

He didn't miss a beat. "Oh, gosh, it's late. I've got to go," he announced. I don't know that I've ever seen someone leave an office more quickly.

The events of that day were memorable in part because they were unique. But almost all of us know the feeling of realizing we have a crisis on our hands. The stakes are high, the stress is enormous, and the path forward is suddenly unclear.

There is no one secret to managing these situations. There is, however, one crucially important question when a crisis hits: How do you make it through to the other side?

In the case of the arrest at Goldman Sachs, it would be hard to overstate how terrifying the circumstances were, especially at first. For one thing, at least at the outset, we weren't sure exactly what was going on, or how much trouble either our partner or the firm might be in. For quite some time, stories had been circulating that Ivan Boesky, one of the leading figures in the arbitrage business, was being investigated for insider trading. It would later be revealed that he had been conspiring with Marty Siegel, a banker at the firm Kidder, Peabody. In almost cloak-and-dagger fashion, Boesky would leave bundles of cash in an alley in exchange for tips from Siegel that were unavailable to the public. Then Siegel would go to the alley and pick up the cash.

Both men pled guilty for their role in the scheme and received prison sentences, which I think was clearly the right outcome. Insider trading is illegal, and for good reason. It undermines public confidence in markets, erodes the public's trust in our financial system, and provides an unfair advantage to those engaged in it. The authorities were right to prosecute Boesky and Siegel for what they had done, and to vigorously investigate the extent of the insider-trading scheme with which they had been involved.

But as would later be revealed, the authorities went too far. In their overzealousness, and spurred by false information Siegel provided in an attempt to reduce his sentence, prosecutors charged several people who were not part of Boesky and Siegel's scheme along with Boesky and Siegel themselves. All sixteen charges filed against Bob Freeman in the aftermath of his arrest would ultimately be dropped.

But at the time, we had no way of knowing how events would play out. All we knew was that one of our partners—and by extension Goldman Sachs itself—was in major legal jeopardy.

We were particularly concerned because the prosecutor targeting us was a young, ambitious U.S. attorney named Rudolph Giuliani. Already, Giuliani was known for dramatic, high-profile arrests and convictions, and there was speculation that some of his methods had more to do with launching his political career than with the evenhanded administration of justice. Decades later, Giuliani's grandstanding behavior and loose attachment to the truth would come to be seen by most observers as antithetical to the rule of law. And just two years after Bob Freeman was first charged, Giuliani would concede that, had he known all the things he subsequently learned, he would not have approved the arrest. But at the time, he was winning an enormous amount of praise for his aggressive style.

Over his career—whether he was pursuing large numbers of people, disproportionately from minority groups, for petty crimes as New York City's mayor; serving as the public face of President

Trump's false claims of election fraud; or investigating powerful and wealthy individuals at Wall Street banks for insider trading—Giuliani also proved adept at attracting major media attention. His investigation of Goldman Sachs was no exception. The morning after I received that frantic call and watched a senator make a hasty exit from my office, *The New York Times* ran not one but two front-page stories about Giuliani's stunning charges.

"The abrupt arrest of three prominent figures on Wall Street," began one story, referring to Bob and two partners at Kidder, Peabody, "indicates that the Government now feels it has the upper hand against insider trading abuses." The story included a chilling—and highly confident—quote from an anonymous source: "You don't arrest the head of Goldman Sachs' arbitrage unit unless you think you have him cold."

The other front-page story was, if anything, even worse. It included, in the fourth paragraph, a single sentence informing readers that all three individuals arrested denied wrongdoing. But surrounding that one sentence were paragraphs packed with detail that described Giuliani's charges against the bankers, including Bob. To anyone unfamiliar with arbitrage, insider-trading law, or Wall Street more broadly, it would have appeared as though prosecutors had an open-and-shut case.

Behind the scenes, we soon became convinced (correctly, it would turn out) that Giuliani's charges were baseless. Months before Bob was arrested, when rumors about the investigation had begun swirling, I had called Arthur Liman, who in those days was probably the premier litigator in New York, and asked him which attorney he would recommend to investigate any possibility of wrongdoing and to help the firm. He pointed us to Larry Pedowitz, who had served under Giuliani as the head of the Southern District of New York's criminal division before leaving for the law firm Wachtell, Lipton.

Larry turned out to be superb. After a thorough investigation, he reported back to the Goldman Sachs partners: there was no indication anyone had violated insider-trading laws or done anything else illegal.

Still, as an experienced criminal lawyer, Larry was far from sanguine. "If you're a target of an investigation," I remember him saying, "there's an 85 percent chance you get indicted. And of those who are indicted, the percentage who are convicted is very high." In other words, Larry cautioned that even though he felt Giuliani's charges were baseless, that might not matter.

(A similar line of reasoning would, a little more than two years later, lead to Bob Freeman's decision to plead guilty to one count of insider trading that had nothing to do with Siegel's plea or accusations, but which was based on unrelated information that came up during Giuliani's subsequent investigation. His lawyers believed Bob had done nothing illegal, but they advised him to plead guilty to a single count and go before a judge for sentencing, rather than face the uncertainties of a jury trial.)

Beyond a single partner's life and career being on the line—which was, of course, important—there was also a real possibility that prosecutors would go further and indict the entire firm. It was not at all clear the firm could survive such a charge. What's more, this occurred when Goldman Sachs was still a private partnership. This meant every partner's personal assets, inside and outside the firm, were at risk. If Goldman was held liable for legal wrongdoing, the partners might not just lose some or all of their stake in the firm—their personal savings and investments, and possibly even their homes, could be seized.

On top of all this, I had reason to be concerned that despite having done nothing wrong, I might find myself next on Giuliani's list. After all, the allegations against Goldman Sachs involved the arbitrage department. I was the former head of the arbitrage department, and I was still the senior partner to whom the department reported. If a politically ambitious U.S. attorney was looking for a bigger fish to fry, I was a logical target.

But even if you're not directly being targeted, all crises are in some fashion personal. They challenge not just organizations, but the individuals within them. Which is why I think the right approach to crisis management begins not with managing the crisis, but with managing oneself.

It's easy to imagine that the best leaders are completely impervious to fear and doubt, no matter how high the stakes. But that's rarely true. In a crisis, everyone has moments of high anxiety or fear. A deciding factor in a leader's crisis response is whether they can control that internal reaction, or whether it metastasizes into the kind of emotional state that affects their behavior and judgment.

I have seen people who are highly capable in most circumstances lose their heads when the stakes and pressure become too high. For example, in the earliest days after Giuliani issued his charges, I went with my co-chief operating officer, Steve Friedman, along with one other partner, to visit our law firm. We were concerned that—despite our full confidence that the firm had not engaged in any illegal behavior—clients might abandon the firm because they wondered if we could remain viable, or because they didn't want to be associated with the kind of situation we found ourselves in. Marty Lipton, one of the most well-known and important lawyers in New York City at the time, had agreed to give us a letter to address these concerns. I don't remember the exact wording, but in essence it stated that his firm had evaluated Goldman's actions and liabilities and did not think Giuliani's charges would be a threat to our viability.

This was a huge development for us—as Steve and I quickly recognized, this letter was something we could show to anxious clients to assuage their fears. But the other partner we had brought to the meeting became overwhelmed with anxiety. He started telling Marty all the reasons he was worried. Then he began fretting that perhaps Marty was making a mistake in giving us the letter, a view that was both unwarranted given the facts and diametrically opposed to the firm's interest.

I hasten to emphasize that this individual was otherwise someone who thought through issues carefully and whose judgment we could ordinarily rely on. In this case, however, the pressure and fear clouded his judgment. It's a situation I've seen repeat itself in a variety of fields.

It's important to note that irrational optimism is just as much a threat to decision-making during a crisis as irrational pessimism. Sometimes people lose their heads by panicking or becoming convinced that the situation is hopeless. But it is also possible, when faced with a seemingly overwhelming wave of challenges and potential consequences, to block out negative information and act as though everything's fine when it really isn't. In a crisis, organizations can't afford to have leaders who engage in either wishful thinking or doomsday thinking.

Keeping your head while being honest with yourself is therefore an essential component of crisis management. In the face of extreme uncertainty, and of possible outcomes that could be severely negative, you may have times when you feel deeply anxious, and perhaps even deeply frightened. But you have to be able to put those feelings aside, both in your decision-making and in dealing with those around you. You must find a way to recognize the reality of the situation, while coping as best you can in the moment.

I remember once, in 2009, I found myself at a reception before a public event with Tim Geithner, who was then the secretary of the Treasury, and Lloyd Blankfein, who was running Goldman Sachs. This was during the Great Recession brought on by the 2008 financial crisis, and both of them were frequently criticized in the press, albeit for different reasons. The public pressure was becoming quite severe. "You just have to kind of separate yourself from everything going on," advised Tim. "Say 'the hell with it.' Go ahead and do what you think is right."

Not everyone can maintain such poise. But those who can, like Tim, are best equipped to be effective in a crisis. These kinds of leaders aren't immune to pressure, but they rely on a variety of different techniques and personality characteristics to keep their heads clear amid chaos and stress.

Perhaps the most common trait of those capable of managing themselves during a crisis is an ability to compartmentalize. They can focus completely on a dire situation in front of them, putting aside anxiety and fear and anything else that might interfere with that focus. And then they can shut that compartment and move on, engaging with other aspects of their work without letting high-stress matters intrude.

Another way of handling pressure is to break down overwhelming challenges into smaller, more manageable tasks and more limited time periods. This is what I tried to do when Goldman Sachs was first targeted by Giuliani. Rather than ask myself, "How am I going to get through this?" I'd ask, "What do I have to do right now? What do I have to do today?" It's perhaps something of a cliché to say that it's important to "take life one day at a time," but it's my experience that during a crisis, the cliché is true.

For example, relatively early in the legal process that followed Giuliani's charges, I learned that I would be called to testify before a grand jury. I was being called as a witness, not as a subject or target of the investigation, but it was still a harrowing prospect. When you testify before a grand jury, you can't bring a lawyer with you, which naturally makes you feel much more exposed than if you had an attorney present. Moreover, even witnesses who are entirely truthful can find themselves in serious legal trouble. In theory, there's no such thing as unintentional perjury, but in practice, if you say something that gets interpreted in a different way than you intended, or new facts come to light that you didn't know about, you can find yourself facing the specter of perjury charges.

I would ultimately appear a total of four times as a witness before the grand jury, and I became reasonably comfortable with testifying. At first, however, I was so concerned about the experience that I considered taking the Fifth Amendment—not because I had anything to hide, but because I wanted to avoid any possibility of accidentally saying the wrong thing. Even after I decided to testify, I remained very worried about what could go wrong. Psychologically, it was extremely difficult to have the prospect of the testimony hanging over my head. But taking things one day at a time, or even one hour at a time, made it easier to handle my work and to help the firm respond to the crisis. I didn't find a way to avoid worrying completely. But by deconstructing my challenges into their constituent parts and focusing on the present, I was able to put my worries to the side and do what needed to be done.

Another crisis-management theory that is easy to understand but hard to put into practice is to keep things in perspective. As pressure builds, leaders can easily overestimate their own centrality in other people's minds. In the days after Giuliani made the arrest at our headquarters, I remember walking around New York and thinking that everybody was looking at me, or that everybody was thinking entirely about the *New York Times* article about a partner at my firm being indicted. But of course this wasn't true. Most of the time, most people are thinking about their own lives. Unless you're part of a truly enormous, all-consuming scandal, whatever attention people pay you and your predicament will be limited and passing. It's important to keep that in mind, because it helps reduce anxiety, which in turn makes it easier to make sound decisions and to go about your life.

Another way of maintaining perspective that I've seen many leaders employ is a sense of gallows humor, which they maintain while at the same time taking challenges extremely seriously and working diligently to solve them. Whether a penchant for this kind of humor is a coping mechanism, an inherent personality trait, or both, I cannot say. But I do think that even in serious situations, it helps decision-makers keep their heads.

Which brings me to the approach to managing oneself during a work-related crisis that I've found most useful, one I like to call "applied existentialism." I'm not referring here to the philosophical school of existentialism, which has its own definitions. Instead, I mean the ability to be fully invested in one's work while at the same time gaining some remove by recognizing that in a truly cosmic sense—in the fullness of time and space—the crisis, and one's success or failure in addressing it, do not matter.

When I was in college, and shortly thereafter, my version of applied existentialism was wrapped up in an escapist fantasy, one that involved sitting in Parisian cafés while living the life of the mind. "If this doesn't work out," I told myself whenever a particularly high-stakes academic or professional challenge arose, "I can always move to the Left Bank." I never seriously considered doing this, but my imagined life in Paris helped me recognize that even a worst-case scenario—say, flunking all my exams—could be mitigated. The world would move on, and so would I.

As I grew older, and the odds of living out my life in a book-filled Parisian garret went from near zero to truly nonexistent, I abandoned my Left Bank strategy for coping with stress. Instead, I began to use a different formulation: "This is highly important right now, but 100,000 years from now, none of it will matter."

This way of looking at consequences and pressures might at first sound empty. If nothing we do will truly matter in the long run, why bother? But becoming deeply invested in my work has never been a problem for me, nor, in my experience, is it a problem for anyone who is effective at what they do. And for me and many others I've observed, that sense of intense engagement is especially true in a crisis. The challenge is not to summon the adequate intensity, but rather to avoid becoming overwhelmed by it.

I've adopted this approach to crises outside my career as well. During the Trump presidency—and since, as Trumpism has continued to expand its influence over the Republican Party—I've been deeply concerned about attacks on our democracy, the continuing disregard of climate change, a lack of concern for the poor, the introduction of white nationalism into modern mainstream politics, and much else. These concerns have led me to become more active in efforts to protect democracy and to spend a considerable amount of time, effort, and financial resources supporting candidates and organizations that have opposed President Trump and his brand of politics.

Yet even before President Trump lost the 2020 election, I avoided being gripped by the kind of psychological duress that preoccupied some people in the circles I tend to be part of. Like them, I felt that Trump and Trumpism present an existential threat to our democracy—and perhaps even to our planet. But I was able to find a mental space that allowed me to remain focused on what I was doing. It might at first seem paradoxical, but by simultaneously investing yourself in and creating distance from your work, you can far more effectively function through a moment of extreme stress.

But applied existentialism—and managing oneself during a crisis—is only a starting point. One must also manage the crisis itself.

Managing during a crisis frequently involves a large number of public statements and communications with stakeholders such as staff, clients, customers, or creditors. But I believe it often begins with something more subtle: walking the floor. It's important to get out of your office and check in with people. The goal should not be to discuss the crisis, although one ought to answer questions about it if asked. Instead, what matters is that everyone feels in touch with leadership. People should know that the leaders of the organization are focused, and that they are paying attention both to the organization and to them as individuals.

Even simple interactions—"How are you doing? What's going on?"—can serve as a reminder that decision-makers are present, calm, and committed to working together through whatever challenges they face.

Of course, in a bigger company or organization, interacting with employees is complicated. And in a world still grappling with the effects of COVID-19, "walking the floor" might sometimes have to be done remotely, which presents a serious challenge. But even figuratively speaking, walking the floor encapsulates much of a leader's role during a crisis, and can include interaction with an organization's managers, meetings with groups, and the various means of communication afforded by modern technology. During times of great difficulty, leadership should be visible, recognizing the gravity of the situation while projecting a sense of stability amid turbulence.

Crisis management is not just a balancing act—it is multiple balancing acts, all of which must be performed at the same time. Among the most important of these is being simultaneously truthful and reassuring. When chaos threatens to engulf an organization, honesty is crucial. It might be tempting to tell people everything will work out perfectly, but if you lose your credibility and the trust of those around you, you lose your ability to lead.

Being honest does not mean that you have to say everything on your mind, or share every piece of information you have access to. If the fate of your entire organization is in jeopardy, you will undoubtedly be deeply troubled. But if you manifest that attitude around others, or if, in an attempt to be completely truthful, you dwell on your worries and fears, it can lead the entire organization into a downward spiral. In a crisis, you can't choose between maintaining credibility and projecting a sense of realistic confidence. You must do both.

As a practical matter, this means that during a crisis I might be less inclined to use the probabilistic language I otherwise find very helpful for decision-making. In the early days of the Giuliani investigation, for example, if someone had asked me, "Do you think Goldman Sachs is going to survive?" I wouldn't have given them a percentage chance, because this would have focused that person's attention on the nonnegligible possibility it wouldn't. At the same time, I wouldn't have said anything I didn't believe. Instead, I would have said something like, "We'll work our way through it. Nothing in life is certain, and we have a very difficult situation. But we've got terrific legal counsel, we've looked at this thing, and we're well positioned to handle the situation and move forward."

Another important element of managing an organization through a crisis is collecting all the facts you can and following them wherever they lead. Understanding what happened, and the potential legal ramifications of what happened, can be extremely difficult. But leaders, and the legal team if there is one, should also set about determining exactly what took place leading up to the crisis.

Conducting a thorough investigation makes it possible that some facts will be uncovered that cast the firm and individuals within it in a less-than-positive light. But there's no way around that kind of problem. In the midst of dealing with a crisis, the only thing you can do is acknowledge that it's impossible to know exactly what a thorough investigation may turn up, and tell everybody to be prepared. It's far better to pursue the facts than to remain in the dark.

Knowing the facts is particularly important if you're going to communicate clearly and honestly with the press, the public, creditors, employees, and all others. In my experience, it's also very important to maintain credibility with the media. In high-profile crisis situations, the media will largely determine how your situation is perceived, both within your organization and externally, and that can have a powerful effect on how well or poorly you fare. Interacting with the press therefore requires a lot of focus, along with a careful balance—you must always tell the truth, though you can refrain from saying everything you know as long as that is not misleading.

Of course, even when leaders deal with the media candidly and helpfully, the press can be unpleasant and oftentimes unfair. I'm a strong believer in the critical importance of a free press, but throughout my career I've felt that even news outlets that strive for objectivity can on occasion—and perhaps too often—sensationalize, exaggerate, take things out of context, and run with views that are poorly supported by evidence. The emergence of social media has amplified all these tendencies by orders of magnitude. But even if there's little you can do to shape a narrative, you have to try. The objective is to get your message across without being dishonest.

When it comes to media relations, much of what I learned came from my time in government. Goldman Sachs was frequently covered in the financial press, at times quite critically, but nothing prepared me for the scrutiny faced by high-level government officials and departments. When I was at the National Economic

Council, I relied on Sylvia Mathews and Gene Sperling to help me navigate interviews. Early in my time in the White House, I would say something to a reporter, and then Gene would say "Well, what he really meant to say was this."

Gene's comment frequently elicited a laugh, but he wasn't entirely joking. It soon became clear that my ability to deal with the media had room for significant improvement. On one occasion, I was part of a joint television interview with Pete Domenici, a New Mexico Republican who was ranking member of the Senate Budget Committee and one of the country's most powerful politicians when it came to economic policy. The interviewer asked something along the lines of "What is the Clinton administration going to do on taxes?" I went into a detailed answer: "We're increasing income taxes at the top end and that will contribute to deficit reduction . . ." Meanwhile, Senator Domenici just kept repeating the same point: "They're raising taxes. They're raising taxes."

When we finished, I thought I had done a very effective job explaining a complicated issue to the American people. "Boy, I did great!" I said to Gene.

"You know what people are going to take away from that?" he replied.

"No, what's that?" I asked.

"He's a nice, smart man and he wants to raise taxes."

Ultimately, on the advice of my White House colleagues, I went to see Michael Sheehan, a media trainer and speech coach who's worked with many of the country's most prominent Democrats, and he was terrific. When we met, I said to Michael, "I can't be anything other than myself."

He answered, "I'll show you how to deal with television. But you never have to be anything other than what you are."

Michael kept his word. Some of what he taught me involved the technical details of the medium. Since TV tends to make you seem less energetic, you're supposed to answer with more inflection than you normally would. And since television tends to make people look grim, it's good to maintain a slight smile, because that will appear neutral to the viewer at home.

Michael also worked with me on sticking to my message while still addressing a reporter's questions. This is a valuable skill, and to the extent I've learned it, I did so from a variety of experts in communications. George Stephanopoulos, who was then President Clinton's top communications adviser, used to say that "every question is an opportunity," and while some questions as stated may not seem very promising, in a sense he was right. David Dreyer, senior adviser to the secretary when I was at Treasury, helped me understand how to make the most of those opportunities. "Whatever you say," he explained, "connect it to the question. And then segue from there to whatever it is you want to say and wherever it is you want to go." In this way, a leader can use interaction with the media to steer the conversation while still engaging seriously with a reporter's own interests and priorities.

During a crisis, being able to deal with the press both honestly and strategically helps get an organization's message across. At the same time, it is important to recognize that even if you do this reasonably well, there is only so much you can accomplish. When George Stephanopoulos stepped down as director of communications and took a new role in the White House, a narrative emerged that he had lost the president's confidence, which wasn't true. He became the senior counselor to the president and was part of almost everything that went on. I remember asking him, "Why don't you just go out and rebut all that?"

"When you have a firestorm," George told me, "you can't do anything about it. The media gets caught up and it doesn't matter whether their narrative is right or wrong or anything else. It's just going to keep going until it peters out."

Something that can help an organization make it through a crisis is maintaining steady leadership—but unfortunately, in a crisis, that's not always possible. For example, about eight years after I became a senior adviser at Citi, the bank suffered very heavy losses during the financial crisis and the Great Recession that followed. Facing a public firestorm, the CEO, Chuck Prince, for whom I have great respect, resigned at the very start of the crisis. When Chuck left Citi, he felt that his position had become untenable, and I think he was probably right. But the lack of stable leadership presented an additional challenge as we tried to address the problems affecting the bank—both for the sake of its employees and shareholders, and because if Citi had not recovered from its severe financial difficulties it could have had a significant impact on the U.S. economy as a whole.

I'll have more to say about my experience at Citi in the next chapter, but as it relates to the discussion of crisis management, I should also point out that crises do not just threaten stability at the highest levels—they make it more difficult to retain talented people throughout an organization. At Citi, there was a risk that the people who could help turn the firm around might leave for other opportunities. One important way Vikram Pandit, who was chosen to succeed Chuck as Citi's permanent CEO, helped bolster morale and retain top talent was to cut his own salary to a dollar per year. I think that helped inspire others to stay and help the bank recover. It also indicated his confidence in the long-term prospects of the company.

In the case of Citi, regulators were also heavily involved. I've worked for both private institutions and government agencies, and I have great respect for people on both sides of the equation. Free markets can function effectively only with proper regulation. That's one reason I would advise someone in the private sector who is interacting with regulators to try to understand the regulators' interest and how to address it, to be completely transparent with them, and to tell them how you're planning to solve problems in a way that will be satisfactory to all parties.

Organizations facing a crisis must also maintain a clear distinction between those who are responsible for the day-to-day handling of the crisis and those who are not. It's important to designate a few members of leadership as the crisis managers, who will immerse themselves in that task—but it's equally important to tell all others to focus on doing their jobs. The organization must ignore distractions to pursue its business.

Putting all this together, it becomes clear that when a crisis hits, you need a plan adequate to the size of the danger you face. You need to decide who's on your crisis-management team; how you're going to handle clients, customers, creditors, employees, or other stakeholders; how you're going to deal with the media; and what the overall strategy is going to be. Yet at the same time, you must limit the extent to which crisis management distracts from pursuing your goals. You need to make sure the plan for confronting the crisis does not consume the organization before the crisis does.

After all, a return to normalcy is the ultimate goal of crisis management. And in some cases, individuals, companies, nonprofits, and even government agencies can emerge stronger than they were before. Lessons learned during one crisis can help prevent or mitigate others. Also, while the cultural aspects of a crisis can tear an organization apart with recriminations and finger-pointing if they are not well handled, the sense of solidarity that can develop during difficult moments can strengthen an organization's culture long after those moments have passed.

It's true that, 100,000 years from now, the ability or inability of a leader to manage grave and unexpected threats will not matter. But in the slightly shorter term, if we're going to handle the most pressing challenges facing humanity, it will be important that decision-makers are able not just to lessen the odds of a crisis occurring, but to handle it when one inevitably does.

· *Chapter VI* ·

HOW DO WE LEARN
FROM WHAT GOES WRONG?

In 1980, the Goldman Sachs arbitrage department—which I was running at the time—achieved a rather dubious milestone. We lost more money in just one month than the entire firm had ever made in a full year.

What happened, broadly speaking, was this: we had a large number of positions whose valuation was affected by the market's widespread expectation that inflation would go up. Much to everyone's surprise, the Fed chair at the time, Paul Volcker, raised interest rates dramatically, which sent inflation down. This meant the market value of our positions suddenly dropped as well—not by a small amount, or in an isolated case, but by large amounts across the board.

The firm held a monthly meeting of all the partners, who at that time numbered about seventy or eighty. As that particular month's meeting approached, I knew what at least one major topic would be: the enormous losses we were facing thanks to my department.

I don't remember exactly what I felt as I stepped into the partners' conference room. But I do recall thinking that the situation we were in—and my attempt to explain it—had the potential to be very difficult. For one thing, almost no one at the firm knew very much about risk arbitrage, which involves estimating the probability that an announced merger or acquisition will go through, and then buying or selling companies' stock based on that estimate. I had been living and breathing risk arbitrage, and it was a major profit center for the firm, but most of my fellow partners were investment bankers, which was a different world. Even John Weinberg and John Whitehead, the excellent leaders who were running the firm at the time, didn't really have a feel for how arbitrage works. They came from the corporate-advisory part of the business and had never been involved in the risk-taking side.

A further complication was that partners were personally exposed to the risks we had taken—as I've mentioned, Goldman Sachs was a partnership rather than a public company at the time. The capital of the firm, and thus the losses my department had incurred, belonged not to shareholders but to the partners.

Given the way my department had dealt a blow, at least in the short term, to the people in that room, it would have been completely unsurprising for them to order me to greatly reduce our exposure or even to unload all our remaining positions to avoid any more damage. I suspect that in most organizations, that's what would have happened, and perhaps my role in the firm or even my job might have been at risk.

But that's not what happened. Instead, we engaged with a pair of important and difficult questions, which all individuals, leaders, and organizations must eventually confront:

How do we learn from what goes wrong? And how should that affect future decisions?

Evaluating past decisions is one of the most crucial elements of decision-making, and one of the most frequently overlooked. A rigorous process of judging one's prior actions is critical to learning lessons that will improve one's future choices. Examining and analyzing past decisions is therefore both important and complex.

Yet remarkably, and worryingly in my view, many people I've encountered don't treat evaluating decisions as a terribly complicated issue at all. Instead, they focus simply, and almost entirely, on outcomes. In markets, they judge traders and investors by how much money they made. In business, they judge CEOs by whether a company had a good year or a bad one relative to the competition. When they elect or reelect presidents, they ask, "Are we better off now than we were four years ago?" I know from personal experience that a Treasury secretary whose tenure coincides with an economic expansion gets a lot of credit, perhaps more credit than he deserves.

When things don't turn out well, the same instinct that leads people to celebrate positive outcomes leads them to assume all negative outcomes are the result of poor decision-making. For example, starting about two decades ago, investment was flowing into what were called the BRICS countries—Brazil, Russia, India, China, and South Africa—based on the idea that these economies were all poised for rapid growth. In the years before the COVID-19 pandemic, serious problems developed in all but China, and many analysts and commentators turned critical of those who had supported the BRICS story and advocated investing in them.

In some ways, this kind of behavior—evaluating decisions based almost entirely on what occurs after those decisions—is part of human nature. (It seems especially prevalent in government, where the media and the opposition party jump into aggressive blame mode when things go wrong.) We pay a great deal of attention to the result that followed the decision while ignoring the quality of the analysis that preceded it.

This is a mistake. At the extremes, the problems with outcome-driven evaluation become obvious. If someone buys a lottery ticket and wins a million-to-one jackpot, many people might be impressed by, or envious of, the winner's good fortune. But almost no one would say investing in lottery tickets is a sound financial decision, or that the rest of us have a realistic hope of emulating the lottery winner's success. Instead, we would recognize the situation for what it was: despite the risk/reward odds being highly unfavorable, someone got lucky.

When it comes to evaluating decisions in nearly every other part of society, however, we tend to take a completely different and less intellectually sound approach than we do when evaluating lottery winners. We ignore the role that fortune plays in generating outcomes. Instead, we act as though there's a perfect cause-and-effect relationship between process and outcomes—that a positive result always stems from a good decision, and a negative result from a bad one.

This way of evaluating decisions isn't just misguided. It's dangerous. If you make the wrong judgments regarding past decisions, you draw misguided conclusions and are therefore likely to make worse decisions in the future, only with even more confidence.

To put it bluntly, the way that much of society performs one of its most important functions—learning from what has already occurred—is broken.

My concern about the way we rely on outcomes does not mean I ignore them completely. But I treat outcomes as only one factor in my evaluation process. I try to focus far more on the soundness of the decision-making analysis and process than on the result.

While there's no need for a Latin term for this, one stuck in my head several decades ago. I often use *ex post*—short for *ex post facto*, Latin for "after the fact"—to refer to evaluating a decision based solely on outcomes. I similarly use *ex ante*—"before the fact"—to refer to evaluating a decision based on the information available at the time, the analysis that led to the decision, and the judgments of probabilities made before the real-world outcomes could be known.

This last point is particularly important. Hindsight is twenty-twenty—or to put it in probabilistic terms, if an outcome has already materialized, the probability of it materializing is obviously 100 percent. But equally obviously, the probability was not 100 percent before the outcome occurred. An *ex ante* approach recognizes that it's important to consider the odds as they existed before—not after—the event.

Many decision-makers who adopt an outcome-driven, *ex post* approach fail to consider two broad ways in which results and decisions can be misinterpreted. The first is that you can be "right" for the wrong reasons—like the lottery winner, you can make an unsound decision that leads to a positive outcome. After all, if you forecast a once-in-a-century event each year, one year out of a hundred you'll be "correct." For this reason, it is not enough to evaluate decisions only when things go wrong. One must evaluate decisions when things go right as well.

Consider a personal choice I made early on in my career. In 1966, after two years at a large New York corporate law firm, I left to go to an investment bank, into a business called "arbitrage" that at the time I knew almost nothing about. Looking simply at how my life turned out in the following decades, an outside observer could conclude that I made a very sound decision. But in fact, I don't think that's the case.

For one thing, I hadn't wanted to go into risk arbitrage at all. I had applied for jobs in research or investment banking. But that was a different era, when financial firms were tiny compared with today and hired relatively few people, and hiring a young lawyer to go into investment banking was highly unusual. As a result, I hadn't gotten any offers outside of arbitrage.

What's more, the little I knew about arbitrage—namely, that it involved analyzing publicly announced corporate transactions and calling financial officers of the companies involved to discuss those transactions—seemed far removed from my experience (and when it came to calling corporate officers, outside my comfort zone as well). Nor had I investigated the business enough to understand that arbitrage involved constantly managing large risks and subjecting oneself to enormous pressures. I never performed my due diligence before embarking on a major career change. I never considered the probabilities that the move might not work. I just dove in.

As it happened, arbitrage was an excellent fit for me, analytically and psychologically. I became comfortable calling officers at various companies, and I found myself well suited to handling the pressures of the work. Also, as I mentioned earlier, arbitrage was a major profit center for the firm despite employing relatively few people. Had I gotten a job in research or investment banking, my career probably would not have been as successful.

But even though everything worked out very well, that doesn't change the fact that my decision-making process was badly flawed. I should have identified and studied the issues in advance, before entering what was then a relatively mysterious and esoteric business.

I was similarly fortunate in my fourth year at Goldman Sachs, when an old-line investment banking firm called White Weld offered to make me a partner if I joined them. I had expected to stay at Goldman for at least a few years, but I figured I'd never become a partner there, so I happily accepted the offer. Then I went to tell the partner I reported to at Goldman Sachs. L. Jay Tenenbaum was furious with me for not coming to him first. But fortunately, he and Gus Levy, who was running the firm at the time, wanted to keep me, and instead of saying the hell with you, they offered to make me a partner at year-end.

As it happened, White Weld suffered significant losses a few years later, when changes in financial market conditions and the industry threatened many long-established firms, and ultimately sold itself to Merrill Lynch. Had I gone there, my career might have been derailed. Goldman Sachs, meanwhile, did very well over time.

But again, just because the outcomes were favorable doesn't mean the way I went about making my decision was wise, or likely to work. I should have learned a lot more about White Weld than I did. And before accepting another firm's offer, I should have gone to L. Jay and Gus, explained the situation, told them how much I respected Goldman, and seen how they responded. Instead, I acted on insufficient due diligence and I took a path that was more likely to make L. Jay and Gus angry and less likely to be successful. I got the best possible outcome, but I didn't go through the best possible process to get there.

The danger of being right for the wrong reasons, and then drawing the wrong conclusions, is especially acute in investing. There's a thoughtful CEO of a highly respected and successful advisory firm for high-net-worth investors who once told me his firm invested heavily in the wake of the market collapse of 2008 and 2009.

"Markets come back," he told me, explaining his reasoning. "They always have come back. And so we bought."

His firm did very well with that strategy, since the markets did indeed come back. But my response to his comments—echoing my approach to tail risk, which I described earlier—was somewhat critical. "I think your thought process was wrong," I told him. "Because what you said was that markets will always come back, and therefore, you decided to buy stock. And while the markets have always come back in the post–World War II period, that doesn't mean they always will come back. The outcome came out right, and it may be that you would have reached the same decision if you had taken the right approach to evaluating the decision, but I don't think you did."

This was not just a matter of semantics, or of not wanting to give undue credit. If the lesson a firm learns from past crises is, "Markets always come back, so we should buy heavily during a crisis," there's a good chance that eventually, that firm will make a dangerous decision, take unforeseen risks, and lose a lot of money.

Of course, in the same way that you can be "right" for the wrong reasons, you can be "wrong" for the right reasons—that is, your reasoning is sound *ex ante*, but the outcome nonetheless turns out to be negative.

Just as with the example of the lottery winner, at the extremes this is a fairly easy concept to grasp. Let's say I offer you a bet: You write down a number between 1 and 10 on a piece of paper. If I guess the number, you give me a dollar. But if I guess any other number, I give you a dollar. You should obviously take this bet.

(A yellow pad would confirm the wisdom of this decision. Nine-tenths of the time, you would make a profit of one dollar. One-tenth of the time, you would incur a loss of one dollar. This means that, on average, you can expect to make a profit of 80 cents on the wager. When added to the dollar you started with, this leads to an expected value of $1.80. If you don't take my bet, you end up with zero profit or loss 100 percent of the time, for an expected value of $1.00, your original amount.)

If I guessed your number and you lost, you might be disappointed, but you wouldn't conclude that you were wrong to take the bet, and you wouldn't hesitate to take me up on my offer again.

Yet when it comes to far more consequential decisions, many people simply don't allow the possibility that someone made a good choice, one that had a high likelihood of leading to a positive outcome, and that some other outcome just happened to occur. Instead, out of a desire to avoid past mistakes, people avoid repeating whatever decision preceded a negative outcome—which, in some cases, may deter them from making a good decision in the future.

I thought about this challenge during the many years I chaired the Goldman Sachs compensation committee. As a practical matter, it was hard to do much when people were right for the wrong reasons—if someone makes a large profit for a firm even though their reasoning and their weighing of risks and rewards were deficient, they expect to see that profit contribution reflected in their bonus. If they don't see it, they tend to get quite upset.

But when circumstances were reversed—when someone had a bad year rather than a good one—I would try, when feasible given the limited time and large number of people working for the firm, to determine whether their poor performance was a result of poor decision-making or the result of a lower-probability negative outcome occurring. I would talk to managers and other people that person worked with, and I would ask them to describe their colleague's thinking. If I concluded that someone was a good decision-maker despite the negative outcome, I would try, at least to some extent, to make sure their compensation reflected that fact.

The ways in which I have attempted to account for the possibility of being wrong for the right reasons—that is, of outcomes being unfavorable even though the approach and thinking were sound—go beyond compensation. In the various organizations I've been a part of, if something went wrong, I tried not to assume that the person who was responsible was at fault. Instead, I sought to determine whether in fact that person made the right call, despite things turning out poorly.

I believe everyone makes mistakes, but this is a separate point entirely: everyone makes good decisions that at first look like mistakes, because they result in bad outcomes. On more than one occasion, I've told a colleague to take back an apology because in my view they made a sound decision, regardless of what happened afterward, and an apology would lead people to learn the wrong lessons for the future.

A recent example of being wrong for the right reasons, this one involving my own investment portfolio, came up a few years ago, during the first months of the coronavirus pandemic. At the time, I thought it made little sense that the markets were not reacting more negatively to the circumstances, so I bought a series of puts—basically a form of insurance—against the possibility of a severe, long-lasting market downturn. In the end, the markets recovered quickly after an initial drop, and I lost the purchase price of the puts. But I still think I made the correct judgment about the risks and was right to take some steps to mitigate those risks.

Another way you can have a negative outcome despite your sound reasoning is to pursue a course of action that has a low probability of success, but a very high reward if that probability comes to pass. Imagine if I returned to you with my number-guessing game, and this time offered you a new bet: if you guess a number I choose between 1 and 10, I pay you $100, and if you guess any other number, you have to pay me a dollar. It is well worth taking the bet—even knowing that nine-tenths of the time, you'll lose.

(For what it's worth, the yellow pad again bears this out. Taking the new bet yields you a profit of $100 one-tenth of the time, and a loss of $1.00 nine-tenths of the time, for an anticipated profit

of $9.10 and an expected value of $10.10 when your original dollar is included. That's far greater than the expected value of not
taking the bet, which remains $1.00.)

Leaders—even leaders of very important institutions—often
fail to recognize that decisions with low odds of success but a
huge potential payoff can be sound. During the 1990s, the Russian
economy faltered badly under President Boris Yeltsin. The Clinton
administration provided the Yeltsin government with financial
resources that were made available in installments, with each in-
stallment subject to progress on the enactment of reforms, but
unfortunately our intervention didn't lead to the economic or political outcomes we hoped for. Shortly after George W. Bush took
office, incoming Treasury Secretary Paul O'Neill criticized the
strategy we had employed in regard to Russia.

The fact that a new administration disagreed with the previous
one didn't bother me. What did bother me, however, was the
argument O'Neill employed: our efforts had not proven successful,
he said, so therefore we had been wrong to try. (When asked why
he approved of our efforts to stabilize the economy in Mexico,
which were similar to our efforts in Russia, he again pointed to
outcomes. "What I liked about it is that it worked," he said.)

I believe this is the wrong way to judge a decision-maker's
actions, or to set one's own course. And with regard to the economic crisis in Russia, I believe we got the decision right, even if
the outcome wasn't the one we had hoped for. We had a thorough
process. We thought through important questions carefully: How
could we support reformers in Russia, and how much would those
reformers benefit from a stabilized economy? What were the odds
that Russia's legislature would enact the reforms that would allow

us to continue the program? What would happen to efforts to foster democracy in Russia if we pulled the rug out from under the government by not offering any support?

Asking these questions left us clear-eyed about the low probability that the program would succeed—we recognized that corruption in Russia was horrendous, that reform was not terribly likely, and that some of the money might wind up in the wrong place.

Yet in the end, we launched an economic rescue attempt knowing it had relatively low odds of success because we concluded the potential benefits to global stability, democracy, and U.S. interests were enormous if it did succeed. To put it differently, when we multiplied the low probability of a positive outcome with the likely impact of that outcome should it materialize, the expected value was still quite high. Once it became clear that Russian legislators were not going to pass the needed reforms, and once we concluded that a large portion of the money was indeed being siphoned into the wrong hands, the expected value of maintaining the program changed, and we discontinued it.

Of course, these were just our judgments of the probabilities and outcomes. Secretary O'Neill could have argued that we overestimated the odds of success, or overestimated the benefits success would entail. While we might not have agreed, this would have led to a productive, *ex ante* discussion about how to evaluate our decision-making. Instead, he ignored probabilities, committing to an *ex post* evaluation that would likely lead to worse decisions in the future.

None of this means outcomes are completely irrelevant. In many cases, perhaps most cases, good decisions lead to better outcomes, and bad decisions lead to worse ones. But to reflexively celebrate positive outcomes and cast blame after negative ones overlooks other possibilities, including at least these four key ones:

First, you could overestimate the probability of a positive outcome, but a positive outcome still materializes.

Second, you could overestimate the size of the benefit associated with the hoped-for outcome, but still get a positive result.

Third, you could correctly estimate the probability of the hoped-for outcome but get an outcome you didn't hope for.

And finally, as I believe happened with our approach to the Russian economy, you could correctly judge that a low-probability outcome has a high potential benefit and therefore a high expected value, and decide to pursue the outcome on that basis, but then the hoped-for outcome does not occur.

If all this makes evaluating one's past decisions sound complicated, that's because it is complicated. The only way to consistently make valuable judgments about past decisions, and to learn the right lessons that will help you make better decisions in the future, is to accept the complexity of an *ex ante* approach.

Of course, one must recognize that the *ex ante* approach comes with temptations of its own. If you make a decision I oppose, and everything turns out well, I might reflexively say that you got lucky, without examining the possibility that you made a sound choice. Because it's impossible to prove beyond all doubt that luck didn't play a role, I could avoid ever having to recognize the soundness of your decision.

Alternatively, when confronted with negative outcomes, the same reasoning can be used disingenuously. If I do X because I predict Y will happen, but Z happens instead, I can always say, "Well, *ex ante*, Y was most likely, but I just got unlucky."

There's a very successful investor I know who, despite his

success, personifies this type of behavior. He always says that something is 55 percent likely to work out. If it works out, he can say he predicted accurately, and if it doesn't work out, he can say he warned you the odds were close to 50–50. While this uses the language of probabilistic thinking, it's not really probabilistic at all. If someone always concludes that they deserve credit for positive outcomes and that they don't deserve blame for negative outcomes, it's a good sign that person isn't being intellectually rigorous.

There's no easy way to avoid the temptations associated with an *ex ante* approach to evaluating decisions. There's only the hard way: by holding oneself to a high standard of intellectual integrity and being as honest as possible when examining past decisions, even if it might lead to conclusions one doesn't like.

Nor is there any perfect test, if an *ex ante* approach to evaluating decisions is taken, to determine whether a judgment was sound or not. Instead, I employ a version of the "reasonable person" standard that applies to many legal issues. In tort law, for example, if you get injured because of conditions on my property, the question becomes: Would a reasonable person have recognized the risk associated with those conditions and fixed them? If the answer is yes, I'm liable, and if it's no, I'm not.

The same approach applies to evaluating the quality of past decisions in two ways. Would a reasonable person, looking at the full set of information available to the decision-maker at the time, feel that the decision was sound or not? Would a reasonable person, looking at the analysis of the information and the decision-making process employed at the time, feel that the approach used to make the decision was rigorous or not?

Additionally, regardless of the answers to those two questions, what lessons would a reasonable person looking at both the decision and the outcome learn that might shape their decision-making process in the future? This question is not relevant to determining the quality of a past decision, because it relies heavily on hindsight. But it's important to ask, because engaging with it can help people make better decisions in the future.

Asking questions designed to rigorously evaluate and learn from past decisions rarely yields a simple answer. To use just one example, I have a friend whom I greatly respect and who is highly experienced with regard to geopolitical matters. To this day, he argues that the decision to invade Iraq in 2003 was a good one, and that it was simply the planning for the reconstruction of the country that was poor.

I take the opposite view, very strongly. But no one can objectively say, with 100 percent certainty, who is right and who is wrong. The best we can do is approach the subject with intellectual rigor and open minds, compare the arguments for our respective positions, and draw the soundest possible conclusions so that we can apply them to any similar situations in the future.

Adding to all this complexity is that what we think of as individual decisions are rarely the product of a single choice or moment. Instead, big decisions are the result of multiple factors, across different lengths of time, all of which ought to be considered if the right lessons are to be learned. And while this is important regardless of the outcome that occurs, it is particularly important to analyze past events when they turned out negatively.

Which brings me to my experience as a senior adviser at Citigroup. As I've mentioned, I joined Citi not long after I left the Treasury Department. For the first several years, the firm did quite well. But then, in the fall of 2007, I got a phone call from Chuck Prince, our CEO. It was a Saturday, and I was sitting in my apartment.

"There's a problem with some of our LBOs," he said. (LBOs stands for leveraged buyouts, a type of financial instrument.)

While it wasn't a good sign that Chuck was calling me at home on the weekend, it was hardly unusual. I figured we would have a meeting, discuss the problem, come up with a plan to resolve it, and then move on to the next challenge.

I was wrong. That meeting was when much of Citi's senior leadership, and I as senior counselor, first learned of a position held by traders in the fixed-income department that would create the most severe crisis in the firm's history. The biggest problem, we learned, was not actually the LBOs. It was a different type of security—a collateralized debt obligation backed by subprime mortgages. These CDOs were divided into "tranches" that carried different levels of risk. Owners of "super senior" tranches were paid back first, owners of "senior" tranches were paid back next, and so on.

As the housing market boomed in the early and mid-2000s, most financial firms were involved in buying and selling subprime CDOs, the same way they might sell stocks or bonds. But at the meeting on September 12, 2007, which Chuck asked me to attend, we were told that Citi had $43 billion of assets backed by subprime loans on its books, a substantially larger position than any other financial institution—and that, for reasons I'll go into shortly, these assets had not appeared on the "risk report" shared with senior management and the board.

I've held roles in a variety of organizations, and I've experienced both good and bad outcomes at nearly all of them. But what happened next at Citi was, by a large margin, the worst outcome that has occurred at a large institution where I was playing a senior role. True, the firm recovered from the financial crisis and the Great Recession that followed, and several other financial institutions did not. But Citi was severely affected, and stabilized only with the help of large, emergency injections of capital from the federal government—more than any other financial institution received during the crisis. The firm eventually paid back its loans and the government sold its stake in Citi, at a profit of $12 billion to taxpayers, but the fact remains: Citi had to be rescued with federal support.

The consequences of Citi's severe difficulties were felt far beyond Wall Street. The firm's shareholders—which included not just wealthy investors but pension funds, union benefit plans, and retirees who had invested through their 401(k)s—were dealt a painful blow.

Citi's troubles became both part of, and a contributor to, the worst global financial crisis since the Great Depression. Millions of people—people who worked nowhere near the financial sector, and who in many cases had not fully shared in the economic benefits of the pre-crash boom years—lost their jobs, homes, and savings. While the economy eventually recovered, it took years for the job market and housing market to bounce back to precrisis levels. It is a tragic but undeniable fact that lives were upended, and in some cases forever changed, by the crisis that Citi played a role in during the time I was there. In addition to the jobs and homes lost, as a result of the crisis countless Americans lost faith in our financial system and in our institutions more broadly. Our entire society is still feeling the effects of that loss of faith today.

Across the financial system—from asset managers and the Federal Reserve to Washington policy-makers and journalists— only a handful of people saw the crisis coming. I regret that I wasn't among them. In hindsight, if I had better seen what was coming, perhaps I might have been better able to call attention to it.

But when evaluating past events, it's important to go beyond asking "What would I do differently if I could go back in time?" and to ask "What should I have done differently *at* the time?" A rigorous analysis of the past—including *ex ante* evaluation of one's judgments—is the best possible way to learn lessons that will help leaders make better decisions in the future. No amount of thoughtfulness can change what has happened. But perhaps it can change what will happen going forward.

The reverse is true as well. If leaders and the public fail to take an honest, complete look at the decision-making that preceded a crisis—if they either ignore what happened or evaluate what happened in an overly outcome-driven way—they make it more likely that the next crisis will hit sooner, hit harder, or both. And as our country now knows from experience, many of the people who will suffer most from a failure to prevent or mitigate the next crisis aren't those on Wall Street or in Washington—they're lower-income and middle-class families whose economic security depends, in a very real way, on sound decisions being made by leaders in government and throughout the financial sector.

It can be bruising, not just intellectually but emotionally, to revisit the past. I've been a public figure, in some form or another, for at least forty years. But none of the criticism I've experienced has been remotely as harsh—in either substance or tone—as that which I received during my final year at Citi. Given the shock felt through every part of our country, and the pain felt by so many people when the economy collapsed, that's not surprising. I was a well-established figure in the financial world and in public policy circles, and a senior adviser to one of the financial firms at the center of the crisis when it hit. It would have been strange if I hadn't been the recipient of a great deal of criticism.

Ultimately, I'm probably not the best judge of which critiques were accurate, and which were less so. Nor is that really the point of asking oneself "What went wrong?" My goal instead is to conduct an analysis of events I was part of as objectively as possible, while recognizing that this is just one person's view, in an attempt to figure out what lessons related to my own decision-making future leaders can learn.

For example, one area where I believe I could have made better decisions in the run-up to the crisis involves Citi's culture. Citi had a culture that was very much oriented toward the short term. The focus was generally on the next quarter, not the next year or the next five years. During my time at Citi, I sometimes encouraged the firm to adopt a longer-term view. But I should have pushed harder to change the culture, and *ex ante*, not pushing harder was a mistake. Going forward, people in leadership in financial institutions should do more than I did to focus their firms on the long term.

To what extent was this kind of short-termism responsible for the trouble Citi faced during the crisis? It's hard to say, because financial institutions of all kinds—with all kinds of cultures—experienced major losses. But perhaps if Citi had been more oriented toward thinking beyond the next quarter, traders would not have taken such a large position in subprime CDOs without doing a more thorough analysis of the long-term risk. Regardless of the extent to which short-term thinking caused a bad outcome in this instance, Citi's short-term focus made bad outcomes more likely to occur, and my decision not to do more to try to change that focus was an error.

Another decision-making error I made in the run-up to the crisis concerned the housing market. As I've mentioned, the CDOs that were at the root of Citi's near collapse were backed by sub-prime mortgages. In the year or so before the crisis, I gave speeches saying that markets, broadly speaking, were likely going to excess, and pointing to specific indicators (for example, that credit spreads had tightened substantially or that American households were taking on unsustainable levels of debt) that might signal impending trouble. But I didn't focus on the housing market in particular.

This is an area where I must be careful not to fall into the trap of outcome-driven analysis. Since the housing market collapse caused the crisis, it would be easy to look backward, with perfect hindsight, and decide that I should have paid more attention to the housing market. Yet I believe that even knowing what I knew then, I should have paid more attention to housing. Some analysts were seeing warning signs in the housing market and trying to point them out. I could have, and should have, asked questions and tried to understand what they were saying, and why.

I'm not suggesting that people in the financial world should have predicted that the subprime housing market was about to fall apart—the vast preponderance of people didn't. But I am suggesting a reasonable person should have investigated the issue in a way that would have increased their chances of accurately foreseeing the crisis. I was not as curious as I should have been.

Not surprisingly, I think Citi's decision to hold $43 billion of

CDOs backed by subprime mortgages was also a mistake—but it's important to understand exactly what that mistake was. Some people concluded that since Citi was holding a $43 billion position in mortgage-backed securities that turned out to be extremely volatile, the firm must have been aggressive about risk. In fact, the reason the bank took a $43 billion position in subprime CDOs was not that it was eager to take on a large credit risk. The bank took its position in subprime CDOs because of the view, which turned out to be severely mistaken, that it was taking on virtually no credit risk at all.

This was because the CDOs held by Citi were from the "super senior" tranche—and because of this, the independent credit-ratings agencies had rated them "AAA," their highest rating. This meant they were considered "money good"—for practical purposes risk free. In fact, AAA-rated securities were thought to be so secure that positions in them were not included on the risk report given to the board and senior leadership. That's why so many of us found out about the CDOs in late 2007 and not sooner.

Even when I did learn about the $43 billion position, I didn't focus on the risk that CDOs with the same credit rating as U.S. government bonds might default. I told the traders I was concerned we were holding $43 billion of anything—there's an old adage that investment banks are in the moving business, not the storage business. I also worried that our position might decline in value if interest rates changed. But I never gave any real thought to the possibility that the value of a AAA security might drop to near zero.

Throughout Wall Street—among the great preponderance of financial institutions, financial journalists, and agencies regulating the markets—to suggest that a security rated AAA had virtually no risk of default had always been seen as not just uncontroversial but obvious. Looking back, I think the collective mistaken assumption wasn't groupthink, in the sense that everyone adopted the same opinion about an issue. Instead, what took place was kind of a group-non-think—almost no one conducted a rigorous analysis of the issue at all.

This leads to some of the most important lessons I believe the crisis should teach decision-makers on Wall Street going forward. Most obviously, just because a security is rated AAA by a ratings agency does not mean it carries virtually no credit risk. I think an investment firm should still treat AAA-rated securities as unlikely to develop serious creditworthiness problems. But a firm should also look under the hood at a security's underlying credit, conduct its own rigorous analysis, and make an independent judgment, because the ratings agencies are not infallible.

There is also a far broader lesson to be learned from what happened at Citi and in the financial system, one that goes beyond the risks associated with AAA-rated securities and touches on the very nature of assumptions.

It's easy for an organization or individual to say they don't make assumptions, but that's never entirely true. For example, hypothetically, an asteroid might hit the earth tomorrow. But most of us don't make contingency plans for such a possibility. Most of us probably wouldn't even recognize that we're making this assumption at all. (When Gus Levy reminded his colleagues at Goldman Sachs to "never assume anything," I suspect he, too, was speaking somewhat less than literally.)

The problem can arise when an assumption becomes so

widespread that we no longer realize we are making it, and we lose our ability to evaluate whether it's reasonable or not. Although it is not impossible that a future crisis will arise from AAA-rated securities turning out to have higher-than-anticipated risks of default, I think it is relatively unlikely, since institutions and others in the financial system will try to not make the same mistake twice. But it is likely that sooner or later, there will be some other widespread assumption that proves faulty and results in a crisis.

Thus, were I advising traders or other position takers at a bank like Citi today, I would—in part because of what I have learned from the 2008 financial crisis—want them to periodically try to identify the assumptions, both large and small, that they might not realize they were making. Most of these assumptions would probably prove uncontroversial. But having a list might, in some cases, allow them to recognize that what appears to be a virtually certain truth is in fact a high-probability outcome that includes a tail risk.

Just as rigorously evaluating and analyzing the crisis holds lessons for decision-makers throughout the financial sector, it holds lessons for policy-makers throughout government.

In the years leading up to the crisis, many leading thinkers in economic policy seemed to believe that a second Great Depression was not just unlikely but impossible. I vividly remember a lunch I had in the early 1990s with Daniel Patrick Moynihan, the legendary New York senator. I deeply admired and respected Senator Moynihan, but during that conversation, he said something that stuck with me during the years since.

"We've tamed the business cycle," he told me. "We'll still have downturns, but we have new policy tools now, and we'll never face another crisis like we did in the 1930s."

It turned out that from the end of the Great Depression until 2007, he was right. But in retrospect, his analysis was based on outcomes—he was arguing, in essence, that because we hadn't experienced a large-scale economic collapse in decades, we had tamed the business cycle. That argument was disproved when the Great Recession hit.

Senator Moynihan was hardly alone in his view. What is remarkable, looking back on it, is not that a crisis like the Great Recession could occur, but that so many economic thinkers were so confident it wouldn't.

If we take an *ex ante* approach to examining collective thinking in the run-up to the crisis, one of the most important conclusions we can reach involves the danger of widespread overconfidence regarding economic policy. Our understanding of policy did indeed grow more sophisticated following World War II, but it was wrong to conclude that the possibility of a systemic crisis had disappeared altogether. When such a crisis hit, our overconfidence made us less prepared than we could or should have been.

In the wake of the crisis, we should therefore recognize that while perfect storms occur rarely, they do in fact occur. And almost by definition, they develop in ways very few people are expecting or anticipating. The job of policy-makers is therefore not just to make crises less frequent and harmful with sensible regulation and fiscal policy—it's to recognize that even infrequent crises are inevitable and to take that into account in their decisions.

I've also thought a great deal about my own decision-making as an economic policy-maker in the 1990s. In 1999, for example, I supported bipartisan legislation to repeal the Glass-Steagall Act, a 1930s-era regulation that separated commercial and investment banking. It was a controversial decision at the time, and some people have since argued that the repeal of Glass-Steagall was a primary driver of the economic crisis that began in 2007.

I've considered and engaged with that idea, and tried to be as objective as possible, and I don't think it's supported by the facts. I've spoken to highly knowledgeable experts in banking law about this, and all those I've spoken to said that by the time Glass-Steagall was fully repealed in 1999, it had been interpreted by the Federal Reserve over many years in ways that would have allowed the banks to do essentially everything they did that, in hindsight, helped fuel the crisis. (Glass-Steagall would have prevented banks from writing or selling insurance, but those activities had little to do with the crisis, or the challenges Citi and similar banks faced in 2007 and 2008.) Even the original Glass-Steagall Act in 1933 would not have prevented financial firms from buying large amounts of CDOs, because that was done through mortgage lending, which the act never covered and which banks had always been permitted to do.

Still, this is one of those areas where, while I am confident in my own view that repealing the Glass-Steagall Act did not cause the financial crisis, I think an exchange of views is very helpful— so long as those views go beyond outcome-based analysis. It's not enough to point out Glass-Steagall was repealed, point out that later the economy collapsed, and from this conclude that the repeal of Glass-Steagall must have caused the collapse. But I believe a broader, intellectually rigorous debate about financial regulation in the lead-up to the 2007–2008 crisis and about what regulations might help prevent the next crisis is helpful for future decision-makers— even if I won't agree with every point made, and even if it's impossible to determine with complete certainty which view is correct.

Another widely raised issue in the wake of the crisis was the role of "derivatives"—a type of nontraditional financial instrument that was poorly regulated in the run-up to the economic collapse, and which, during the crisis, threatened the solvency of the insurance giant AIG. I have long believed that it is important to regulate derivatives more strongly because of the exposure they create for investors and their potential for destabilizing effects. When I was co-senior partner at Goldman Sachs, I went to the Chicago Board of Trade to ask it to impose stricter margin and capital requirements, which would limit investors' ability to buy derivatives using borrowed money and would also require banks that bought and sold derivatives to hold more capital in reserve. Later, when I served at Treasury, I continued to be in favor of derivative regulation—although I also felt that it required a complex policy approach, and that certain approaches could do more harm than good.

Ultimately, despite my concerns, I never got the chance to focus deeply on derivative regulation because issues like the Asian financial crisis took priority. In 2010 the Dodd-Frank financial regulation bill imposed new rules around derivatives, which I agreed with, although I thought the bill should have gone further with increased margin and capital requirements.

More broadly, I think that going forward, policy-makers should do more so that regulation keeps pace with innovation in the financial sector. And I think the financial industry should, broadly speaking, support this idea, not just because it will reduce the economic hardship from future crises, but also because Americans are more likely to trust the financial sector if they believe it is adequately regulated. A similar logic led me to support the creation of the Consumer Financial Protection Bureau as part of Dodd-Frank in 2010.

Trying to carefully and comprehensively analyze what happened during the Great Recession—and learning from past decisions more broadly—is not as simple or viscerally satisfying as relying solely on outcomes. But it is worth the added effort, complexity, and uncertainty. If one's goal is to learn lessons that lead to better decisions in the future, then the right approach to evaluating both negative and positive outcomes is not just useful but essential.

Which brings me back to that partners' meeting at Goldman Sachs more than forty years ago, not long after my department had lost an enormous amount of money. At first, I remember being quite uncertain how the partners would respond. But what I said was this: "The reason we're showing these losses is that, because of the Fed's decisions to raise interest rates, the structure of the market has changed. Rather than just focus on the outcomes at the moment, let's reexamine the expected value analysis on each of our positions in light of that change. If a position still isn't expected to yield a positive value, let's reduce or more likely eliminate it and accept our loss. But where positions meet that test—if the expected value remains positive, after rigorous reevaluation—let's not just keep those positions. Let's consider increasing them."

The management committee, and the partners more broadly, agreed to allow me to take this approach. We broke out the yellow pad, going through every one of our positions based on the new realities—such as the change in inflation expectations, the change in markets, and the change in earnings outlook—and then asked ourselves in each case, "Should we sell or not sell?" In some cases, we even added to our existing positions.

Very few organizations would have gone along with such an

idea after such a negative outcome. But the partners at Goldman Sachs did. And fortunately, in this case, we didn't just wind up cutting our losses. When the markets recovered, the sound decision—and the right approach to evaluating and learning from past decisions—led to a very positive result.

Chapter VII

AN EMAIL FROM ELIZA

As I look back on my life and career, many of the moments I remember most clearly, and that I suspect have most influenced my views on decision-making, involve someone raising an insightful but challenging point. One such moment occurred at a Goldman Sachs partners' meeting more than half a century ago.

It was early in 1971, not long after Goldman Sachs had issued commercial paper for Penn Central, and subsequent lawsuits surrounding Penn Central's bankruptcy had threatened to put our firm out of business. (This was the same set of legal troubles during which I'd gone to Gus Levy with concerns about his initial choice of lead attorney.) While the danger to the firm had largely passed by the time the partners' meeting took place, the episode was still on everyone's mind. At some point, one of the other young partners, Richard Menschel, raised his hand:

"Did we not look at Penn Central properly," he asked, "because it was a client of the senior partner?"

By senior partner, Richard meant Gus—who was in charge of

the firm, and who was therefore also running the meeting. I don't remember exactly what Gus said in response to Richard's question, but I certainly remember the tone in which he said it. To put it mildly, he was not pleased.

Yet despite his initial outburst, Gus didn't hold a grudge. Through his actions, if not his immediate reaction, he demonstrated an openness to engaging with Richard's concerns. Not long after our meeting, Goldman hired highly experienced independent credit analysts as consultants to examine the way we issued commercial paper. The consultants then made meaningful recommendations regarding the firm's process. In the end, the firm improved the way it did business, in large part because of Richard's challenging question.

I've been fortunate to be part of many meetings—and many institutions—that didn't just allow but actively encouraged people to express views at odds with the group consensus or the opinion of the ultimate decision-maker, even if they might make people uncomfortable. I vividly remember sitting in the Cabinet Room or Roosevelt Room with President Clinton and other top advisers as matters of economic importance were being discussed. If everybody was veering in one direction, or everyone was agreeing with him, the president would step in and ask someone to make the opposite case: "What's the other side of the story? What would the people who are opposed to this say? If we're wrong, why are we wrong?"

As I've discussed elsewhere, fostering this type of exchange of views in government and politics can be even harder than it is in the private sector. The high levels of transparency in many aspects of government may at times be useful, but they can seriously impede candor. Also, those involved in government receive far greater scrutiny and criticism in the media and from their opponents than ordinarily occurs in the private sector, which can make people more reluctant to acknowledge error. Finally, even in closed-door meetings, the greater probability that someone might leak an uncomfortable question or argument to the press, something that happens far less frequently in corporate life, can chill the discussion of views.

Yet what struck me was that despite these challenges, President Clinton created an atmosphere in which you felt comfortable asking questions, disagreeing with him, or even criticizing his past decisions. Everyone worked together to determine the best way forward. You would raise a point, counter an argument, test a proposition—and then all of a sudden you'd realize the guy you're arguing with has a title, and that title is president of the United States. Even though the president was the most powerful person on the planet, you never felt like you were working *for* him. You always felt like you were working *with* him.

I tried to create similar environments in the meetings I ran at the National Economic Council and later at the Treasury Department. Our debates were genuinely intellectually engaging, which is not always the case when the stakes are so high. Alan Greenspan, the chairman of the Federal Reserve, once described these meetings as almost like graduate seminars, so much so that he enjoyed coming over to Treasury to participate in them. I think it was precisely the elements of our debates Alan found enjoyable— the difficult questions raised and differing opinions aired and encouraged—that gave us the information and understanding necessary to make the best possible decisions.

I look back on these environments—a partners' meeting more than fifty years ago, the Clinton White House, our policy debates at the Treasury Department—with fondness and appreciation.

And I think they highlight one of the most important requisites of sound decision-making: a commitment to what I think of as "unfettered discussion."

My opinions on this subject have been shaped by a variety of writers and thinkers whose work I've read, the professors I studied with in college and law school, and the students I engaged with intellectually in those years. They have also been shaped by more recent experiences, including many discussions with people I have known and worked with who have disagreed with me, sometimes vociferously so.

These interactions have been valuable for several reasons. First, they've caused me to consider new ideas. Second, in some cases they've caused me to change my mind. Third, they've provided intellectual sparring partners—requiring me to better identify issues, evaluate arguments, and make a case to defend my views. This helped make me a better decision-maker, because if you're going to make the best possible yellow-pad assessments of probabilities and outcomes, you need to be well informed—and the way to be truly well informed is to have a full-fledged, honest, unvarnished exchange of views, including disagreements and discussions on all relevant issues.

Put simply, I believe that individuals, organizations, and societies that permit, protect, and encourage the open exchange of views make better decisions than those that do not.

This is one of those ideas that may at first appear straightforward, particularly in a country and culture guided by the spirit of the First Amendment. Yet in my experience, fostering unfettered discussion is, in practice, neither simple nor easy. For as long as I can remember, creating an environment in which people can openly state and discuss their views has been one of the greatest challenges facing decision-makers—although in some ways that challenge has never been so great as it is today.

Before going further, it's important to examine what "unfettered discussion" really means. After all, no conversation is truly limitless. In the United States, the Constitution both prohibits government restrictions of speech and articulates a broader principle in favor of free expression, yet even the First Amendment comes with a narrow but real set of caveats. A speaker cannot directly incite violence, commit libel, or engage in public obscenity in the name of free expression. I think those are reasonable constraints.

In addition to that relatively narrow set of explicit restraints on our speech, all discussion is bound by a set of implicit social conventions. For example, if you consistently say things that are completely irrelevant to the topic being discussed, or lie in order to support your views, or attack people personally, then someone might stop including you in their discussions. Such an exclusion would not be an attack on the idea of unfettered discussion. It would simply mean that the person in question is choosing not to engage in discussion with you.

What I mean by unfettered discussion, then, is not about defining the limits of what can and can't be said in each moment and setting, and instead about an overall approach. When I refer to a discussion or decision-making process as "unfettered," I mean that those engaging in it are allowed to express their views, even if those views are troubling or unpopular.

I suspect some people's mental image of an "open exchange of views" resembles a shouting match, but I think it's the opposite: creating a culture where unfettered discussion can flourish begins with encouraging mutual respect. Like most people, I believe individuals ought to try to treat each other considerately, and should give each other the benefit of the doubt unless it is clearly not warranted. These are not just matters of politeness or civility. If you start with a presumption that others are acting in good faith, and are confident that the same presumption is being extended to you, you are far more likely to say what you really think and to be open to others saying what they really think as well.

This is crucial, because in my experience, cultivating the most productive possible discussions requires openness: recognizing complexity and uncertainty, encouraging thoughtful disagreement and the discussion of uncomfortable topics, and ensuring that leaders' views aren't treated as off-limits or infallible.

Another component of intellectual openness—and of protecting unfettered discussion—is creating an environment where people are comfortable acknowledging gaps in their knowledge. Too often, saying "I don't know" is seen as a failing. This attitude discourages individuals from asking questions for fear of exposing any lack of knowledge, which increases the likelihood that the group and its leaders will be inadequately informed and their decision-making will be faulty. Conversely, recognizing gaps in knowledge and looking for more information better positions individuals and organizations to make good decisions. As my friend Richard Haass, the president of the Council on Foreign Relations, says, "'I don't know' is a verifiable statement."

Intellectual openness creates an environment where people can work with the leaders to make the best decisions, where they feel that their views are respected in the decision-making process, and where they have permission to ask one of the questions discussed in the previous chapter: "What went wrong?"

This is particularly important when the answer to such a

question might challenge the decisions made by a CEO or other member of senior leadership—as Richard Menschel did in his question about Penn Central in that partners' meeting. It's not hard to see why such questions are seldom asked. Too often, chief executives, or other powerful individuals, aren't used to being questioned, especially by people junior to them. In some cases, they create an intimidating atmosphere that discourages challenges. In other cases, the people who might be in a position to challenge the leader simply assume the leader doesn't want to be challenged.

But if leaders won't engage with difficult questions or admit mistakes, it makes evaluating a decision extremely difficult. Organizations cannot learn from their mistakes if there is an operating presumption that senior leadership cannot make them or doesn't want to hear about them.

When I held leadership positions at Goldman Sachs, I wanted everyone to feel free to ask the kind of question that took courage for Richard to raise in 1971. An environment where difficult questions can't be asked and discussed honestly is likely to become seriously dysfunctional. Yet I suspect these kinds of dysfunction too often occur in organizations, if for no other reason than that people in those organizations can be reluctant to scrutinize past decisions, especially when made by senior leaders.

Even when organizations are willing to evaluate the quality of past decisions (including those made by senior leaders) using rigorous analysis, they too often focus on figuring out whom to blame. That's generally counterproductive, because once people know management is looking for a scapegoat, they may engage in self-preservation rather than self-evaluation. This, in turn, leaves the decision-maker without the benefit of whatever insights the group might otherwise have uncovered.

Creating an environment in which people feel comfortable acknowledging a mistake is not just supportive but practical. It helps leaders understand what happened and improve future decision-making. People need to trust that they won't be unfairly penalized or, even worse, lose their job or their responsibilities.

For this reason, I have always been reluctant to impose negative consequences on people for making bad judgments, so long as the individual involved engages in a candid examination of what went wrong in order to learn from it. If someone makes a series of bad judgments, that is a different story. But after a single mistake—even a big one—or the kinds of occasional mistakes that are inevitable when issues are complicated, I tend to say, "Such is life" and focus on improving our decisions in the future.

This leads me to another important point about fostering unfettered discussion: it greatly helps to have challengers who are happy—perhaps even, at times, a little too happy—to ask difficult and provocative questions that might sharpen the decision-making process.

A productive challenger is not someone who is difficult for the sake of being difficult. Some people love to engage in sophistry, raising issues even if they're not well grounded. Such frivolous devil's advocates are hardly helpful. But to have someone disposed to raising otherwise unrecognized or uncomfortable issues, or even remote but realistic possibilities—to saying, "You know, there's only a small chance of this happening, but have we considered it?"—can be tremendously valuable.

Challenging prevailing wisdom, and raising difficult and controversial questions, may be the type of thing you are psychologically wired either to do or not to do. Many people fall into the latter category. They may have many other strengths that contribute greatly to decision-making, but they are just not disposed to asking uncomfortable questions, taking issue with a leader's view, or posing questions they think might expose a gap in their own knowledge. In contrast, I've found that the best challengers seem made for the role. Some of them can be somewhat difficult personalities from time to time. (Jacob Goldfield, my occasionally shoeless colleague at Goldman Sachs, was a born challenger.) But I've always felt that the benefits an intellectually rigorous challenger brings to discussions and decision-making greatly outweigh the possible costs involved.

No matter how smart or impressive the group of people you've assembled, you need someone who will test you and your thinking. Even when there's lively discussion within a group, rather than immediate consensus, it's important to include the kind of minds that will get outside of whatever the discussion is and see possibilities others might not. And that in turn requires not only being willing to hire such people, but proactively seeking to hire them, and then maintaining an environment where they feel comfortable operating in this way.

This doesn't mean challengers' ideas are always good. It does, however, mean we shouldn't reflexively reject what they have to say. Good decision-makers don't need to agree with challenging opinions. But they do need to listen to them.

Finally, and perhaps most important, decision-makers who seek to promote the free exchange of views should be wary of chilling effects, which in practice curtail others' abilities to express their opinions and ideas.

In this context, I think it's worth revisiting Gus's outburst in 1971. It's likely that, in a slightly different company with a slightly different culture and leader, a reaction like Gus's could have had a chilling effect on future discussions among partners. Imagine if Richard had been technically free to speak up at the meeting, but he knew that by angering the senior partner he was putting his continued success in the firm at risk, or he felt that other partners would attack him personally for raising an uncomfortable topic. The impact of this kind of chilling effect is difficult to measure—but that doesn't make it any less real or consequential.

Consider what chilling the expression of unpopular ideas does to an expected value table. If some considerations are off the table in making judgments about probabilities and outcomes, the odds of making the best decisions are decreased, often substantially so.

I think many people too often either ignore questions of whether their actions might chill open discussion, don't care if their actions create a chilling effect, or underweight the negative impact a chilling effect might have.

It is precisely because of the high costs of chilling the open exchange of views—and the enormous benefits of protecting it—that I think of protecting the open exchange of views not just as a helpful approach to decision-making, but as a powerful guiding principle leaders should do everything possible to adhere to. In theory, all potential courses of action can be examined on the yellow pad. But in practice, except in the most extreme circumstances, I don't believe that curtailing open discussion or stifling views I don't agree with should be considered as viable options.

Applying this powerful guiding principle in the real world is often difficult, and sometimes quite controversial. In 2006, for example, Iranian president Mahmoud Ahmadinejad visited New York City. Traditionally, the Council on Foreign Relations invites many visiting foreign leaders to engage with its membership at its

New York headquarters, regardless of how unfriendly those leaders are to the United States.

But this visit was different, because Ahmadinejad was well known for being a Holocaust denier. The idea that he might be invited to a prominent and well-regarded institution sparked substantial opposition. After much debate, the council's leaders decided to go ahead with the meeting. They believed that the event would allow participants with interest and influence in foreign policy to better understand—and, importantly, question—an adversary's views.

I wasn't personally involved with the decision, but I believe it was the correct one. The council made some changes to the format of the event around the margins to reflect the nature of the speaker and his views. (For example, while Ahmadinejad was invited to speak, he was not invited to share a meal with council members, as that would have seemed too social.) Extending the invitation came with a cost—Ahmadinejad was given a forum with influential New Yorkers in which he could express his false, harmful, and loathsome ideas. But ultimately, decision-makers at the council recognized that upholding the principle of protecting an open exchange of views provided powerful long-term benefits that far outweighed the costs.

Thus far, I've mostly talked about the importance of discussions in business, government, and public policy. But I think the same idea extends to all elements of society—and in particular to schools and universities, which are the places where I and so many others acquired a foundation for navigating the world and, ultimately, for making decisions that affect and hopefully improve it.

There is nothing new about fierce debates over how much to allow unfettered discussion and a spirit of open expression on campus. In 1958, when I was a sophomore at Harvard, a white supremacist and antisemite named David Wang was invited to deliver a set of controversial (and in my view, repellent) remarks. On one hand were people like Herbert Milstein, the president of the Harvard Liberal Union, who argued that "a liberal society should allow free discussion." On the other hand were critics who felt that Wang should be barred from expressing his views on campus. Wang's remarks were even interrupted by a bomb threat.

Yet while this debate existed when I was a student, its intensity appears to have increased to a point where a difference in degree has become a difference in kind. The contours of the debate about free expression at universities have also changed, and I believe not for the better.

A few years ago, I received an email from my granddaughter Eliza. She was a sophomore at Harvard at the time, the same age I was when David Wang was invited to speak.

Eliza was writing me about some group that had invited a white supremacist to campus. An op-ed in the *Harvard Crimson* argued that the university should allow the white supremacist to speak and allow listeners to decide for themselves whether they agree or disagree and why. Eliza did not agree with the op-ed, and she told me so in her email.

I don't find it surprising that many people, particularly those of Eliza's generation, might take such a view about allowing the on-campus expression of a white supremacist's ideas. When I entered college, civil rights seemed to be steadily, though much too slowly, advancing. Today's college students are living in a very different moment. The prominence of extremist ideology, including white nationalism, appears to be growing rather than receding. Misinformation, dishonest arguments, and dangerous conspiracy theories can—thanks in part to social media—spread with unprecedented speed.

Still, I maintain a different view. I sent an email back to Eliza saying that I agreed with the person arguing in favor of allowing the white supremacist to speak. I tried to elaborate on the idea Herbert Milstein had laid out decades ago, that a liberal society should allow free discussion. Not only did I feel that listeners should be allowed to decide for themselves what to make of the white supremacist's views; I also felt there was a possibility that hearing those views might help them understand why the speaker thought that way and what his underlying motivations may be, which might in turn help someone effectively argue against his views. Moreover, understanding a heinous ideology might better enable a society to reduce its appeal by addressing its root causes.

Finally, I wrote Eliza, if we don't live by the spirit of the First Amendment, then maybe the next time it's not the white supremacist who can't speak, but the person with whom you agree who is silenced.

Sometime later, I brought all this up with Harvard's president emerita, Drew Faust. Drew has always been clear that she believes protecting free expression is a guiding principle, so I expected her to immediately agree that I was right and Eliza was wrong. But to my surprise, she said the issue was more complicated than I was making it out to be.

"There's another problem here," she said. "If the white supremacist speaks on campus at Harvard, then the white supremacist has the imprimatur of Harvard. And while it's true Harvard is not endorsing the views, it does create the problem that people see this person advocating those views on a Harvard platform, and it might give the kind of respectability to those views that they don't deserve."

I must admit that until Drew made this point, I hadn't really considered some of the ways in which the costs and benefits of allowing people with repugnant beliefs onto a well-known campus may have changed since I was a student. Perhaps the biggest new factors are social media and the wide availability of video online. If someone gives an inflammatory speech at Harvard today, the target audience is not really the students who can debate the speaker's views. The target audience is the millions of people who might watch the speech on the internet, and who may confuse Harvard's willingness to allow the expression of differing opinions with an endorsement of the remarks themselves.

The kinds of complexities I just described do not change my view that protecting unfettered discussion is a powerfully important principle. But real-world applications of principles still involve judgment calls, with trade-offs that deserve to be considered in the decision-making process. When Drew commented on Eliza's email, she was using the figurative yellow pad, thinking through possible courses of action, weighing costs against benefits, and trying to mitigate the former while maximizing the latter.

But—and I believe this is crucially important—as decision-makers carefully think through these kinds of issues, they should give appropriately heavy weight to the principle of protecting free expression. And they should consider the full range of costs that come with curtailing expression, not just through explicit prohibitions of certain types of views, but also through chilling effects that make people afraid to share opinions and ideas. It doesn't matter whether the institution in question is a university, a government department, an investment bank, or anyplace else: in an environment where everyone is walking on eggshells, an open exchange of views is not really possible.

I'm deeply concerned that in many cases, this type of harmful chilling effect is not just a theoretical problem, but a real one. I suspect that compared with a few decades ago, or perhaps even a few years ago, many people—of all ages, at a variety of stages in their careers, in academia, businesses, and nonprofits—are far more afraid to share views, or even to discuss issues, that would not too long ago have been seen as well within the bounds of the acceptable.

It's important to recognize that protecting free expression does come with costs, and that some kinds of speech, or the expression of certain views, impose larger costs than others. That's particularly true when speech seeks to diminish groups of people, unintentionally adds to a sense of oppression and pain, or actively communicates hate. All of this is very real, and like so many burdens in our society, these costs are not borne equally—which reflects grave inequalities in our past and present that need to be forcefully addressed. Given these circumstances, I don't think it's surprising that some people feel that the best way to resolve some of the most difficult challenges we face might include chilling the open exchange of views or curtailing the expression of certain opinions. But as real as the costs of protecting unfettered discussion may be, I continue to think that they are far outweighed by the benefits.

Almost none of the speech I've described in this chapter is directly bound, or protected, by the Constitution. But I think the First Amendment—in addition to being a powerful declaration of rights—reflects a sound set of principles: that at the end of the day, allowing even the most offensive speech will protect all people's right to speak at times when their views are unpopular; that an exchange of views can lead those with just and virtuous causes to sharpen their arguments; and that the best answer to almost all types of bad speech is not to deny, silence, or ban them, but to refute them.

More broadly, as I mentioned in my email to Eliza, there is no way to ensure that the people drawing lines around what type of speech is acceptable will agree with you. They may in fact decide that your ideas are the ones that ought to be suppressed.

Recently, we've seen worrisome examples of exactly this kind of behavior. Extremist politicians across the country have passed bills that would require the government to fire teachers for exposing students to ideas lawmakers disagree with concerning gender identity, sexuality, or racial issues. Many of those same lawmakers have attempted to ban books they don't like from libraries and school curricula. This has both a direct impact and a chilling effect, because it leaves educators unsure which ideas or material will make them a target of government censorship.

This is unfair to teachers. It's also unfair to students. We need to give young people a chance to fully explore and understand our society, in order to prepare them to navigate our society effectively as adults.

The trend toward government censorship that we've seen domestically is being increasingly experienced internationally as well. In regimes where democracy is struggling or nonexistent, government critics are harassed, arrested, and sometimes murdered. State-run or state-affiliated media is promoted, while media unfriendly to the state is targeted economically or simply shut down. In some cases, state-run companies refuse to do business with companies or individuals who express opinions they disagree with or who call attention to facts that run counter to their government's official position. This is a way of using autocratic countries' global economic clout to coerce speakers into accepting their positions and to chill free speech worldwide, not just within those countries' borders.

To discourage this kind of political pressure, both domestically and internationally, it is important to demonstrate a firm commitment to the guiding principle that the open exchange of views should be welcomed and encouraged. By articulating and upholding their commitment to unfettered discussion, even when it's highly difficult, institutions—including universities—can help defend a principle that is increasingly under threat.

Of course, even if university administrators are determined to protect rather than curtail free expression, they have difficult judgment calls to make and difficult questions to ask themselves. How do they determine which ideas and scholars have academic merit and should be embraced by the university, and which do not? What constitutes unacceptable verbal harassment of a faculty member, student, or administrator, as opposed to unwelcome but legitimate expression? How should colleges approach building community? How can the university fulfill its role as an environment that fosters the intellectual and academic lives of its students and faculty, and create a culture where students and faculty feel that an open exchange of views is welcomed and productive not just in theory but in practice?

There is no one right answer to these questions. But I do think that as university administrators engage with these questions, they should do so with a powerful presumption in favor of an open exchange of views. Their default position ought to be that discussion helps rather than hurts society.

Some people might point out that I personally experienced many of the benefits of unfettered discussion, and relatively few of its downsides, reflecting a place of privilege. That's true. I've had many advantages in my life, and many people have felt the costs of others' free expression more acutely than I have.

But I don't believe today's students, regardless of their background, will be better off if we deny them the chance to engage with a wide variety of different ideas and views, including those that are uncomfortable or that reasonable people find abhorrent. We should help students deal with the added stresses and complexities of university life as best we can. But that effort doesn't require us to sacrifice the liberal tradition underlying our universities—the exchange of ideas and views in pursuit of better understanding all aspects of the world we live in. Our goal should be to make sure everyone receives the advantages that come from intellectual inquiry, while recognizing that some people can be more adversely affected by its downsides than others.

I believe that the long-term benefits of fostering unfettered discussion outweigh the costs. To put it another way, if today's graduates leave campus without the intellectual disposition and skills to grapple with difficult questions as they face challenging decisions, their schools will have done them a great disservice. And the consequences of such a failure will be felt far beyond the campus, because universities are where so many of tomorrow's leaders develop their approach toward the challenges and decisions they'll face later in life. If leaders lack the ability to evaluate arguments and are not comfortable dealing with uncomfortable questions and opinions, I believe our entire society will be worse off.

The reverse is true as well: when leaders are comfortable dealing with uncomfortable opinions, they are more likely to effectively confront the challenges they face. I remember one meeting during the Clinton years when we were all sitting around in the Cabinet Room. I believe the subject of our discussion was foreign assistance, but I don't remember many of the specifics. What I do recall is that President Clinton wanted to do things one way, and I, along with a few others, wanted to do things a different way. The discussion was never personal or disrespectful, but it became very heated.

After President Clinton had made his decision and everyone had begun to leave the room, I remember someone who was fairly new to the administration turning to me in surprise. "He's the president! How could you engage with him that way?"

"We tell him what we think," I replied. "That's what he wants. It's just how we operate."

Throughout my life, I have been very fortunate to work with many groups of people, and in many organizations, that have operated that way. It's my hope that decision-makers in future generations will be similarly fortunate.

Chapter VIII

NOT EVERYTHING
IS THE ALAMO

There are some things we can't do," I told President Clinton. "For example, we can't agree to cut the capital gains tax." I was in the Oval Office, along with several of the president's other advisers. For months, we had been discussing how best to approach the 1997 budget, the president's first since his reelection. With Republicans in control of the Senate and the House, we knew we would not be able to pass a bill that contained only our priorities. We would need to make concessions if we wanted to reach any kind of meaningful agreement.

At the same time, we felt strongly that some policies should not be considered, even in the context of a broader deal, and that one of these policies was cutting the capital gains tax rate. Having spent decades in markets and investments, I had long thought that lowering capital gains taxes—taxes on income resulting from the sale of a stock or similar asset, as opposed to taxes on salary or wages—did little, and probably virtually nothing, to increase savings or investment, instead simply reducing the amount of revenue the federal government receives. This lost revenue either would increase deficits or would have to be made up for by cutting spending or raising other taxes.

I was not alone in my opinion. President Clinton's economic advisers shared the view that cutting the capital gains tax should be off-limits. So did the president himself. When he picked up the phone and called Trent Lott, the Senate majority leader and the lead budget negotiator for the Republicans, he was well prepared.

For a few minutes, matters appeared to be going smoothly, with the president and the senator exchanging views on their priorities. Then, rather abruptly, President Clinton put his hand over the phone. "He wants to cut the capital gains tax," he said.

"Well," I replied, "that's one of the things we can't do."

President Clinton nodded, and then returned to the call.

He and Senator Lott had some back and forth, and then President Clinton spoke. "Yes, Trent, I understand. We're going to cut it."

Perhaps, to some, this kind of story illustrates Washington's lack of principles. I felt cutting capital gains tax rates was a bad idea, the president's other advisers felt cutting capital gains tax rates was a bad idea, the president felt cutting capital gains tax rates was a bad idea—and yet, in order to pass the budget we wanted to pass, we conceded to the other side's demands and did it anyway.

But what I saw in the Oval Office shouldn't discourage anyone from having faith in our political process. Just the opposite. I believe what I saw in the Oval is an example of exactly what it takes for our democracy to work—a commitment to effective governance when negotiating with people who don't share your views, and a willingness to engage in the give-and-take of compromise.

More broadly speaking, our government, and indeed our society, cannot thrive if our political system cannot function. And our political system will not function if our leaders cannot find ways to work together and move forward even when they disagree.

Politics and governing have never been straightforward or perfect. Neither have the people who engage in them. But in recent decades, something important seems to have changed, giving rise to a question that was seldom asked during the first sixty or so years of my life.

How do we restore functionality to our political process before it's too late?

The 1997 budget agreement was an example of a functional political process at work. I believe the benefits President Clinton was able to secure—including the creation of the State Children's Health Insurance Program, a new tax on cigarettes to raise revenue and discourage smoking, an additional $1.5 billion for the food stamp program, the restoration of disability and health benefits for hundreds of thousands of immigrants who had arrived legally in the United States, and serious deficit reduction—greatly outweighed the harm of acceding to Trent Lott's demand that we cut the capital gains tax.

Yet in more recent decades, the kind of scene I witnessed—two leaders with opposing views engaging in give-and-take, accepting some measures they didn't like, and ultimately obtaining an overall agreement they *did* like, both substantively and politically—has become rare. For the most part, our elected officials from across the ideological and partisan spectrum seem unable or unwilling to come together to address major national challenges.

This puts our entire country at risk. America has great economic strengths that position us to succeed over the long term. But to realize our potential for strong, sustainable growth and widespread economic well-being, we must meet hugely consequential policy challenges. And that in turn requires us to restore the effectiveness of our political system.

To younger readers of this book, a political system that fosters effective government might be hard to imagine. But this was not always the case. Walter Mondale, who served for twelve years in the Senate in the 1960s and 1970s before becoming Jimmy Carter's vice president, once told me that when he was in Congress, people fought and argued fiercely.

"The difference," he said, "was that most members of the Senate were basically committed to the idea of governing. And so, at the end of the day, we would work together to find something that we could agree on. Not on every issue, and not every member was willing to do it, and there were some things that we never could agree on. But more often than not. And that's what's missing today."

In other words, fifty or sixty years ago, politicians from opposing parties fiercely disagreed with one another, just as they do today. They sought to be reelected and to defeat members of the opposing party, just as they do today. But they were nevertheless able to work together to accomplish important legislative objectives much more frequently.

In the 1980s, our political system was still functional. Republican President Ronald Reagan and Democratic House Speaker Tip O'Neill were famously able to come to agreements that advanced the country's interests, on issues ranging from the budget to immigration, despite their very different policy views. In 1993, when I arrived in Washington to serve as director of President Clinton's

National Economic Council and prepared to work on our inaugural budget, I assumed I would find a similar level of bipartisan cooperation. I imagined that we'd develop our views, Republicans would develop their views, and then we would work something out.

Instead, there was a stone wall. Not a single Republican voted for our 1993 budget, which passed with slim margins in both the House and the Senate. I had been involved in politics for a long time before joining the administration. I came to Washington thinking that, at the end of the day, people were more often than not going to work together to do what they thought was the right thing for the country. It turned out to be very different than I expected.

In retrospect, it's possible that my time in Washington coincided with the start of a fundamental shift among many political leaders away from a commitment to effective government. It wasn't just our budget that faced unprecedented, lockstep opposition. So did our attempt at health-care reform, despite early pledges on both sides to work together.

When Newt Gingrich became Speaker of the House in 1995, the level of political combativeness increased even further. Gingrich and his caucus attempted to coerce President Clinton into agreeing to their budget proposal by threatening to force a default on our nation's debt. This plan was ultimately thwarted with novel measures we took at the Treasury Department, but it nonetheless represented a dangerous escalation of partisan hostility. As a next step, Gingrich shut down the government later that year.

Yet despite the growing toxicity, leaders who disagreed fiercely were willing to work together across party lines in the Clinton years in areas when they felt it served their political purposes or policy goals. A lot happened as a result. We passed NAFTA. We banned assault weapons. We balanced the budget. We vastly increased the earned income tax credit and expanded the Head Start program. We ratified the creation of the World Trade Organization. We had substantial increases in many other areas of public investment, while reducing our deficits and ultimately balancing the budget for the first time in thirty years. And much else. While there was a great deal that didn't get done, Washington was able to bridge divides through give-and-take to move forward on many fronts, even as the atmosphere grew increasingly partisan and contentious.

Despite some recent bipartisan accomplishments, such as the 2021 infrastructure law and 2022 technological competitiveness bill, that kind of ability to function on a bipartisan basis seems substantially diminished today. If our government consistently fails to recognize and promote the common interest, it creates a downward spiral. I remember Ron Klain, who served as chief of staff to Vice President Gore and went on to become chief of staff to President Biden, saying to me five or so years ago that we were in a vicious cycle. Ineffective government, he said, leads to declining economic conditions for many people, which undermines confidence in democratic governance and increases support for nationalism and populism instead of sound policy. This in turn leads to even less effective government and poorer economic conditions, and on and on, in an ever worsening feedback loop.

A fundamental and foundational challenge facing America today is breaking that vicious cycle. We must reestablish a government effective enough to address our challenges even when there is strong disagreement about key issues.

Having been around politics for roughly five decades, I am

under no illusions about how difficult restoring a functional political process is likely to be. One source of this difficulty is that issues in government are genuinely complex. Once, in a conversation with the political strategist and commentator Paul Begala, I remarked that effective government was the critical requisite with respect to our country's future. He replied, "Effective government in pursuit of what?"

He raised an important point. While debates in the private sector are often complicated, they generally involve questions of means rather than ends. The strategy might be multifaceted, but the primary objective is relatively straightforward: to increase profits over time. Defining the objectives of government is far less simple. Different constituencies, policy thinkers, regions, and individual leaders have their own views and interests, which are all legitimate from their perspectives.

My purpose here is not to provide the answers as to how to restore functionality to our political process, though I do have some thoughts. Instead, my hope is to contribute to our overall understanding of how our system does and doesn't work, to describe the problems as I see them, and to identify what I see as the broad requisites for effective government.

To that end, I would argue that three things are necessary for our political system to succeed: the willingness to make politically difficult decisions; grounding decisions in facts and analysis approached with intellectual integrity, while recognizing that politics will always be involved; and engaging in the give-and-take of principled compromise.

Those outside politics and governance often assume that meeting these requirements is easier than it actually is. For example, when you speak about elected officials, at least in the world of business and markets where I've spent most of my life, you often hear people say that they're all motivated by politics and not the good of the nation. The implication is that politicians ought to be making decisions regardless of the political consequences, and that anything else is disappointing and perhaps even cowardly.

Yet this attitude is no more correct than calling all business-people greedy for seeking to make money. Politicians, like all individuals, have multiple motivations. There's the desire to promote the common good, however one defines it. There is also more personal self-interest, which in politics means the desire to get elected and reelected. Many politicians probably think that in a broad sense, the two objectives come together—to have the chance to make good policy, you must first win elections—just as many businesspeople probably think that by pursuing the success of their activities they are also promoting the success of the economy.

Lloyd Bentsen, who preceded me as secretary of the Treasury in the Clinton administration, once remarked to me in the Oval Office that "good policy is good politics." President Clinton used to make a complementary point, that the politics have to be as good as the policy, or the policy will never happen.

But on some key issues, the politics of good policy are very challenging, however well the message and strategy may be designed. Improving our political system requires us to understand and address this dilemma: How should politicians handle politically difficult decisions in order to meet our most difficult policy challenges?

The answer isn't simple, and it involves recognizing, rather than disregarding, the conflict that elected officials may face. Asking politicians to "put politics aside" and ignore their sense of self-interest will never yield the desired result. After all, as one leading senator once said to me when talking about business-people who criticize politicians for being political, "A politician's job is to get reelected."

One area where good policy and good politics frequently diverge was identified by Margaret Thatcher when she was asked why leaders in major democracies didn't do enough to control the long-term costs of government pensions. "They are very aware of the impending crisis," she said, "but their attitude is this: It's not going to hit on my watch. So why should I take the pain for someone else's gain?"

Policy-makers can, and often should, take steps to reduce short-term costs in order to make their proposals more politically feasible. But there's no way to get around the fact that the combination Thatcher described—long-term gain and short-term pain—defines many of the most serious challenges facing our country and our world. Taking aggressive action against climate change, for example, is necessary to save the planet from catastrophic harm over the next several decades. But any job losses, or increased costs in sectors involving energy, would be felt quickly. (This would be true to some extent even if, as some claim, the net effect on jobs would be positive in the short run due to increased activity in clean energy and other areas.)

The converse of Thatcher's statement is true as well: politicians are often too willing to make decisions where the benefits are short-term and the costs are long-term. For example, rather than abide by the principle of fiscal discipline, it's far easier to spend money or cut taxes without finding a way to cover the cost, thus delivering immediate results to constituents while letting future officeholders deal with the consequences of increased debt. On a state level, it's tempting for leaders to drain a rainy day fund in order to provide increased pensions and benefits for state employees, knowing that the bill will come due on a successor's watch.

The more cynical voters become about politics, the harder it can become for politicians to prioritize the long-term. This is because when elected officials call for short-term sacrifice in order to realize a long-term gain, their constituents may assume that they will bear the costs, while someone else will reap the benefit. In many cases, this isn't true—but the widespread *belief* that it is true further disincentivizes politicians from risking short-term pain for the sake of long-term gain.

Yet failing to address climate change, and setting spending and taxes at unsustainable levels, are not acceptable options if our country is to succeed over time. Which is why an important skill that leaders ought to possess—and that our political system ought to reward—is the ability to make the benefits of politically difficult decisions resonate with people. Too often being called a politician is seen as a negative, when in fact it's a skill set that is essential for our system to work.

I witnessed an effective example of this kind of skill in 1998, when members of President Clinton's economic team were trying to figure out how to spend an unexpected budget surplus, the first in thirty years. Republicans wanted to spend the money on tax cuts; we wanted to use it to pay down the national debt. We were confident that over the long run, our plan would prove more beneficial to the country.

But the president told us that he could never make the case to the American people that debt reduction should be a higher priority than tax cuts. The first involved long-term, little understood, and complicated benefits such as lower interest rates, less risk of financial market disruption, improved business confidence, greater resources available for public investment over time, and greater resilience for dealing with a future financial or geopolitical emergency. The second involved lower taxes.

Then John Hilley, who was at the time the White House legislative director, came up with a clever formulation: "Save Social Security First." Rather than talk about deficit reduction, President Clinton could frame his deficit reduction plan in terms of protecting a program that Americans both understood and supported. The connection was somewhat tenuous, but I believe it was defensible enough on policy grounds that it was not intellectually dishonest. And by making deficit reduction appealing to the short-term political interests of members of Congress who would be needed to legislate the desired outcome, "Save Social Security First" helped the president make the right decision for the long-term interests of the country. Getting the politics right made good policy possible.

Unfortunately, it seems to me that in recent years, some well-meaning reforms have made it harder to create an effective political strategy. Take, for example, measures cutting down on what is known as pork barrel spending. For most of the twentieth century, and the first few years of the twenty-first, it was common to offer lawmakers job-creating infrastructure projects—roads, bridges, and much else—in their districts or states to secure their support for sweeping pieces of legislation.

These local earmarks were at times abused by lawmakers, particularly when they were issued excessively and in secret. But on many other occasions, they were a small price to pay to bring politicians' local and individual agendas into alignment with a larger purpose that was in the nation's interest. The overall benefits of these bills could easily outweigh the relatively minor misallocation of resources involved in the pork. For example, say a bill was likely to help the overall economy. Party leaders could attempt to persuade a member of Congress to support the bill by promising a local project.

But in 2010, good-government and small-government activists worked together to abolish earmarks. In theory, this reform was meant to improve the effectiveness of government. In practice, eliminating earmarks may well have significantly reduced the capacity of our political system to address major challenges, without any major corresponding gain. This is an example of how putting purity ahead of pragmatism can be the enemy of good government. (Earmarks were reinstated, with tools to guard against their abuse, in 2021. I believe this was the right decision.)

Another example where reforms can go too far, undermining the political system they're intended to protect, is transparency. Some level of transparency is a good thing: allowing government to operate in secret would badly undermine public accountability and oversight. At the same time, when negotiations and deliberations are required to be conducted in front of cameras or the media, rather than behind closed doors, they become an opportunity to score political points rather than to reach agreement, which renders a candid exchange of views and of negotiating positions impossible.

Consider a conversation that took place in 1995, when I met with Guillermo Ortiz, the finance minister of Mexico, during the Mexican sovereign debt crisis. The assistance the U.S. government had arranged in partnership with the International Monetary Fund wasn't working, and we were extremely concerned. So Guillermo flew to Washington. I initially said, "You're doing what you need to do, but it's not working, and we're thinking we may need to pull the plug."

In the end, however, the meeting (along with a discussion with Leon Panetta, which I mentioned earlier) convinced us that we should continue the program. If the conversations Larry and I had with Guillermo and Leon had been public, we couldn't have had the exchange of views that enabled us to think through the issues and to make a sound decision based on what we learned. The United States—not to mention Mexico—would have been worse off.

Another reason good politics has become increasingly divorced from good policy in recent years is the much-discussed breakdown of our campaign finance system. I have been engaged for decades in raising money for Democratic candidates and for ideas I support, and I think that kind of engagement can be largely constructive. However, our campaign finance system is hugely counterproductive in many important respects. Massive fund-raising requirements, and the time that elected officials have to spend fund-raising, deter many good people from running for office and take up a great deal of time that those who do get elected to office could otherwise spend governing. All this has become worse as the amounts required to run have become greater.

Finally, much fund-raising, especially on the corporate level, is driven by narrow private interests. And the Supreme Court's extremely unfortunate *Citizens United* decision in 2010, which allowed individuals and corporations to contribute unlimited sums to political causes, has created the opportunity for wealthy donors to exert unprecedented influence over our leaders. Perhaps someday means will be found to remedy these conditions, such as through public funding sufficiently attractive to induce candidates to either forgo or greatly limit fund-raising. (Nor is *Citizens United* the only recent example of how the Court's decisions can greatly affect major issues in our society in ways that are seen by many as activist or politicized. How we should think about this, and how our political system should react to this, will be major issues going forward.)

Another way in which political decisions have become more difficult over the last few decades is the increased importance of primary politics as opposed to general-election politics. Bob Kerrey, who was elected to the Senate in 1988 and served two terms as a Democrat from Nebraska, told me some time ago that he could name a dozen moderate Republican senators whom he could work with during his time in the Senate, but who today could no longer win their party primaries. I think a similar dynamic might be at play, though to a much lesser extent, in the Democratic Party as well.

My complaint is not with primaries in general. If those further to the left or right want to unseat a lawmaker whose views are closer to the center, they should have the chance to make their case, and vice versa if moderates want to unseat a legislator from their party's left or right wing. My concern, however, is that voters in party primaries tend to come from the extremes compared with voters in general elections, and many primaries exclude independents and members of the opposite party. Politicians concerned about winning primary elections—particularly in today's primaries, where each party's extremes are better organized and better financed than they were several decades ago—will therefore be more likely to adhere to the goals of those extremes and less likely to engage across political and policy divides to draw broader support.

Structural reforms to our political process could help realign incentives, so that a commitment to effective governance becomes more likely to help officeholders get elected and reelected. But reforms, however comprehensive, cannot change the reality that for government to be sufficiently effective, politicians, on at least some occasions, must be willing to make decisions that may be unpopular.

During my time in government, elected officials made a substantial number of politically difficult decisions, knowingly taking on the attendant political risks for the sake of a broader policy goal. NAFTA, for example, was quite unpopular with the base of the Democratic Party, yet many members voted for it (understanding that it would not be perfect, and would need to be adjusted) because they rightly believed it would contribute to our overall economic well-being. Similarly, the passage of our 1993 deficit-reducing budget included a small gas tax increase and some small cuts to popular programs, both of which many Democrats in Congress viewed as politically troubling. But taken as a whole, the measures in that budget helped set the stage for years of strong growth, millions of Americans being lifted out of poverty, and economic gains across the income distribution.

Today, politicians seem far less willing to take political risks than they were when I served in government. Some of this increasing reluctance to make politically unpopular decisions probably stems from the changes to our political structure that I highlighted earlier—the decade-long disappearance of earmarks, the end to many limits on campaign contributions, the increased importance of primary politics, and so on.

Changes in the nature and structure of the media have greatly contributed to political dysfunction as well. The mainstream media, which, for all of its faults, has for the most part been committed to intellectual integrity and provided reasonably reliable reporting and well-thought-out opinions on public policy, has declined in influence. Meanwhile, cable TV and social media have become powerful forces fomenting partisanship, enabling the spread of misinformation and allowing politicians to communicate directly with their base and bypass reporters who might hold them accountable.

But the character and culture of our politics, independent of these factors, matter as well. In my experience, politics is like any other field: leaders set a tone and general direction, but trends can take on a life of their own in a kind of snowball effect. When someone who runs for office on a thoughtful platform is defeated by a candidate who panders to the extremes, that can accelerate a downward spiral, influencing who decides to run in the future and how candidates and elected officials speak and act.

Over the past forty years or so, I have seen bad behavior beget worse behavior. If America is to be successful in the twenty-first century, that trend must be reversed. Leaders from all fields in our society ought to recognize that whatever their views may be, and however great their differences may be, we will not succeed unless we are willing to do what is necessary to make our political system work.

Of course, embedded in the idea that our political system must improve to advance the common good are deep, difficult questions. Who defines "common good"? Who's to judge what is bad policy and what is good policy? While I have strong views about the direction our country should take on some issues, along with more uncertain views on others, I recognize that all issues are complex and that views different from mine can have legitimate points on their side and should be considered seriously. By extension, thoughtful, well-meaning people who disagree with me will support their positions as strongly as I support mine.

It would therefore be both unreasonable and unhelpful to say that my opinions are objectively correct and shouldn't be debated. Instead, it's far better—crucial, even—to ground political debates in facts and analysis, with a commitment to intellectual integrity.

Yet too often, that is not how issues are approached. I recall a conversation I had in the 1990s with Orrin Hatch, a Utah Republican who served in the Senate for forty-two years. Orrin was a committed public servant and a very decent person. We were discussing the capital gains tax, the same issue that President Clinton and Trent Lott discussed in the Oval Office in 1997. Orrin insisted that cutting the tax would lead to greater economic growth.

"I don't think the evidence supports that view," I replied. I went on to say that with the exception of a few outliers, studies showed that decreasing the capital gains tax rate has little effect, if any, on either savings or investment, meaning it reduces government revenue over time without creating real public benefit in return.

What happened next surprised me. I expected Orrin to present his own analysis, to rebut mine, and then perhaps cite some studies or economists who supported his views. But instead, he put aside the idea of an evidence-based discussion entirely. I forget the exact words he used, but it came down to, "Cutting the capital gains tax grows the economy. Trust me."

Other politicians may claim to be engaged with the facts, but in practice they too often assert without evidence that the facts support their views, rather than basing their views on the facts.

Take the 1993 budget agreement. By 1998 or 1999, the general view among most economists was that President Clinton's policies had played a substantial role in creating excellent economic conditions. But as I recall it, Bill Archer, the Texas Republican who chaired the House Ways and Means Committee at the time, refused to acknowledge this. Instead, he argued that if we had followed a different path and not raised taxes, conditions would have been even better.

I liked Congressman Archer personally. And I can't definitively prove he was wrong about the policy, because the kind of counterfactual he offered can never be disproven with certainty. But imagine if, instead of applying his broader views about taxes to critique the 1993 deficit reduction program, Congressman Archer had taken a different approach. If he had looked at the reasoning behind the program, and then seriously evaluated what actually happened according to independent, nonpartisan economists, he might have reached a facts-and-analysis-based conclusion that could more soundly inform his thinking on future policy decisions.

This is not to say the congressman and I would have found ourselves in agreement. In a democracy, disagreement is inevitable. But it is vital that those disagreements be resolved with genuine facts and analysis, not competing ideologies and ungrounded opinions.

Intellectual integrity in politics and policy-making is vitally important. In 1992, shortly after the election, President-elect Clinton's team was down in Little Rock, and Leon Panetta, the incoming head of the Office of Management and Budget, was going over the numbers in the budget that was being prepared. I remember very clearly that the president-elect said to Leon, "You know, I'm willing to argue with people about policy all day long. But I don't want anybody ever to attack the integrity of my numbers." He understood that while there will always be fierce debate around big decisions, those debates must be rooted in reality.

This commitment to intellectual integrity is one reason President Clinton always relied on the nonpartisan Congressional Budget Office's assessment of his agenda during his two terms. Sometimes we were happy with the CBO's estimates of the projected costs and benefits of a policy proposal; other times we didn't like their reasoning and thought they were wrong. Yet regardless of our own opinions, we accepted their conclusions and operated on that basis, because they were a nonpartisan arbiter and broadly accepted as such.

Partisanship will always be part of politics, but a firm commitment to an intellectually honest process can make cooperation between parties much more likely. The late Marty Feldstein, who chaired the Council of Economic Advisers under President Reagan, once said to me that he believed that if he as a conservative sat down with a liberal economist equally committed to the spirit of give-and-take, they could reach agreements on the vast majority of the nation's issues. That might be a bit of an exaggeration. But Marty's point was that if politicians were a little more willing to develop their views based on the evidence—rather than starting with positions and then adapting the evidence to support them— our system would be far more functional. I think he was correct in that view.

Throughout my career, I've encountered many other conservatives who share Marty's commitment to, and respect for, intellectual integrity. Alan Greenspan is a Republican with whom I've disagreed on some issues, but he doesn't use numbers that aren't real. Neither does Arthur Brooks, the former head of the American Enterprise Institute, a conservative policy organization. In fact, a few years ago Arthur reached out to the Hamilton Project to discuss this topic.

"You're a think tank made up predominantly of Democrats," he said, "and we're a conservative think tank. But we both agree on the importance of the integrity of facts. How does a democracy survive if we don't have that? So let's do a joint event." And so in March 2017—six weeks after the inauguration of Donald Trump—we did.

Unfortunately, it seems that politicians have become less likely to adopt Arthur and Alan's commitment to intellectual rigor. I believe this is partly because of changes in the media. When I served in government, I was often critical of journalists, and I think some of those criticisms were warranted. But whatever their faults, the three nightly news anchors, along with the Sunday morning shows and the most prominent elements of the print media, expected factual integrity—and had immense influence on public opinion. Senator Daniel Patrick Moynihan famously said that "everyone is entitled to his own opinion but not to his own facts." Broadly speaking, journalism reflected Moynihan's perspective.

Today, on the other hand, it does appear that everyone is entitled to their own facts—or at least can create their own facts, whether they're entitled to them or not. If you don't agree with the view of reality put forward by the journalists at *The New York Times*, *The Wall Street Journal*, and network news, you can find a different "reality" that expresses a worldview you agree with on cable TV or social media. The much-diminished presence of trusted and trustworthy authorities in the media, with a corresponding loss of accountability for those who mislead and deceive, is one reason the political consequences of falsifying or distorting facts and analysis are lower than they were two or three decades ago.

I imagine that in our current political environment, it must be especially tempting to disregard facts and analysis. It would be easy to say, "If they're making up alternative facts for their side, we'll make up facts for our side." But this is a path to perdition. If you believe leaders should make sound decisions—and if you believe government can and should make a positive difference in people's lives—then intellectual integrity in our political debate is essential.

Which brings us to another fundamental reality of our democracy. Even if we restore a greater commitment to integrity around facts and analysis, elected officials often will still have different views based on different interpretations of the facts, different analyses, different judgments, different value choices, and different politics. This is why, throughout our history, almost all major legislation has required a willingness to compromise in order to move forward.

This willingness to compromise is what Walter Mondale referred to when he told me that in the 1960s and 1970s, people would have fierce arguments yet still come together to pass laws. But it is critical to recognize that what Vice President Mondale was referring to is not just what politicians often call the search for common ground. Common-ground negotiations are, in theory anyway, quite simple. Imagine that two politicians, one Democrat and one Republican, compare their positions on a variety of issues, find that they agree on a handful of them, and then decide to act on those limited areas of agreement and ignore everything else. That would be a common-ground agreement. On one hand, neither side is compelled to do anything it disapproves of. On the other hand, much is left unaddressed.

The kind of compromise Mondale was talking about involves true give-and-take. Each side makes concessions—doing things it doesn't agree with and may even consider counterproductive—in order to achieve a broader agreement that both think is on balance beneficial, substantively and politically. Give-and-take is not about finding common ground. It's about moving forward in the absence of common ground. That's what I witnessed in the Oval Office in 1997.

Willingness to compromise does not mean one lacks conviction. For example, I believe strongly in fiscal discipline, and that principle has guided my views and decision-making. But as a policy-maker, I have been willing to support proposals that were not as fiscally disciplined as I would like, provided I felt the gain was worth the cost.

The ability to be true to one's principles while still engaging in compromise is something I used to discuss with Larry Summers when we were at Treasury. Sometimes during tense negotiations, it would become clear that, while our reasoning on an issue or policy had not changed, we would have to give ground in order to achieve a larger purpose, or because we had no choice and opposition was futile.

For example, in the late 1990s a group of lawmakers began advocating measures they claimed would make the IRS more user-friendly, but which we thought could in practice undermine the effectiveness of IRS revenue collection. At some point, despite our concerns, the momentum in favor of the change became unstoppable. In such moments, I often reverted to the same phrase.

"Larry," I would say, "not everything is the Alamo."

For leaders to be effective, and for our political system to function, there must be room for each side to be guided by principle, but all-out last stands must be the rare exception, not the rule. Unfortunately, in recent decades, our political system seems to have become less capable of producing such compromise than it did when I served in government. Principles that once helped frame the give-and-take of a negotiation are now too often considered inviolable, with disastrous consequences for our country.

Consider tax cuts. Small-government conservatives, and those who believe that lower tax rates are the most powerful tool for promoting growth, have long been in favor of lower taxes. But starting in the mid-1980s, and accelerating through the 1990s and 2000s, more Republican lawmakers agreed to something called the Taxpayer Protection Pledge. In signing the pledge, political candidates and elected officials committed to never, under any circumstances, raise income or corporate taxes in the future. By 2011, more than 238 members of the House of Representatives—all but six of the chamber's Republicans, along with two Democrats—had signed.

The tax pledge is a quintessential political bright line, or as it's also commonly called, a litmus test. It takes what was once a strong policy preference—a desire to lower taxes—and recasts it as a principle that cannot be compromised under any circumstances. In 2011, at a primary debate for the Republican presidential nomination, the candidates were asked whether they would support a hypothetical deficit-reducing agreement that would allot ten dollars of spending cuts for every dollar in increased taxes. If you believe in lower deficits and smaller government, as the candidates at the debate claimed to, walking away from such a deal should be unthinkable. But because even an agreement so clearly in their favor would violate the litmus test, every one of the potential Republican nominees said they would refuse to accept the deal.

In other cases, rather than refusing to accept a given position, elected officials might categorically refuse to work with an entire party. For example, after Barack Obama took office, it appeared as though some leading Republicans in Congress refused to strike any kind of meaningful deal with Democrats, even on issues that had previously been bipartisan. (This sentiment was expressed most notably when then–Senate Minority Leader Mitch McConnell said, "The single most important thing we want to achieve is for President Obama to be a one-term president.")

Litmus tests existed when I served in government. But they seem far more prevalent today. The result is that compromise is becoming harder and harder to reach.

Here I should note that the proliferation of inviolable principles, and thus the rejection of compromise, is particularly ill suited to the objectives most Democrats share. For those of us who believe government has a critical role to play in growing our economy and improving people's lives, being unable to reach agreements should not be an acceptable outcome.

So how can we determine when and how to compromise? How are we to know which issues really are the Alamo, and which are negotiable? Like so much else in life, the more you think about this, the more complex it seems. But I think the bottom line is that inviolable (or nearly inviolable) principles should be the infrequent exception rather than the rule. The preponderance of the time, probabilistic thinking and an expected value–mindset allow for the nuance and complexity that the bright-line approach lacks. The yellow-pad approach to compromise, in other words, is most likely to lead to optimal outcomes.

Consider a hypothetical example involving an otherwise liberal candidate for Congress who supports the National Rifle Association. Some might argue that this is exactly the right time to apply a litmus test: if a candidate supports the NRA and its policies that increase the amount of gun violence in this country, you shouldn't support them. I am personally in favor of stronger regulations on guns, which means that in most cases I wouldn't support an NRA-backed candidate.

But let's say that, by supporting a handful of NRA-endorsed candidates, Democrats' odds of winning control of the House of Representatives, and therefore of securing a majority for a whole host of issues Democrats care about, including gun-safety legislation, would go up by 10 or 20 percent. In this hypothetical situation, the yellow pad would allow that context to be considered, where a bright-line approach would not. And in such a situation, it does seem to me that the yellow pad would lead to a far better outcome, which would be backing a few gun-friendly candidates in exchange for a meaningfully increased chance of a Democratic-controlled Congress.

Similarly, a yellow pad allows far more nuance—and in my opinion better decision-making—when it comes to deciding whether to seek a compromise with certain people. Consider a remark I heard Joe Biden make at a fund-raiser early in the 2020 presidential campaign, about how he had found ways to advance proposals he cared about by working with Herman Talmadge and James Eastland—two former southern Democratic senators who were ardent supporters of white supremacy and Jim Crow, which Biden abhorred. Few people in the room gave Biden's comment much thought, and indeed, not long after, Representative John Lewis said he agreed with Biden that it was worth trying to negotiate with people whose views you found repugnant. Yet Biden's remarks generated a firestorm.

Like most people, I find Talmadge's and Eastland's views repellent. In fact, were I to take an expected-value approach to negotiating with them, I would add a number of costs that might typically go overlooked. For one thing, there's the harm I would do by legitimizing, even in a small way, people who have dedicated much of their lives to a despicable cause. For another, there's the long-term reputational cost of being associated with someone whose views are widely (and in my view, rightly) considered vile. These added costs would indeed make compromise less likely.

Yet if, even after taking all these costs into account, a compromise still appeared likely to be beneficial, I would take it. I certainly wouldn't reject negotiations out of hand, before even finding out whether a worthwhile deal might be reached.

This approach to principled compromise suggests that walking away from a negotiation should be a last resort. In a situation where it seems compromise can't be reached, the focus should then be on trying to change the circumstances—the political incentives, policy options, perhaps the facts on the ground—in a way that reshapes the expected-value calculations and allows for a more successful effort at a sensible, principled compromise.

I do not believe that restoring the willingness to compromise will solve all of our country's problems. Yet I believe that through principled compromises, we could make great progress on the preponderance of issues that matter most to most Americans.

One can hope that the political system is able to heal itself, at least to some extent. If leaders emerge who succeed politically with a commitment to effective government that resonates with voters, we could see a snowball effect as politicians adjust their political calculations in that direction. And that could begin with politicians at the federal level, or with governors and mayors who show that seriousness about governing works electorally.

But I believe we are likely to have effective government only if all of us—from every sector of society—do a far better job coming together to restore it. Business must recognize that having a political system capable of tackling big challenges is in its interest. Civil society groups and nonprofits must recognize that restoring effectiveness in government is crucial for all of us, no matter the issues we most care about. Perhaps most important of all, voters must recognize that the willingness to be intellectually honest and to compromise are crucial qualities in a leader—and they must demand those qualities from candidates who hope to earn their support. It is the job of all of us to do whatever we can—from voting and interacting with candidates and elected officials to making decisions about whose campaigns to support and which causes to associate ourselves with—to reverse the trend toward dysfunction in our political process.

Would all this be enough? To what extent would these kinds of changes in our political culture motivate structural reforms, and to what extent do we need structural reform to create the conditions for cultural change? I wish I knew the answers, or even could state my views with a high degree of confidence. But I don't and can't. There has always been a gap between how we hope our system of government will function and how it actually functions. It is dismaying to watch that gap grow wider and wider, and even more dismaying that there appears to be no clear way to reverse the trend.

Yet I have lived long enough to see seemingly inexorable trends reversed. To use just one example, when I was in college, there was a widely held view that the Soviets were winning the Cold War. It didn't work out that way. A situation can go years or decades without improvement, and then for whatever reason an inflection point arrives and things change dramatically, rapidly, and for the better.

It is hard to predict when or why these inflection points may occur. But the fact that America's system of government has become less functional over the past few decades does not mean that it is doomed. Instead, I hope—and think history suggests—that there will likely be opportunities to change the direction of what many see as a seemingly inexorable trend that puts our country at risk. We must remain alert to those opportunities, so that we are prepared to seize them when they arrive.

Chapter IX

LABELS ARE NO
SUBSTITUTE FOR THOUGHT

About a decade ago, I met the CIA station chief in China. I had gone to Beijing for a conference, and Jon Huntsman, the former Utah governor then serving as U.S. ambassador, invited me to his residence. As we were discussing the two countries' respective trajectories, he introduced his colleague from the intelligence community.

Turning to the station chief, I asked him to describe the prevailing point of view within the Chinese government. What he said—and the bluntness with which he said it—stuck with me.

"They think they're entering the station, and we're leaving it."

At the time, I was hearing some version of the first half of this idea—that China is entering a period of unmatched global influence not unlike the one the United States has enjoyed since World War II—expressed frequently as either a prediction or a concern, both from China experts and from leaders in the American business community. More worryingly, the second half of this idea—that America's best days are behind it—seems more pervasive today than at any time I can remember.

The challenge we face is not just about our economic status relative to China or any other country, but, far more important, about our own long-term outlook. A growing number of influential leaders and experts, and many in the public at large, worry that along with increasing political dysfunction and social friction, the United States is inevitably heading toward increasingly disappointing economic growth over the longer term.

I don't know that I've ever been described as Pollyanna-ish about anything, particularly regarding economics. But while our country faces tremendous challenges, I don't share the pessimistic views that now seem to be gaining traction.

I believe America has tremendous long-term economic strengths. We have a dynamic and entrepreneurial culture, strong research universities with established pipelines to commercialize their research, flexible labor and capital markets, the rule of law, better age-related workforce demographics than other major economies, vast natural resources, and much else. I would rather engage in economic activity—for example, starting, investing in, or running a business—in the United States than in any other country. If we put in place measures to more broadly share the benefits of economic growth, there is more potential for workers to experience a steadily rising standard of living in America than anywhere else.

We are well positioned to succeed. But whether we realize our potential or muddle along economically with increasing social strife will depend on the decisions we make as a country.

This has always been true to some extent. Yet it is truer now than at any point I can remember. In the post–World War II decades, we were an unparalleled economic giant. That insulated us, at least in certain ways, from the potential consequences of subpar decisions. But that's no longer the case. Other countries are competing more assertively, and while our overall role in the global economy is still unmatched, the gap between the United States and other nations has shrunk. If we fail to make sound decisions moving forward, it's unlikely that our structural advantages, considerable though they are, will be enough to provide prosperity over the long term.

In other words, our economic future will be decided in large part by our collective answer to a question I've been engaging with, in some form or another, for more than half a century:

What approach should we take toward the most important policy challenges we face?

As different policy ideas have gained and lost popularity over the decades, I've thought about how one's basic approach toward policy-making ought to change over time. And I think the answer is that it shouldn't. When it comes to the specifics of policy, rather than the overall way one thinks about policy-making, flexibility is important. One should always be learning from the past and applying it to the present. When circumstances change, new facts come to light, or new analytic insights are developed, policies should change to reflect them. But I believe that even as policy positions change, the keys to sound policy-making do not.

Growing up, I never imagined that so much of my adult life would be spent thinking about what these keys to sound policy-making are. For me, and I would guess for many people, my interest in politics came before my interest in policy. My grandfather

Samuel Seiderman ran one of New York City's most influential Democratic clubs, back in the days when those types of organizations still mattered.

My mother adored her father, and I looked up to him as well. Though it is hard to know exactly where one's interests come from, his influence may well be what sparked my interest in politics from an early age. Even after I began my career in markets, I knew I would want to find ways to get involved politically as well.

As I began to engage more politically, did I ever consider doing so as a Republican? The short answer is no.

Partly this was because I came from a family of Democrats. But as I established my own political views independent of any family background, I continued to feel closer to the mainstream of the Democratic Party than the Republican Party. I had no moral belief in large government or small government, but as a practical matter, I felt our economy could be successful only if a strong and effective government functioned side by side with a market-based economic system, addressing the issues that markets by their nature won't address effectively.

I also held the subjective view that government has a moral imperative to provide for the general well-being, which means helping everyone, especially those in low-income communities, achieve a decent standard of living and share broadly in the benefits of growth. (I thought this was greatly in our economic interest as well, since helping low-income communities reduces public costs in the long run, boosts productivity, and increases social cohesion.)

I don't hold every policy view generally ascribed to Democrats or reject every policy view generally ascribed to Republicans. But fifty years after I began to get more involved in politics, I still feel that my views are much closer to those of most Democrats than those of most Republicans. And while both parties have extremes, even when I disagree with policy prescriptions held by some members of the Democratic Party, I often relate to their broad objectives (for example, access to health care, reducing inequality, or fighting climate change). My disagreements with the extremes of the Republican Party, on the other hand, generally involve both means and ends—and these disagreements have intensified over the past several years, even more so in the wake of efforts to overturn the 2020 election.

Yet while I'm a lifelong Democrat, I believe policy debates often rely too heavily on partisan or ideological labels to simplify complex questions. For example, the average Democrat is significantly more likely than the average Republican to support higher taxes on the wealthy to fund important functions of government. I share that view. But when it comes to the policy specifics—What effects do various types of tax increases have on economic growth? How much revenue should we seek to raise in order to provide important public services? Exactly how should these tax increases on the wealthy be structured?—party affiliation does little to provide constructive answers.

Ideological labels are frequently not just reductive but counterproductive. A few years ago, I suggested to a leading Democratic policy thinker—someone who's served at very high levels in government and whose intellect I respect—that we needed a cost-benefit framework for thinking through regulatory reform. He responded by saying, "We need a progressive approach to regulatory reform."

Broadly speaking, this person and I have similar policy views, but I bristled at his language. In my view, one ought to decide on a goal, and then try to figure out what policies most effectively advance it. If you make the soundest possible decisions regarding regulatory policy, and those decisions are coincidentally labeled "progressive" (or "moderate" or "conservative" or anything else), then the label is irrelevant. If you reject the soundest possible decision in favor of one that could better fall into a certain ideological category, then guiding the decision using a label is actively harmful.

In my experience, the most important distinction when discussing policy is not between liberalism and conservatism, progressivism and centrism, partisanship and bipartisanship, reform and institutionalism, or anything along those lines. The most important distinction is between those who accept that policy issues are complicated and think through them carefully based on facts and analysis approached with intellectual integrity, and those who do not. Dogma and shorthand can make the complex seem simple, but they undermine sound decision-making.

Edward R. Murrow, one of the finest journalists of his era, once said, "Our major policy obligation is not to mistake slogans for solutions." In a similar vein, I believe that where policy is concerned, labels are no substitute for thought.

In practice, it's quite difficult to balance the endless complexity of interconnected policy issues with the need to make decisions. When I first got to the Treasury Department, and Sylvia Mathews began her new role as my chief of staff, she asked me, "What are your priorities?"

"Oh, my priorities? That's easy," I replied. Then I listed about thirty items.

"You can't have thirty priorities," she said. To which I said, "Yes

I can. They're all my priorities." I suspect she may have wanted to strangle me.

As a practical matter, Sylvia was right that you can't do thirty things at once. Yet I think I had a point as well. Policy-makers should always keep in mind that no prospective action or decision exists in isolation. Everything relates to everything else.

This is why a well-run policy-making process is so important: it can enable leaders to acknowledge complexity without being overwhelmed by it. Such a process must be grounded in the recognition that nothing is certain and that all decisions involve weighing probabilities and trade-offs. But there are additional aspects of a thoughtful approach to policy-making that avoids the influence of labels, allows for nuanced and careful thinking, and enables leaders to make sound decisions.

The policy-making process should start by defining objectives. A surprising amount of the time, decision-makers begin to evaluate choices before making a real effort to determine what goal, or goals, they hope to accomplish. The act of explicitly and rigorously describing one's objectives can help bring the entire team together and provide a disciplined framework for thinking through decisions. Leaders should know what they hope to accomplish before they decide what they're going to do.

Another crucial element of policy-making is adopting the right approach toward experts. Disregarding experts can be disastrous. But "listening to the experts" is complicated. For one thing, experts can be wrong in their assessments and predictions, in part because they can become bogged down in their models and theories and lose sight of real-world factors that models don't capture. Also, experts often disagree with one another—there's rarely a clear expert consensus to follow.

Instead of relying completely on experts, or dismissing them, I believe policy-makers should strike a balance. They should listen carefully to experts, work hard to understand their views, and then make their own judgments. At Treasury, for example, we had an outstanding group of both economists and highly knowledgeable non-economists who could identify and refine key questions, develop policy or decision options in response to those questions, and lay out analysis and facts to help guide my decisions. As my colleagues expressed their views and judgments, I would often ask them to explain the opposing view to theirs, or to mine, in order to broaden the discussion and to identify possible flaws in thinking.

I didn't need to be as knowledgeable about economics as the economists I worked with. (Although it was certainly helpful to work with a deputy secretary who was one of the nation's leading economists.) But it was critically important that I was conversant with the economic concepts that informed their thinking, so that I could engage in serious deliberations. If someone brought up a point or an argument in a meeting that I didn't fully understand, I didn't mind displaying my ignorance. I would ask them to explain what they meant.

Listening carefully is an important skill, and not only when in the presence of experts. In my experience, the best policy-makers tend to be excellent listeners. That doesn't mean they're easily swayed, but it does mean that they fully engage with others' opinions. A good listener will process what you say and then give you a well-reasoned response, whether in agreement or disagreement.

Good listeners aren't necessarily polite listeners. Larry Summers, for example, will tell you quite bluntly when he thinks you're wrong. But if you ask him to repeat your opinion back to you, he'll be able to demonstrate that he understands exactly what you were talking about, even if he disagrees. And if you ask him to make the best possible case against his own position, he won't give you a flimsy straw man—he'll lay out cogent, detailed arguments.

Policy-makers should also think carefully about *when* to make a big decision. Often, a leader must choose a path forward quickly. Not choosing would itself be a choice, because other options would quickly become unavailable. But in many cases, leaders can delay a choice, not out of fear or undue hesitancy, but in order to gather more information or see how circumstances develop. I call this "preserving optionality."

One way to preserve optionality is simple: Ask yourself, "Do I have to make this decision right now?" If the answer is no, figure out what, if anything, would help you make a better decision later. But leaders can also preserve optionality through other means. They can make a decision that addresses urgent concerns but doesn't lock them into a course of action for the long term. Or they can choose the course of action that keeps open the greatest number of options in the future. (In this way, I'd argue that preserving optionality is what I did by going to law school. I thought it unlikely that I would want to practice law, but law school seemed to be good preparation for a wide range of career choices.)

Another important aspect of effective policy-making is the ability to simultaneously consider both politics and policy. One reason I believe many people who go from business into government struggle with the transition, and often fail to make it successfully, is the added level of complexity I referred to earlier. Unlike in business, policy decisions almost always involve large groups of stakeholders and competing interests. No matter what any policy-maker—even the president—would like to do, it's generally necessary to get a large amount of buy-in before a policy can be put into place.

I believe that the politics should be in service of the policy, not vice versa. But politics and policy need to be considered together in decision-making, because as I've said before, if the politics can't be made to work, the policy becomes difficult or even impossible to implement effectively.

At the same time, political concerns can be used disingenuously to oppose a policy option. If someone opposes a decision, but doesn't have a particularly persuasive argument against it, they might dismiss it as politically undoable rather than engage with it on its merits. There's no easy way to avoid this problem. The only solution is to have teams and leaders committed to evaluating both politics and policy with intellectual rigor and integrity.

Policy-makers should also apply cost-benefit analysis to policy options. It may seem rather straightforward that if a policy's benefits outweigh its costs, the measure should be adopted, and if not, it should not. But few things are that simple. For example, not all variables can be readily quantified. What is the value of a human life? Or a clean stream? Or an abstract notion such as freedom? Even when something can't be readily quantified, that doesn't make it any less real, and it should still be included in a cost-benefit framework.

Another complexity policy-makers must engage with involves the time horizons over which costs and benefits will be examined. Some policy ideas that are highly beneficial in the short term might be highly costly in the long term, and vice versa. One way of thinking about this is to decide on what is known as a "discount rate" as you make your expected-value calculations. For example, a gain of one hundred dollars might be deemed to be worth one hundred dollars if it is realized tomorrow, fifty dollars if it's realized a decade from now, and twenty dollars if it's realized twenty years from now.

Second- and third-order costs and benefits must be considered and weighed as well. Let's say a policy would be beneficial but would substantially reduce the political appetite for enacting a different, even more beneficial policy later on. Is the net benefit positive or negative?

Policy-makers must also avoid the temptation to examine only the benefits of a policy while avoiding the subject of its costs. In 1982, Ted Kennedy was thinking about running for president a second time, after challenging Jimmy Carter in the 1980 Democratic primary, and I went to see him speak. He was an excellent orator and a prominent voice in the Senate, and I shared his concerns about education, combating poverty, and much else. I remember being quite impressed. "What he's saying really makes sense," I thought.

But when he finished, I realized he'd never said anything about how he was going to pay for his many proposals. My concern was not that he proposed a payment method I disagreed with, or that I felt lacked fiscal discipline. My concern was that he had not proposed a payment method at all. Either he hadn't thought about how to pay for things, he didn't want to deal with the politics of paying for them, or he figured the topic wasn't important enough to include in his speech. I decided that just wasn't going to work, and I declined to get involved in his campaign.

Another important thing to keep in mind when conducting cost-benefit analysis is that sometimes even the "best" decision won't lead to a positive result. Some policy-makers find this hard to accept. I remember being in the Situation Room with another senior official in the Clinton White House. Larry Summers and I presented a series of options, all of which were likely to lead to negative outcomes. "There must be a good answer," the official said.

"No," we replied. "There isn't."

Larry and I weren't implying that all choices were equal. We were, however, saying that in some cases, every possible course of action is likely to end badly. Put differently, every choice available, including doing nothing, is likely to result in significant negative consequences.

In such cases, it's not productive to continue searching for a "good" choice. You simply have to recognize that all choices are bad, or perhaps even terrible, and search diligently for the least bad.

For example, when facing the Mexican financial crisis, we recognized that one option—intervention in the form of lending funds to Mexico—could create what is called "moral hazard," because lenders might then assume we would intervene in other emerging-market debt situations if those countries ran into trouble. This belief could lead lenders to extend credit without appropriate discipline, increasing the probability of future trouble. Similarly, other governments might assume that the United States would bail them out if they made unsound choices about borrowing. These would be bad outcomes.

Yet the other option, doing nothing, would lead to bad outcomes, too. We felt that failing to intervene would likely lead to severe and prolonged duress in the Mexican economy, contagion to other emerging-market countries as concerned creditors withdrew from them as well, and an adverse impact on the American economy. No matter which course of action we pursued, the costs could be substantial, with some form of negative consequences likely to be felt. But we felt that intervention was the least-bad choice, so that's what we recommended to the president.

Fortunately, when it comes to our overall economic outlook and the policy agenda we ought to adopt in the coming decades, we do have good choices available to us. And after many decades immersed in economic policy debates, I think the course of action that gives us the best chance to harness our long-term advantages—an approach I've seen work very effectively for Americans across the economic spectrum before, and that I believe can work again—is one often referred to as "inclusive growth."

In my view, at the heart of inclusive growth is the idea that economic growth and broadly shared economic well-being are interdependent objectives. It is not possible to provide an acceptable and rising standard of living for our people, overcome poverty, or otherwise adequately promote the general welfare without relatively strong growth over time. It is true that policies I tend to support—such as higher taxation on the wealthy in order to fund public investment and social safety net programs—transfer money from those with the highest incomes and wealth to middle-class and lower-income families. But as a practical matter, redistribution can accomplish only so much. Healthy growth is necessary for job creation, a lower unemployment rate (which tends to increase wages), and the fiscal resources necessary for public investment.

At the same time, it would be a mistake to focus on growth without regard to the broad-based distribution of prosperity. In the long run, that won't work either. Among its many other benefits, widespread economic well-being creates greater consumer demand. It provides workers with more financial capacity to obtain education and training that contribute to higher earnings and increased productivity. It can also build broad public support for market-based economics and trade liberalization. Just as growth is necessary for widespread well-being, widespread well-being is necessary for strong and sustained growth.

A second observation that undergirds inclusive growth is that, in the post–World War II era, no country has been able to achieve consistently strong economic growth without a foundational commitment to a market-based economy. China began substantial economic improvement only in 1978, when it embraced crucial elements of market-based economics. (It has reiterated this commitment frequently, though its current situation and future trajectory are complex and uncertain.) And while the Nordic countries, sometimes held up as a model for socialism, have higher taxes and much stronger social safety nets than the United States, they have market-based economies—that is to say, private ownership of the means of production—as well.

I don't "believe in free markets" in any kind of moral or ideological sense. But the evidence clearly shows that markets are the best system for achieving economic growth.

Yet there are many critically important issues that markets by their very nature cannot and will not address effectively, from poverty and widening inequality to climate change and more. We will succeed over time only if we have a strong and effective government to do what markets won't.

We can't choose between growth and a more equal society. We need both. We can't choose between governments and markets. We need both.

When describing what achieving inclusive growth might look

like, I find it helpful to divide the role of effective government into three main areas. The first area is public investment. Market forces are highly effective at encouraging investment in areas where the returns on investment accrue to the investors, especially when those gains are likely to materialize in the short or medium term. But when returns on investment accrue primarily to the public, or when those returns might take a long time to be realized, markets are unlikely to adequately invest.

As a result, one of the primary roles of a strong and effective government is to fill the large gaps left by private investing, spending public funds on investments that promote the general welfare and grow the overall economy. To list just a few examples, we should build much more public infrastructure, for both the transportation of people and goods and the movement of information via high-speed networks. (While President Biden's bipartisan infrastructure law was a significant step forward, even more investment is needed to fully make up for lost time.) We should also greatly increase public support for basic and applied research and development. Government research has led to an enormous number of innovations, from radar and GPS navigation to smartphones and the internet, that have improved lives and vastly contributed to the American economy.

Other public investments both contribute to economic growth and serve the vital purpose of providing a social safety net. Among their other benefits, for example, Medicare and Social Security make older Americans less likely to fall into poverty. This isn't just good for them and their families. On a broader economic level, it helps maintain demand in markets and provides popular public benefits that can contribute to support for our market-based economic system. In a similar vein, antipoverty measures reduce costs to society and increase productivity, thus providing a high rate of return on investment to taxpayers.

Even if these measures had no economic impact, I still think they would be well worth the expense, because I believe government should help support the most vulnerable members of society. But as I have pointed out to more conservative friends and colleagues on many occasions, you don't have to share my subjective opinions on the role of government to believe in the importance of publicly funded social programs. You merely have to recognize the enormous benefits these programs bring to the economy overall.

Of course, large public investments come with large public costs, and those costs must be paid, either by raising revenue, borrowing money, spending less somewhere else, or a combination of all three.

How should the government pay for the investments it ought to make? This question brings us to the second major role of an effective government in promoting inclusive growth: setting sound fiscal policy.

Fiscal policy is not always considered a scintillating subject. My wife, Judy, suggested I call the following portion of this chapter "Slog Through It." But fiscal issues are probably the area of economic policy with which I've been most closely associated throughout my career, and I feel it's important to discuss the topic in at least some detail.

This is especially true because fiscal policy positions are frequently oversimplified. Nuanced issues are reduced to a binary struggle, mischaracterizing people as either "fiscal hawks" (or sometimes "deficit hawks") who believe in low deficits, and "fiscal doves" who believe that relatively unconstrained borrowing—and thus higher deficits—can be undertaken without adverse effects.

I'm generally lumped in the "hawk" camp, but this is one of those cases where labels obscure as much as they illuminate. It's true that I believe in fiscal discipline, which is to say that I think we should be careful about what we spend public money on and how large we allow the federal debt to grow relative to the overall size of our economy. But I'm not against debt or deficits per se. During the Great Recession, and more recently at the start of the coronavirus pandemic, I spoke and wrote about the need for robust relief and stimulus measures funded by deficit spending to offset the shortage of private demand in the economy.

The most important divide, in my view, is not between fiscal hawks and doves. It's between those who think rigorously and carefully about questions surrounding fiscal issues and those who act as though these questions have easy answers.

It seems to me that a growing number of politicians, policy-makers, and even a handful of academics now fall into the latter camp. At the extremes, they might argue either that we should lower deficits no matter the long-term social or economic costs, or that we can borrow unlimited sums of money indefinitely. A less extreme version of the former approach, but hardly a more rigorous one, is claiming to believe deficits matter, just not when it comes to one's own political priorities, such as tax cuts on the right or public spending on the left.

Some of the people who don't think rigorously about fiscal matters might end up taking policy positions similar to mine. But I feel I have much more in common with someone who disagrees with me on policy but engages carefully with the relevant issues than I do with someone who doesn't engage thoughtfully with those issues but happens to agree with me on policy.

For example, some economists argue that while we can't indefinitely increase our debt relative to the overall size of our economy (usually referred to as our "debt-to-GDP ratio"), we still have a lot of room to go. And that argument was made even more forcefully when interest rates had been low for many years, before they began rising in 2022.

Many of the economists and experts who make this kind of argument have thought this issue through. They and I would agree on basic points. First, there is some limit to how much debt the United States can accrue. Second, this limit cannot be precisely ascertained ahead of time because it depends, among other factors, on the psychology of markets, business confidence, and how willing the markets are to lend the federal government money.

But I nonetheless disagree with their conclusions. This is not because I am a deficit hawk in some ideological sense. It's because, in my judgment, running higher deficits over a long period would be much riskier than these economic policy thinkers believe.

In fact, I think even our current longer-term fiscal trajectory—which is to say, our current projected debt-to-GDP ratio—creates a web of serious and interrelated risks. Basic economic theory suggests that governments should borrow and spend more money during downturns, to make up for lost consumer and business demand, and should reduce their debt-to-GDP ratio during periods of economic strength by lowering spending, increasing revenue, or both. But in recent decades, we too often haven't followed that strategy. Instead, we've run large deficits in both good times and bad, ratcheting up our debt-to-GDP ratio to the highest level in our country's history, other than in the immediate aftermath of World War II.

This creates the possibility that markets will be less willing to lend the Treasury money during a future downturn, which would leave us far less economically resilient. Our high levels of borrowing now could also leave us less able to make deficit-funded public investments in the future, either because market interest rates would react adversely to the increased borrowing, because of a lack of political appetite to make those additional investments, or both. (Deficit-funded public investment can have enormous importance, but the benefits of those investments still must be weighed against the risks that the deficits create, including the risk of significantly higher interest rates or even of a financial crisis, either of which would make such investment unsound or impossible.) While excessive borrowing and spending are not the only causes of inflation, they can contribute to inflation by overheating the economy.

As I write this, inflation is a major concern for American consumers, workers, and policymakers. But inflation is not the only risk associated with unsound fiscal policy. There are others, including the potential weakening of the dollar, foreign capital withdrawal from our markets, and possible market concern about future inflation or about future imbalances between our economy's supply of and demand for savings. For all these reasons, an unsound fiscal course could lead interest rates to rise significantly at some unpredictable time. At the extreme, that could produce a financial crisis.

In January 2021, Peter Orszag, the former director of the Office of Management and Budget, the Nobel Prize–winning economist Joseph Stiglitz, and I contended in a paper that there was "deep uncertainty" with respect to future inflation and interest rates. I think events have borne that out. The broader point is that there is always great uncertainty with respect to these conditions, even after long periods of quiescence on inflation and interest rates, and that should be taken into account in calculating the risks of deficit funding for spending or for tax cuts.

It's important to remember that fiscal conditions can have psychological effects that models don't fully capture. In the early 1990s, for example, concern over our country's fiscal sustainability, and the uncertainty it created regarding our country's economic policy more broadly, undermined business confidence in the capacity of our political system to meet our challenges. That created a drag on investment and hiring and thus on the economy overall.

The risks associated with unsound debt-to-GDP ratios and deficits did not materialize for a long time, although our deficits probably decreased support for public investment in recent years, and in 2022 the economy experienced substantial inflationary pressure due in part to deficit spending. And while there is no certainty about whether current fiscal conditions are out of sync with fundamentals, the fact that our current debt-to-GDP ratio is at historic highs—near its highest level since 1946—suggests at least the possibility of a harsh correction sometime in the future.

But whether I'm right or wrong about the probabilities of these risks materializing, they aren't risks we need to take. Before the coronavirus pandemic, federal tax revenues as a percentage of GDP were well below the historical average for a full-employment economy, and even further below where they were during the economic boom of the 1990s. Rather than borrow more money for still unmet infrastructure needs, antipoverty programs, and other worthy investments, we can raise the necessary funds via progressive tax increases and gradually improve our intermediate and longer-term fiscal trajectory. (I use "progressive" here in an economic rather than political sense, to describe taxes where the burden falls disproportionately on those with the highest incomes and wealth.)

Nor is raising revenue the only way to improve our fiscal picture while continuing to make much-needed public investments. Our country's current ratio of national health-care costs to GDP vastly exceeds that of other developed economies, with no better health outcomes. This means we have an opportunity, in theory at least, to reduce health-care costs, which would reduce the costs of federal health-care programs without sacrificing patient care.

To sum up, I believe that instead of continuing to incur the risks associated with the current longer-term trajectory of our debt-to-GDP ratio, we should invest wisely, increase revenue through progressive taxation rather than relying so heavily on borrowing money, and reduce costs where possible through greater efficiency, in order to give us more room to pursue a wide variety of necessary public programs. I don't think a fiscal policy agenda that adopts such an approach is either hawkish or dovish. But I do believe such an agenda would best position the American economy for long-term success.

Beyond raising and spending funds, there is a third role I believe government must play, which is to address what I call "structural issues." This is a bit of a catchall—and there's some overlap, because many structural issues also involve greater public investment. But broadly speaking, I'm referring to the issues other than public investment that can be effectively addressed only through governmental action—either legislation or executive-branch rulemaking.

One such issue is regulation. Too often the deliberation in this area involves questions of quantity—"How much regulation should we have?"—rather than the merits of proposed or existing regulation. Even when regulations are considered on the merits, the debate is often relatively undisciplined and ideological. That is why I think we would be well served by applying a rigorous cost-benefit framework.

Some past administrations, including President Clinton's and President Obama's, have tried this, and while they met with only limited success, future administrations should continue trying, because the gains could be enormous. (To increase the chances of success, we should significantly increase the staff and resources available to the federal Office of Management and Budget, where regulatory review is housed.)

Some of my fellow Democrats are skeptical of a cost-benefit approach to regulation because it has been used in the past to allow businesses to avoid rules that would be in the overall public interest, and they worry it would inevitably be biased toward business in the future. But if policy-makers consider the full range of costs and benefits—such as whether regulations reduce economic inequality and the future costs of climate change—I don't think this would be the case. For example, given the enormous economic damage that would be done by unmitigated climate change, taking a cost-benefit approach should lead to strengthening, not weakening, environmental regulation.

In the financial sector, a cost-benefit approach would similarly lead to more effective regulatory policy, while making the need for such regulations clearer. I believe that markets go to excess because of greed and fear. From the time I took on a more senior role at Goldman Sachs, which is when I began considering market risks in a more comprehensive way, I supported financial regulations designed to make systemic market failure less likely.

A lack of effective financial regulation invites serious problems including market manipulation, a decline in the creditworthiness of systemically important institutions, and a lack of appropriate consumer protection. Finally, effective financial regulations have the second-order benefit of increasing support for our market-based economic system, because they increase the likelihood that most people will feel that the system benefits them and isn't taking advantage of them.

This last point about maintaining public support for our market-based economic system is frequently overlooked. Take, for example, labor policy. Many CEOs I know oppose unions. I think that's a mistake. If CEOs want to maintain support for market-based economics, flexible labor markets, trade liberalization, and all the other priorities for a successful economy, the American people must feel these policies are working for them. Unions can play a critical role in doing that by better bringing more of the benefits of economic growth to all sectors of society. I think this effect is positive in and of itself. But even if you disagree, broad-based participation in the benefits of our economy will build support for sound economic policy, which is in companies' interest.

As with climate change, my views on the importance of reducing income inequality have changed in recent years. A few years ago, Heather Boushey, an economist who has advised many Democrats and was later chosen by President Biden to be a member of his Council of Economic Advisers, came to my office to talk with me about the subject. At the time, I believed that while widely shared economic well-being was a central objective of sound economic policy-making, reducing economic inequality per se—that is, narrowing the gap between the top and the bottom—was not.

But Heather presented a set of ideas I had not heard before. As inequality expands, she argued, the wealthy lose their sense of having a stake in many aspects of society and in policy outcomes that affect the country as a whole, such as public education, universal health care, and combating poverty. Because the wealthy also have disproportionate political influence, their sense of disconnection could lead the country to not pursue those policy outcomes as fully as it should, thus causing more people to feel the system isn't working for them, which erodes support for market-based economics. In addition, rising inequality can increase social friction. Heather convinced me that even if standards of living were steadily improving for people across the income distribution, income inequality would still threaten the effectiveness of our government, the strength of our economy, and the cohesiveness of our society.

My conversation with Heather is, in my view, an example of why applying cost-benefit analysis to structural issues is not a centrist approach, or a progressive or conservative one. It's common sense. Doing one's best to fully understand the impact of proposed measures, and reflecting that understanding in one's decisions, is required for sound policy-making. And what I think are the most commonly employed alternatives to a rigorous cost-benefit approach—basing decisions on whether they are construed to serve an ideological cause or on opinions not thoughtfully grounded in facts and analysis—are highly detrimental.

Yet even if a cost-benefit framework is adopted and supported throughout the federal government, there will always be structural issues that are difficult to deal with, both politically and substantively.

A good example is trade. The long-standing theory that undergirds much trade policy involves comparative advantage. In simple terms, each country's economy should produce the goods and services it can produce at a lower cost than other economies. Then the different economies trade to get the benefit of one another's advantages. This leads to cheaper imports and increases competition for domestic producers, lowering prices and allowing consumers to raise their effective purchasing power. It lowers input costs for producers, creates export opportunities for American firms, gives consumers a wider range of choices, and spurs the innovation that comes from an open exchange of goods and ideas.

But in real life, trade policy is difficult to manage effectively. In part, this is because trade tends to result in small gains for a large number of people, while resulting in high, very visible costs for smaller groups. Let's say allowing foreign imports causes the price of a common household appliance used by tens of millions of Americans to go down by twenty dollars, but also causes a far smaller number of workers who make that appliance to lose their jobs. A traditional economist would likely point out that this trade-off results in a net gain. A behavioral economist, noting that human beings tend to value the avoidance of loss far more than they value the acquisition of gains, might say the situation is more complex. And politicians, who are unlikely to receive credit for slightly cheaper appliances but are likely to be blamed for lost jobs, might argue that the benefits of trade are outweighed by the costs.

The solution, it seems to me, is neither to abandon trade nor to ignore its costs, but to find ways to mitigate those costs to the greatest extent possible with a broad array of effective programs. And a fair look at the last several decades of trade policy suggests that we have fallen far short in this regard. Greatly expanding our efforts to help people dislocated by trade and technology to reenter the workforce and secure a fair standard of living would bolster the productivity of our population, improve economic growth, and promote widespread economic well-being—all while substantially improving the politics of trade.

We should also take measures to ensure that the benefits of trade aren't being artificially inflated. Left unchecked, countries can engage in unfair competition to drive down their costs of production by flouting generally accepted international trade norms—for example, by providing generous government subsidies to manufacturers of certain goods. In the short run, that might mean even cheaper imports for American consumers. But in the long run, this will distort global economic conditions and could lead to us artificially hollowing out our productive capacity for the goods in question. Then, when we no longer have the ability to compete, the country that at first drove down costs could gouge prices, hurting American consumers further.

Other countries can also bring down the cost of goods relative to ours by adhering to weaker labor and environmental standards than we do. I'm a strong believer in both labor rights and environmental protection, but whether to include labor rights and environmental provisions directly in trade agreements is the subject of long-standing debate.

In theory, no country should get a trade advantage because of weak environmental standards or weak labor laws, such as by unfairly disadvantaging workers' ability to collectively bargain. On the other hand, it may not be possible to use trade agreements to spur other countries to raise their standards to our level. If the United States walks away from a trade negotiation, it doesn't prevent trade agreements from happening. It just means that the country or countries in question create their preferential arrangements with other partners and leave us on the outside.

Regulatory policy and trade are just two examples of complex structural issues that policy-makers must address. Along with addressing many of the issues discussed in this book, such as reforming the criminal justice system and reducing the risks of climate change, inclusive growth should extend to areas such as K–12 education policy and funding; job-training programs to prepare our workforce in the twenty-first century; overcoming poverty; reforming our immigration system to provide an inflow of workers who contribute so much to our economy while creating pathways to citizenship; and much more.

Of course, even if policy-makers wholeheartedly embrace inclusive growth—through expanded public investment, sound fiscal policy, and action on structural issues—economic policy-making will still be the subject of contentious debate. What are the things that markets do well on their own, and what do they fail to do adequately? Which areas should have priority in public investment, how much should we invest, and how do we pay for it? How can structural reforms solve major challenges caused by, or left unsolved by, market forces? What are the best ways to reduce economic inequality?

There are no simple answers. Different people, approaching these subjects with intellectual honesty, rigor, and the best possible policy-making process, might nonetheless arrive at very different places. But at least we would be asking the right questions. And I believe that if we put aside simplified labels and ideological categories and focus on the kinds of results we hope to achieve, we will find far more areas of agreement and opportunities for give-and-take compromise than the current state of our policy debates would indicate.

Chapter X

FOUNDATIONAL QUESTIONS

We all agree that Hitler was the personification of evil. But here's a different question: Is our view provable in an objective sense?

Asking this question does not always make you popular. This was particularly the case in the early 1960s, fewer than twenty years after the end of World War II. Yet when I was at law school, I frequently found myself in the student lounge, asking this and other similar questions. Some of my fellow students were happy to engage me in discussions on these subjects. Others were simply not interested in a question that seemed to have an obvious answer.

Even in rooms full of thoughtful people, I've found that a certain type of definitional or philosophical question is seldom raised. For example, in the Clinton White House, I remember a group of the president's advisers once gathering in the Roosevelt Room to discuss issues related to urban policy. Different people weighed in with different ideas about how to support cities, how to grow the economy in cities, how to provide adequate social services in cities, and so forth. As was generally the case in the administration, it was a lively discussion. Finally, I raised my hand.

"What," I asked, "do we mean by 'city'?"

The reaction I received in the West Wing was, quite possibly, the reaction I will receive from readers of this book. Some people were curious about why I had asked such a question. Others may have thought that the question was irrelevant or the answer was obvious. But gradually, we began to discuss what "city" really meant. Were we talking about metropolitan areas? Areas governed by mayors and city councils? Areas with a certain population density? Areas designated as cities in accordance with state-established criteria?

The optimal approach toward urban policy, it turned out, depended in many ways on what one defined a city to be. Yet for whatever reason, in our Roosevelt Room meeting we had skipped that step. We had engaged in a highly consequential policy debate without explicitly defining what we were debating.

I believe this sort of thing happens more frequently than most people realize. Even those who put in place a strong, intellectually rigorous decision-making process frequently skip what is sometimes a critical step: asking foundational questions.

Foundational questions are not always necessary. In fact, the great preponderance of thoughtful and well-informed decisions are made without them. But when foundational questions *are* important, they are often crucial to the decision-making process. In these cases, going below the surface is highly practical. It helps you to form better judgments and to better advocate for the judgments you form. If you don't ask foundational questions in these cases, certain high-stakes debates will be held—and the decisions that follow them will be made—on shaky ground.

There's no checklist for determining when foundational questions are helpful, but when one is making a major decision, it's worth stopping and saying, "Is there a foundational question we should ask?"

There are several reasons foundational questions are overlooked, even when asking them could be extremely helpful to decision-makers. First, foundational questions can frustrate people because they often turn areas of seemingly straightforward consensus into subjects of complicated and time-consuming discussion. To go back to my example from the Roosevelt Room, if two people share the view that New York and Detroit are both cities, they might feel they don't need to probe any deeper.

Asking foundational questions can also sometimes be perceived as stating an opinion, rather than raising a subject for discussion. When, in law school, I asked whether we could prove in an objective sense that Hitler was evil, I wasn't expressing my own view in regard to whether he was evil. Like most people, I believe Hitler was evil incarnate. But it is possible, and often important, to both strongly hold a belief and be willing to examine it. In that case I was trying to raise the question of what saying someone is evil really means.

Finally, decision-makers frequently ignore foundational questions because they don't think they have the time to engage with them. "What is a city?" sounds, perhaps not coincidentally, like something that might be asked in the student lounge at a law school. The kinds of people meeting in the Roosevelt Room, or any other place where high-stakes decisions are being discussed, might feel their time is better spent on more urgent, specific matters.

But while I can think of many reasons foundational questions are frequently ignored, I continue to think that in a small but extremely important number of cases, it's a mistake to ignore them.

Of course, this raises a foundational question of its own: What, exactly, is a foundational question?

I would define a foundational question as one that explores an issue that would not ordinarily be part of a discussion, but upon which that discussion rests. From this, it follows that foundational questions have several distinctive characteristics.

First, foundational questions broaden and deepen a conversation, while still relating to the decision at hand. "What is a city?" was a useful—as opposed to a merely interesting—question because of the context in which it was asked: a discussion of urban policy.

Foundational questions tend to involve concepts rather than specifics, but they can't be too far removed from practical details. A few years ago, I was told by a Harvard professor who knows a great deal about how scientists think that it cannot be proven in an ultimate, metaphysical sense that what we perceive as reality exists. That's a fascinating line of inquiry. But "What if our perceived reality doesn't really exist?" is not a useful question for most discussions; the real-world decisions we make are going to be the same whether we engage with it or not.

Foundational questions are also defined by the way in which

they are asked: seriously and in a spirit of genuine inquiry. They certainly shouldn't be used as rhetorical devices. If someone asks a question just to prove how smart they are, show off the fact they thought of something someone else didn't, or derail someone else's line of argument, then that question is unlikely to lead to a productive discussion. It is also quite likely to be seen, understandably, as obnoxious.

John Whitehead, who became a co-senior partner at Goldman Sachs after Gus Levy died, seemed to understand the value of foundational questions in business. He often liked to ask, "What purpose does our industry serve?" He would then express his own view: the financial sector is the intermediary between the providers of capital and the users of capital.

Some people might agree with John. Others might not. But regardless of how one answers, it is an important question to ask if one is interested in financial markets and the policies that affect them. Take the issue of regulation. Earlier, I noted that I'm a strong believer in effective regulation of the financial sector, including margin and capital requirements to limit leverage, regulation of derivatives, corporate disclosures, and consumer protections. And I also believe that having a view of what purposes financial markets ought to serve better enables you to design regulations to serve those purposes.

In other cases, foundational questions can reveal and challenge assumptions, even among very thoughtful groups of people. In 2013, former British prime minister Gordon Brown asked me to join a commission on human rights that he was chairing, and which was sponsored by NYU and partly funded by the Carnegie Corporation's UK Trust. I have always found the former prime minister smart and thoughtful, so I was happy to say yes. He assembled a wide-ranging group to engage in the commission's project, which was to reexamine the 1948 Universal Declaration of Human Rights and suggest ways to update it for the twenty-first century.

The commission communicated frequently over the phone and via email, as well as occasionally meeting in person. Most of the other members had spent much more time than I had thinking about human rights, and I found our discussions spirited and thought-provoking.

At the same time, I remember being struck by the feeling that something important was being taken for granted. There was a lot of argument about whether access to the internet is a human right, whether rest and leisure is a human right, and so on. But as our discussion went on, I began to feel it was important to ask some bigger-picture questions. When the initial draft of our report was circulated internally, I wrote to the commission and asked:

"What are human rights? Where do they come from? What do they ultimately mean and what are they grounded in?"

Some members of our group were happy to engage with these questions. Others may have felt that I was being a bit presumptuous.

But while I knew I was asking provocative questions, my goal was not to provoke. I would imagine, for example, that everyone in our discussions agreed that access to the internet is a benefit that as many people as possible should be able to enjoy, and that universal internet access would lead to broad gains for society. But is internet access a human right? That question is worth discussing—but without first examining what human rights are or where they come from, it's very difficult to discuss that question in a productive way.

I also suspect that some people, upon hearing me ask "What are human rights and where do they come from?" would assume I don't believe strongly in human rights. That's not the case. I believe human rights are enormously important, that governments should protect the rights of their people, and that governments, NGOs, and international institutions ought to promote those rights around the world. At the same time, as my questions to the group suggested, I believe human rights have a subjective rather than an objective basis. In my view, the list of human rights is not written in the sky—it's a human-made construct. I believe in human rights because that is how I would like to live and how I think society should be, rather than because I think that they exist independently of the people who discuss and define them.

This is not to say that people shouldn't hold, or advocate for, strong views about the nature of human rights, whether those views come from a philosophical orientation, religious faith, or anywhere else. Where I think some people go wrong is in assuming their own moral standards are universally self-evident. One can have a great deal of confidence in the rightness of one's own views while still recognizing that others have different views.

This fact—that people have a wide variety of perspectives—ought to be taken into account in the decision-making process. On the human rights commission, for example, we were seeking to expand the Universal Declaration of Human Rights in a way that better protected those rights around the world. That meant it was important to ask not just what a group of people selected for a human rights commission might believe, but also what people from different nationalities, religions, and perspectives might believe. My view was that, while we didn't have to agree with those opinions, we did have to recognize they existed—and in some cases, consider how to factor them into our decisions about what to include or not include in our conception of human rights.

In addition to helping me form opinions about areas like human rights, asking foundational questions has helped give me the flexibility to change or further develop those opinions over time. A decade ago I would have said that while human rights were important to protect domestically, and while human rights abuses in other countries were tragic and worth advocating against, the state of human rights around the world did not affect America's national interest in a meaningful way.

Today, however, my view has changed. Over the last few decades, the human rights records of major countries, from Russia to Saudi Arabia and China, has been growing steadily worse. It now seems to me that the erosion of human rights poses a risk to our own national security in the United States, and that a world in which major powers have more respect for human rights is less dangerous than one where they do not. I also think we have had, and will continue to have, a greater chance of cooperating constructively on economic issues, climate change, and other pressing challenges with countries that share a baseline commitment to human rights.

Having said that, I still believe we should out of necessity be pragmatic. If I were a U.S. government official negotiating with a Chinese counterpart, for example, I don't think I would make our relationship with China dependent on its treatment of the Uyghur minority—not because I approve of that treatment, which I certainly don't, but because I think there's very little we can practically do to change it. Our self-interest lies in a constructive relationship with China with respect to climate change, nuclear weaponry, trade and investment norms, and much else. But I do think that, while we should be realistic about whether and how much we can influence China to change its policy toward the Uyghurs, if China were to do so it would provide a better basis for a constructive relationship.

Finally, I believe that considering foundational questions makes one a more effective advocate. Let's say that I knew I was about to meet with a high-ranking official from a country with a poor human rights record, and that the subject of human rights was likely to come up. If I were a moral absolutist, my arguments in favor of respecting human rights would, no matter how profoundly expressed, become largely circular: "We should respect human rights because it's important to respect human rights."

On the other hand, as someone who believes in morality while also believing that morality has subjective rather than objective grounding, I would likely be motivated to prepare a more thorough case. I would probably try to pull together a group of people who could take an expansive view of the history of human rights, how they've benefited the United States, and how they have or have not existed in and benefited the other country throughout its history as well. I would then try to prepare myself as well as possible to make the argument that respect for human rights is both a question of right and wrong, and a matter of national self-interest. I don't know that in this hypothetical scenario, I would be persuasive—but I do think I would likely be more persuasive than someone who thinks human rights are objectively provable and self-evident.

As our society fiercely debates topics where we once had broad consensus, the importance of foundational questions has only increased.

For example, many Americans, especially young Americans, are questioning the social and economic value of market capitalism with an intensity I rarely encountered from young people in the 1990s, or even in the early 2000s. As I've made clear, I don't think there's anything wrong with being skeptical of, or even rejecting, capitalism. But I do think any examination should include foundational questions that can better inform one's judgments.

Take the debate over the role of corporations in society, which is part of a debate over capitalism as a whole. Some people believe large corporations are beneficial to society. Others believe they're harmful. I wouldn't suggest that my own engagement with this question has allowed me to form a provably correct opinion, since no view on this type of issue is right in a completely objective sense.

But my concern is that some people on both sides of it may have reached their positions without thinking deeply enough about a foundational question: "What role should corporations serve?" And I do think asking foundational questions has allowed me to explore the issue and form my opinions in a more thorough and nuanced way.

While I believe corporations should pursue long-term profitability within the boundaries set by law, I am not a market fundamentalist. My view is and always has been that strong and effective government—one that taxes corporate profits and individual incomes to make public investments, maintain an effective social safety net, provide sound fiscal policy, and meet our other challenges—is essential for our society to succeed. In that context, there are hugely consequential issues around maintaining competitiveness, preventing fraud, reducing inequality, combating climate change, and much else that markets cannot address adequately on their own and that government can and must take on.

At the same time, healthy economic growth—coupled with sound policy—is essential if a society hopes to create jobs, raise standards of living, and create a tax base large enough to fund public investment and protect our geopolitical interests. I believe that history and economic theory strongly suggest that a prerequisite for generating strong economic growth is having companies that seek to increase their long-term profits.

In other words, corporations pursue long-term profitability because it is in their interest. At the same time, when they succeed in that goal, it is in society's interest because they contribute to overall economic growth, which can raise standards of living and make more revenue available for public investment and social safety nets. Those benefits are not sufficient to justify all corporate behavior—corporations must function within a framework of sensible and appropriately strong policies to regulate companies, tax profits and individuals, and invest public funds wisely—but they shouldn't be ignored or undervalued.

My view that corporations should pursue long-term profitability is also rooted in my belief that, while corporations are very good at generating economic growth, they are not nearly as good at solving major social problems on a global or national level. Part of this is an issue of size. Even large companies that can influence huge supply chains can make only a limited difference relative to the magnitude of our challenges. They simply don't have the reach and scale of government. They also don't have access to the levers that can most effectively address the most pressing issues in our society. Even a giant company like Walmart or Amazon can't impose taxes or regulations, or make government-like public investments.

Private businesses also face incentives that make them poor candidates for taking on major national or international challenges. They will always have strong incentives to put the interests of investors, shareholders, and owners above broader social objectives. Many corporations tout a social mission, but I doubt that many of them would sacrifice material portions of their profits in service of that mission.

Importantly, longer-term profit motives align with public-interest objectives more frequently than many realize or appreciate. For example, some companies can reduce energy costs over time by switching to cleaner energy. Others can enhance their brand, and thus increase revenue, by expressing a set of values in line with those of their customers—whether through a public statement by a CEO, a marketing campaign, a firm's social media presence, or some other means. In recent years I have also heard business leaders say that if companies place themselves on the right side of the debate over climate change and take action to show they are serious about the issue, they'll be better able to recruit talented young employees. In these cases, acting on climate is in a corporation's long-term profit-making interest. In other words, while some forms of engagement with public issues might create controversy that harms a company's profits, other types of engagement with public issues could build trust with customers, win goodwill in a community, or create a competitive advantage for a brand.

I also think that, in a narrow set of cases—where a non-financial consideration is so overpowering as to be a difference not just in degree, but in kind—the corporate profit motive can be outweighed. For example, if I had been running a corporation after Vladimir Putin launched his invasion of Ukraine in early 2022, I think I would have chosen to cease doing business in Russia.

I suspect there would have been many good reputational reasons for this decision, including the fact that many employees might choose not to work for a company that was seen as enabling Putin's atrocities and nuclear threats. But even in the absence of those considerations, Putin's conduct was so reprehensible, and the threat his invasion posed to the world so urgent, that I would make an exception to my typical view that long-term profit motives should drive corporate behavior.

Yet even this example demonstrates the importance of strong and effective government. Companies could have an impact on Russia's economy or Putin's foreign policy through their individual choices. But those choices could not come close to matching the impact of government policies. While I recognize that there can be exceptions to the idea that corporations ought to seek long-term profitability, and further recognize that determining what qualifies as such an exception is a judgment call, I believe these exceptions ought to be exceedingly rare.

I do not, however, share the libertarian view that corporations should maximize long-term value for shareholders and government should do as little as possible. In fact, my view is diametrically opposed: I believe corporations should pursue long-term value for shareholders and government should proactively do whatever markets can't or won't, including passing legislation and issuing regulations to limit what corporations can do.

In other words, my opinion that corporations should take a

limited role in solving major societal problems goes hand-in-hand with my opinion that government should be doing much, much more.

Applying this conceptual framework in the real world raises its own set of difficulties. For example, what happens if the government, for whatever reason, fails to play its role and leaves major responsibilities unfulfilled? What happens when the most cost-effective way for corporations to maximize profitability is to impede the government's ability to function on behalf of the general public, for example via lobbying?

These questions have grown more urgent in the last two decades. I don't have the answers to them, although certain structural changes, such as campaign-finance reform, would clearly help. I also believe that in the absence of clear answers, asking and deeply engaging with these kinds of questions will give decision-makers the best chance of addressing them in the ways that most benefit society. For example, if allowing corporations too much influence over policy would put them in a role for which they're not well suited and make government less effective, it would follow that reducing corporate influence in politics would be in society's best interest. Similarly, it might make sense for corporations, CEOs, and employees to take the presence or absence of functional government into account when deciding whether to take actions that align with broader social goals, while at the same time being careful not to underestimate the potential value to society that broad economic growth fueled by corporate activity can create.

Another once-settled debate that has in recent years taken on new dimensions and greater urgency concerns the fate of democracy itself. To those of us who believe in democracy, and appreciate the importance of protecting it, merely raising a foundational question on this subject can be uncomfortable. Asking "Is democracy always, under all circumstances, the best possible form of government?" leaves open the possibility, however remote, that the answer might in some cases be no. At a time when many countries around the world are trending away from democracy, and the same forces driving this global trend are threatening the United States, that's a troubling proposition.

Still, I think the question is worth asking. I care a great deal about preserving democracy, I'm deeply concerned by the threats to it that have emerged at home and abroad, and I would not want to live under any other form of government. Yet just as I think it is important to acknowledge that human rights are not written in the sky, and to consider the implications that flow from that idea, it is important to ask ourselves whether, in an absolute or universally self-evident sense, democracy is better than other forms of government.

I believe in democracy because I believe it provides the best possible chance of government serving the public interest, and because it best allows for a set of basic freedoms I would not want to relinquish. But my opinion that democracy is better than other systems, however firmly held and however well supported on moral and practical grounds, remains an opinion rather than an unquestionable fact.

Acknowledging this is important, because it can help decision-makers and policy thinkers consider exactly what about democracy makes it preferable to other forms of government. But it also raises the possibility that, if faced with a choice between the least effective versions of democracy and versions of authoritarian government that effectively provide favorable economic conditions and social stability, some people might choose the latter over the former.

My own view is that democracies must be effective at improving the lives of their citizens in order to gain popular support and remain stable over the long term—and that, when this condition is met, democracies are far preferable to authoritarian systems for a variety of practical reasons. I think history has so far borne this out, especially as it relates to economic growth and widespread economic well-being. Democracy alone cannot explain the success or failure of an economy, and all democracies are imperfect. Yet the fact remains: the vast majority of modern economies with the highest overall standards of living and the greatest levels of stability are democratic.

(In this context China is a complex case. On the one hand, it is an autocratic country that has been extremely successful at growing its economy, lifting people out of poverty, and developing modern industries in many areas over the past four decades. On the other hand, it faces tremendous economic and social challenges of its own, and it remains to be seen what rate of growth it can achieve going forward and whether it can raise its people's overall standard of living to that of European countries or the United States.)

In some ways, economic competition from other, more autocratic countries only underscores the ways in which "effective" and "stable" are important modifiers when it comes to democracy. After all, if you think that democracy is always better than any other system of government, no matter what other conditions may exist, you likely view the choice facing nations as binary. Either they're democratic, which is good, or they're not democratic, which is bad.

The real world is more complicated, even for those of us who believe democracy is a far superior form of government. For example, once we recognize that not all democracies are inherently effective at providing meaningful benefits to their people or weathering political turmoil, it becomes less surprising that so many countries that have tried to transition to a democratic form of government, or had democratic government thrust upon them, have been unable to sustain democracy over time. The practical question that naturally follows is: What conditions make it more likely for an effective, stable democracy to emerge?

Many experts have spent a great deal of time considering this question and grappling with the implications. I remember speaking in 2011 with Richard Haass, the president of the Council on Foreign Relations, when millions in Middle Eastern countries were rising up against autocrats during the Arab Spring. The impression I got from Richard and others like him was that these movements—while inspiring and hopeful reminders of the desire for greater freedom and opportunity—were unlikely to end well, as turned out to be the case. But it seems to me that many others inadequately weighed the question of what conditions best allow for an effective, stable democracy, and thus drew overly optimistic conclusions.

A similar, oversimplistic view of democracy seemed to take hold in the aftermath of 9/11. Had we recognized that effective, stable democracies are not easy to create and not always welcomed, the United States might have acted with more humility in the early 2000s. But instead, in part because of a belief that democracy was objectively superior, and could therefore be established and sustained among nearly any population, we spent the better part of two decades trying to turn Iraq and Afghanistan into stable, functioning democracies and being surprised when that task proved extremely difficult.

Finally, a recognition that democracies must be stable and effective in order to provide the benefits we typically associate with that form of government ought to inform the way we think about government within the United States. Our future as an effective, stable democracy is far from certain. It's hardly surprising that a growing number of young people doubt whether democracy can deliver on its promises. Additionally, over the last few years, we have seen unprecedented attacks on the right to vote, on the nonpartisan administration of elections, on the right of the people (rather than state legislators or other politicians) to choose presidents, and, on January 6, 2021, on the peaceful transition of power. All these attacks put our democratic system at risk.

If one assumes that democracy is somehow preordained as the best form of government, it would be easy to conclude that effective democracies will always sustain themselves indefinitely, and that the current state of American democracy is thus no cause for alarm. But this would be a vast oversimplification of the issues surrounding democracy. It would likewise overestimate the probabilities to assume that America's system of self-government is certain—or even extremely likely—to survive without a meaningful course correction. Asking foundational questions does not undermine belief in democracy. On the contrary, it ought to motivate us to act far more urgently on that belief.

This is true of foundational questions more broadly. In a world full of conflict, at a time when decisions often must be made extremely quickly, it would be tempting to conclude that engaging with deeper questions—having debates that precede the debates—is a luxury we can't afford. I think it's the opposite. In a world full of rapidly evolving threats and challenges, asking foundational questions might be one of our most important tools for getting difficult decisions right.

Chapter XI

THE HUMAN FACTOR

Between 1980 and 1990, CEO salaries rose 212 percent. In many cases, CEO compensation rose even when corporate profits and wages did not. By the time President Clinton took office, executive pay had become a major political issue, and fairly early in the administration we had a debate over whether and how to address it.

I remember expressing the opinion that, while I personally believed many CEOs were being compensated more generously than was merited based on their performance, these were private companies and it was not the government's role to determine how much they paid their executives. I acknowledged that curtailing executive pay was politically popular, but I thought the policy argument against restrictions was powerful and should prevail. Others argued that, for both political and substantive reasons, the administration ought to involve itself in the effort to curb executive salaries. Ultimately, their view won out. The president signed a law barring businesses from deducting money spent on salaries above one million dollars from their taxes.

The new rule did indeed have a major impact on the way CEOs were compensated. But rather than limiting overall compensation, it simply prompted companies to change the way compensation was handed out. They began awarding executives less cash, but more stock options, which were not covered by the new tax changes. In a rising market, these options often became worth far more than the salaries they had replaced. A policy meant to curb the rise in executive compensation instead helped to dramatically accelerate it. From 1995 to 2000, thanks in no small part to the growing popularity of stock options, the average yearly compensation for the CEOs of America's largest public companies grew by about 260 percent. During the same period, average worker pay grew by just 5.6 percent.

The debates we had over executive compensation were rigorous. At some points, people even raised the possibility that corporations would increase the extent to which they compensate employees with stock. Yet looking back, to the best of my recollection, no one involved with the decision ever anticipated the scale at which corporations would come to rely on options for executive pay, or the possibility that a booming stock market might—when coupled with the increasing use of options—widen rather than narrow the compensation gap between senior executives and average workers.

The proponents of the tax-code change didn't realize what would happen, of course. But opponents of the decision, myself included, made the same oversight. If I had suspected the new rules around compensation were likely to accelerate the rise in total executive pay, I might have added that to the list of reasons I opposed them. But I never anticipated the consequence that actually came to pass.

In many ways, the group of people assembled to discuss executive pay during the Clinton administration took the yellow-pad approach I have described throughout this book: bringing together people with different views; attempting to measure costs and benefits; addressing a complicated issue with intellectual rigor and integrity; and estimating probabilities and outcomes. But we didn't adequately focus on a crucial question: If we limit companies' ability to pay employees more than one million dollars per year, which those companies rightly or wrongly want to do, how are they likely to try to get around this thing? In other words, we used a figurative yellow pad. But the outcome took us by surprise because we left something important out.

That something might be best described as the human factor—the way human psyches, human behavior, and human nature change the likelihood of certain outcomes occurring. If decision-makers who are committed to a yellow-pad approach want to get that approach's full benefits, they must ask a pair of important questions:

How will human beings respond to our decisions in the real world? And how is our own human nature likely to affect the decision-making process?

I'm not surprised that decision-makers frequently overlook the human factor when evaluating options and estimating probabilities. When I was starting my career, asking questions about psyches and their relationship to behavior was often seen as a purely intellectual exercise, the domain of poets and philosophers rather than leaders of real-world organizations. While behavioral economists have been systematically exploring these questions in recent decades, decision-makers still often don't engage with them as deeply as they should. Part of the reason may be that such questions are impossible to answer with a high degree of confidence.

Yet I think addressing the human factor, despite its amorphous and uncertain nature, is an essential activity for decision-makers hoping to make the best possible choices.

Take the question of whether people and societies are motivated more by a desire to promote the greater good or by a desire to promote their self-interest. This is one of those debates that will never be fully resolved: human beings aren't all one thing or the other, and there's no way of proving any given view to be correct. Yet I think engaging with this question, and developing a view on it, is important for anyone who hopes to evaluate and choose among different courses of action.

My own view is that, while I've known plenty of people in my life who can be relatively altruistic, most human beings tend to prioritize their own perceived self-interest, or their group's perceived self-interest, above promoting the greater good. (Or, quite commonly, they conflate their self-interest with the greater good.)

Moreover, if you look back through history, those with the means and unchecked ability to do so have frequently acted to take advantage of, conquer, oppress, and otherwise exploit others. It is a record that contains a tremendous amount of brutality toward other human beings.

There is also an indirect way in which people—even those with good intentions—tend to prioritize their self-interest: with some measure of indifference to those in need. To the best of my knowledge, no affluent person I know, myself included, gives enough money to charity to have a materially adverse impact on their way of life. Most people in developed countries—not just those with the greatest wealth, but throughout much of the income scale—could give more than they do to address poverty at home and abroad, or urge their representatives to support more foreign aid and humanitarian assistance. Many of us care about the greater good and are quite generous, but our actions (or lack thereof) suggest that at least in this respect, we value self-interest even more highly.

To secure their perceived self-interest, some people are inclined to act in unethical or even illegal ways. I would guess that in financial markets, if there were no authority or possibility of being held accountable, more people would engage in fraud or other deceptive behaviors in order to advance their finances and careers. (This would create a major problem for the entire financial industry and for society as a whole—one reason I believe the industry has a strong stake in effective regulation.) Without clear rules and strong enforcement of those rules, those inclined to behave in an unprincipled manner would have a significant advantage over their more principled colleagues, and their behavior would undermine public confidence in markets.

I can't objectively say my view of human nature is right or wrong. What I can say is that a considered view of the extent to which people are typically motivated by altruism as compared with self-interest should inform the decisions one makes. When evaluating a proposed course of action, decision-makers should ask themselves, "What view of human nature would have to be correct in order for this proposal to make sense?"

If a given course of action will have a high expected value only if people behave altruistically, and you believe people are more motivated by the pursuit of self-interest, then you ought to seek a different course of action. And of course, the reverse is just as true.

Relatedly, it can be helpful to ask what implicit view of human nature is represented by a decision, and whether that view aligns with your own. In retrospect, this is something we didn't really do when debating executive pay during the Clinton years. In choosing to address the issue rather narrowly, via a tax penalty on salaries, the administration was taking an implicit stance that corporations would not continue to pursue their perceived self-interest by finding new ways to increase their executives' total compensation. To me—and admittedly, with the benefit of hindsight—that does not seem a very realistic or thorough assessment of human nature.

If we had not overlooked the human factor, we might have more seriously asked ourselves important questions. How likely are companies to try and find ways around this new rule? How would a company that wants to get around the new rule do so? And knowing this, what can we do to close potential loopholes in advance? But we didn't ask these questions, at least not in any meaningful way, and as a result the purpose of the legislation was not achieved.

One's view about human nature can also influence the way one attempts to spread principles and culture through an organization. When I started at Goldman Sachs, Gus Levy strongly believed that the firm should treat all clients as partners, always giving them full and honest advice and acting in their interest. He could have phrased this idea using altruistic language. (For example, "Treat everyone fairly.") Instead, he often used a phrase that implicitly presented a different view of human nature:

"Be long-term selfish."

Gus was not phrasing his admonition in terms of right and wrong. But his words had the kind of effect an ardent moralist would likely approve of. For example, let's say a client was seeking guidance about whether they should make a transaction, and the people working on the matter believed the transaction was unwise. If they were thinking only in terms of short-term interest, the best course of action might be to recommend going ahead with the transaction in order to collect a fee. But over the long term, it would be far better to give the client sound advice even at the cost of that fee, thereby deepening the relationship, building trust, and gaining repeat business over many years. And, just as important, that was the way to feel good about yourself and about what you were doing.

Gus's focus on the long term addressed the human factor in another important way. The natural inclination—for individuals, and by extension for organizations—is too often to overweight the short term. Corporations face pressure from markets, investors, and other forces to prioritize their performance in the next quarter above their performance over time. Given the realities of the stock market, resisting such pressure can be hard to manage for a corporation, and meeting that challenge as well as possible requires a carefully thought-through communications strategy, among much else. But corporations that are able to plan beyond the short term increase the chances that they'll perform well over time.

The same dynamic applies to government and policy-making. Decision-makers have short-term incentives to enact programs that spend money immediately and leave the question of payment for some time in the future, and unfortunately, that is often how politics works. But these kinds of decisions can prove counterproductive and make it more difficult for government to be effective over time. (Again, the challenge is to do the best one can in developing a politically resonant communications strategy.)

Gus's maxim was a way of curbing the natural tendency toward caring too much about the immediate future and not enough about the long term. This is important, because a probabilistic approach should seek to maximize expected value *over time*. The amount of time is one of the issues decision-makers must discuss and determine. Part of asking "What decision is likely to produce the best outcome?" is asking "Over what length of time?" If decision-makers overlook the latter question, they run the risk of defaulting to short-term thinking.

Of course, maximizing expected value over time will often involve immediate action—but even in these cases, the long term should be given appropriate weight. A good example is the large, deficit-funded stimulus and relief legislation that passed in 2020, shortly after the beginning of the COVID-19 pandemic. In addition to supporting the legislation because I thought it would alleviate a great deal of suffering, I argued that as a matter of fiscal policy, while the relief plan would add to our deficit and debt, the economic crisis that might result from a failure to pass a relief bill might well increase our debt-to-GDP ratio even more over time. (The question was and remains whether we have the fiscal discipline to enact offsetting surpluses when times are better, or whether we continue to run large deficits.)

Another human factor important to sound decision-making

involves judgments about rationality: How rational or irrational are people, and in what ways?

Decision-makers should try to behave as close to rationally as they can—that's the point of probabilistic thinking. Yet it is also important for decision-makers to recognize that most people, and most groups of people, do not behave purely rationally. Or to put it slightly differently, and perhaps more accurately, people frequently disagree as to what is rational and what is not.

I remember Richard Menschel giving me some very good advice early in my career at Goldman Sachs: "Never attack somebody's gods." Richard was referring not to religion, but to people's broader sense of identity. If people feel as though the prospect of change threatens their identities, they'll reject that change even if it could greatly benefit them in other, more concrete ways.

I've encountered examples of this phenomenon throughout my career. When I was part of the Clinton administration, I remember asking Gene Taylor, who was then a Democratic representative from Mississippi (he eventually left the House in 2011, and subsequently changed parties), why his constituents cared so much about guns. His reply had nothing to do with hunting, or self-defense, or any other approach that argued the benefits of gun ownership outweighed the risks.

"You don't understand," he told me. "That's the number one issue in my district." I don't remember the exact words he used, but what he explained to me was that gun ownership was almost akin to a type of religion, something fundamental to his constituents' sense of self and beyond the realm of what I would consider straightforward analysis.

I don't happen to derive my sense of self in that particular way, but I think the attitude Gene Taylor described is very human. We all have our gods. And change can become far more difficult when it involves attacking those gods.

Sometimes taking that difficult route is unavoidable. But if it is possible for a decision-maker to choose a course of action that is respectful of people's defining beliefs, commitments, and sense of identity while still pursuing important changes, that is the wiser choice.

Change almost always requires buy-in, whether from employees, shareholders, the general public, or some other group. A senator once told me about a secretary of the Treasury he encountered long before I entered government. The senator told me that the secretary came to Capitol Hill, arranged a meeting with the Senate Finance Committee, and said, "These are your instructions." Needless to say, that didn't go over well with the senators. It would have been far more productive to recognize that, even if they agree with an administration's policy agenda, most senators care deeply about their role as part of a coequal branch of government. Saying, "This is what we think we ought to do, and these are our reasons" would have been likely to result in a better outcome than trying to hand down an edict and hoping that United States senators do what the Treasury Department tells them to.

The way you describe a proposed change can also be important. For example, one can acknowledge the significance of a given issue to someone else's identity before advocating for one's own position. In other cases, it might even be worth making a meaningful concession, solely to avoid challenging someone's deeply held beliefs.

To go one step further, decision-makers should take this lack of complete rationality (or the lack of a universally agreed-upon definition of rationality) into account as a factor when determining expected value.

Not long ago, I met with a Democratic member of Congress who has served in national security positions overseas. This person told me he felt his background helped insulate him from political attacks and improved his chances of getting elected and reelected. I suspect he's right that a small but meaningful number of voters who would otherwise vote Republican will consider voting for him primarily because of his national security background. I think this is somewhat irrational for many of those voters. In my view, while national security experience is valuable, the differences between the agendas of the two parties are great enough that it wouldn't make sense to support the candidate of one over the other for that reason alone.

But if I were choosing which candidate to support financially or vote for in a primary, I would take voters' potential for irrationality into account. I might support someone whose views I generally agreed with, and who had what I judged to be the more electable background, over someone whose policies I agreed with even more, but who I felt had less chance of being elected. In other words, after considering the human factor, I would accept what I view as a less-positive outcome in exchange for a higher chance of that outcome occurring and thus a higher expected value.

Perhaps some people would accuse me of betraying my principles for making a decision this way. Perhaps others would point out, accurately, that "electability" has in the past been used to justify opposing women and people of color running for office, and would therefore be skeptical of the very concept. But I don't think it's a betrayal of one's principles to consider the likelihood of a desired outcome occurring, and to accept that the likelihood will be influenced by the human psyche. In fact, I would argue that if decision-makers fail to take the human psyche into account and assume that people will act rationally (at least as they define it), they are more likely to make a decision that does not lead to a hoped-for result.

As for the concern that influential figures in politics may deem a candidate electable or unelectable because of bias rather than a genuine and thoughtful assessment of the probabilities, I think this is worth taking seriously. But the answer is not to ignore discussions of odds just because they might be conducted in the wrong way. The answer is to conduct those discussions the right way—with honesty, rigor, and discipline. Decision-makers must make the best judgments they can about probabilities, and in doing so there are no shortcuts to, or substitutes for, intellectual integrity.

Another way decision-makers must take the human factor into account is to remember that they themselves are human. When they're making decisions, they are being influenced by their own psyches, and they should consider exactly what that means, and what it might imply for their decision-making.

For example, most of us—even those most committed to thinking probabilistically—have a tendency to take the familiar for granted. It is easy to embark on a course of action confident not just about what you can change, but about what you can leave unchanged. But unanticipated developments occur, and they occur more frequently than many people realize.

One reason for this is that it's very hard to predict how other people, who are influenced by their own psyches, will react to one's decisions. I remember on one occasion at Goldman Sachs, we put a very capable partner on the management committee. Almost immediately, another high-level partner in the firm, who was also extremely capable but whom we did not add to the committee, came in, said he was offended, and quit. I'm not sure that, had we known that elevating the first partner would cause the second to quit, we would have done anything differently. But we didn't adequately consider that possibility. And this lack of adequate consideration is, in my experience, quite common. Most people are inclined to underestimate the ripple effects of their decisions.

I've also seen a related problem: decision-makers correctly anticipate a broad category of outcome, but they underestimate the magnitude of the outcome by such a wide margin that it is as though something completely unexpected has occurred. In the Clinton years, for example, we concluded—correctly—that new trade agreements and technological automation would create powerful benefits. At the same time, we recognized that trade and technology could disrupt local economies and result in downward wage pressure and lost jobs for a significant number of people. President Clinton discussed these challenges in his speeches advocating trade liberalization.

But while we were correct that the net benefits of trade and technology would far outweigh the costs, the magnitude of those costs was nonetheless higher than we expected. Given enough time, we would have tried to counteract the adverse effect on jobs and wages through tools such as an expanded social safety net, a higher minimum wage, further enlarging and increasing the earned income tax credit, and much more investment in programs around job training, lifelong learning, and job placement. The administration had even developed detailed proposals to address these issues. But after we lost control of Congress, it was no longer possible to put these ideas into practice.

These two cases—promoting a partner to the management committee at Goldman Sachs and evaluating trade policy and the effects of technological innovation for the United States—involved very different types of decisions. But in both cases, we made a set of implicit assumptions about what would remain the same in the future, and those assumptions turned out to be wrong. I've spent much of my life thinking, talking, and writing about how nothing is certain. But even those of us who acknowledge the ubiquity of uncertainty often underestimate just how uncertain things really are.

There are at least two ways one can compensate for the instinct to take the familiar for granted, and preempt the unexpected developments and unintended consequences that often occur as a result.

The first is to do more work than might initially seem necessary in order to more fully anticipate what might happen in the future. I've written about the importance of having a variety of different perspectives and opinions in a meeting or group, but it is also important to push all members of that group to stretch their imaginations and ask themselves whether they have truly considered all the potential outcomes. Sometimes the answer will be yes. But other times you will realize that your expected value table was incomplete because an outcome that had a meaningful probability of occurring was overlooked.

For example, there is little doubt that to meet the needs of its people, the American economy must change in significant ways. Among much else, we still need far better programs to enable workers displaced by technology and globalization to reposition in our economy. We also need to improve social safety nets; make sure workers have a fair ability to opt for collective bargaining;

and reduce economic inequality both by increasing the incomes and net worth of those at the bottom of the income scale and as a byproduct of public investment and deficit reduction funded by raising the taxes of those at the top.

Still, because of many factors—including flexible labor and capital markets, an entrepreneurial culture, vast natural resources, a tradition of openness to immigration, the rule of law, the strength of our universities and their ability to commercialize their research, and favorable age demographics compared with other developed countries—Americans alive today have only experienced a dynamic economic culture and an economy that, despite its very real problems, grows at a healthy rate over time. While considering ways to adapt our economy to the needs of the twenty-first century, we must be careful not to take these advantages for granted, or we risk losing the economic dynamism and growth they help create.

I think policy-makers and advocates too often don't consider the possibility that they are taking the familiar for granted, and that in doing so they might be ignoring potentially adverse economic impacts of their proposals. In many cases, the risk that a given policy decision will jeopardize our economic success might be low. But by rigorously identifying situations in which the risk is higher, decision-makers can either accept that consequence, find ways to mitigate that risk, or pursue other courses of action that have a higher expected value.

I don't think market-based economics is sacred, although it's a system I believe very strongly in. People should be free to vigorously argue about, for, and against it, examine its failings, and come up with what they think are the best possible reforms.

The importance of this debate is especially clear given how

unequally the benefits of our society are distributed and how many people are left behind. But even when placed in that context, I think those who want to dismantle or move away from our market-based economic system, rather than improve it, underestimate its overall benefits.

We need to figure out how to address the shortfalls in our economy and society without losing the fundamental strengths that create so much potential for all of us.

A second way decision-makers can respond to the natural tendency to take the familiar for granted is to recognize that, even after trying to identify and assign probabilities to all possible outcomes in advance, unexpected developments are more likely to occur than most people think. Generally speaking, a yellow-pad calculation assigns specific probabilities to specific outcomes, and those probabilities add up to 100 percent. But it might be worth assigning some percentage chance to a different, vaguer outcome: "Something else."

The chance of that "something else" occurring is likely to be higher than most people would at first care to recognize. Everyone is wired differently, but as a general rule, if your initial inclination is that there is a 10 percent chance some unforeseen, major consequence will occur, you would be wise to assume you're underestimating that probability. Because most people do. To expect the unexpected may seem like a contradiction. But to acknowledge that there is a more-likely-than-expected chance of something unexpected occurring is both consistent with probabilistic thinking and central to effective decision-making.

It's difficult to plan for these unforeseen consequences and developments, precisely because one does not know what they are. But by allowing for a greater possibility of the unexpected, one can at least make decisions with an appropriate degree of humility and prudence.

For example, when President Clinton left office, the United States was running a large budget surplus and was projected to continue running surpluses well into the future. One approach would have been to use much of that surplus to pay down America's debt, increase our capacity for public investment, and improve our ability to respond to a future downturn. But instead of adopting that approach, the incoming administration argued that our fiscal position was sound and would likely remain so for some time, and that we could afford a very large tax cut.

My own view was that the economic case for paying down the debt was much stronger than the case for tax cuts, and I expressed as much in a *New York Times* op-ed. But leaving that debate aside, after the 9/11 terrorist attacks, our fiscal position deteriorated in a way that would not have happened had we not enacted such large tax cuts. The administration's economic policy team can't be faulted for failing to see the future, but their statements and actions suggested an overly confident view of the likelihood that Clinton-era budget surpluses would continue well into the future.

One more way decision-makers should compensate for their own human nature is to recognize the tendency to think in binaries rather than thinking statistically. In some ways, statistical thinking is just an extension of probabilistic thinking. While yes-or-no questions are pleasingly simple, approaching questions in ways that allow one to make judgments based on probabilities or percentages will improve one's odds of making an optimal choice.

Along with avoiding yes-or-no questions, another important aspect of statistical thinking is the careful examination of what numbers really mean. An especially common mistake is to focus only on the numerator and to ignore the denominator. For example, shortly after the first COVID-19 vaccines were introduced, people frequently published articles saying, "X number of vaccinated people were infected with COVID," without making clear the overall size of the vaccinated population. Without denominators, numerators are just anecdotes masquerading as data.

The best way to deal with the human tendency to think in binaries is to address that tendency directly in the decision-making process. If individuals come across a yes-or-no question, they should ask if it might be more productive to ask a sliding-scale question instead. And when one hears a number used to make an argument, one should always ask whether a denominator is needed, and how different possible denominators might change the way the numerator is interpreted. Numbers and statistics are vitally important tools for decision-making—but without careful analysis they provide false comfort and certainty rather than useful information for estimating outcomes and odds.

There's an old saying that "Change is the only constant." Yet in recent years, the pace, intensity, and character of the change we are experiencing seems different from anything I have witnessed before. If change has at times proceeded in a linear fashion, today that gradual progression seems to have been replaced by sudden, jarring leaps.

During such an unsettling moment, it might seem easy to brush aside the questions I have discussed in this chapter—What motivates people? How rational are groups and societies? How do our own psyches affect our decisions? How can we avoid taking the familiar for granted or the natural tendency to think in binaries rather than statistically?—as tangential to the real work of shaping the coming decades.

But I think with the stakes so high, the benefits of taking the human factor into account are, if anything, greater than ever. We are living in an era full of serious dangers and severe potential consequences of our actions. We would do well to be taken by surprise as rarely as possible.

THE CASE FOR ENGAGEMENT

About forty years ago, my wife, Judy, and I took a short vacation to the Bahamas. At one point during our trip, we went to a place called Deep Water Cay. I brought my fishing rod along—the same kind of rod and spinning reel I had used since I was a boy growing up in Miami Beach. But once I got out on the water, I saw somebody doing something I had never seen before. Instead of launching a lure toward the fish, he was throwing long, graceful loops of line out over the water.

"What's he doing?" I asked our guide.

"He's fly-fishing," he replied.

"Well, how do you do that?" I asked.

He had a fly rod with him, and he offered to let me try it. I've never had a spinning rod in my hand since.

I can't quite explain why fly-fishing has been such a rewarding part of my life over the last four decades. It's an almost mystical experience. For me, casting a fly is an art form, one that took many years to even begin to understand, and which I know I'll never perfect. Combine that with reading a river to figure out which pool might hold trout, or scanning saltwater flats for wary bonefish, and I sort of meld into what I'm doing.

Like nearly all fly-fishing enthusiasts, I practice catch-and-release—and the number and size of the fish I catch isn't the most important part. Instead, it's that fly-fishing becomes its own world, separate from all of life's other pressures, concerns, and consequences.

While I've been fortunate to fish in many different places, my favorite is probably Montana. Maybe it has something to do with the character of the country and its waters, and the feeling I get walking along a gravel bar on a river's edge. Maybe it's just that I've been going there for a long time, long enough that my favorite rivers have carved out a special space for me emotionally.

Whatever the reason, I started fishing in Montana more than twenty-five years ago, and, until recently, never missed a summer. But then, in 2021, Montana was hit by an overlapping series of environmental disasters—heat waves, heavy wildfire smoke coming in from other states, low water levels—that would have been hard to imagine when I first started traveling there in the 1990s. Warmer water began stressing the trout, and sometimes even killing them. As water levels dropped, some of the state's iconic rivers were temporarily closed to fishing. It was the kind of scenario that brought to mind Al Gore's warning in his office some twenty-five years earlier. For anglers—and more important, for the many local people and businesses who rely on them—it was an extremely difficult season.

There was also a specter of something more fundamental happening that summer, something that went beyond the economic or personal consequences that came with months of extreme weather. At one point, I spoke with a friend who runs a Montana environmental group about the disaster they were experiencing. Conservationists are, by nature, aware of how much we have to lose. Even so, I was struck by how deeply unsettled he seemed. He was struggling to figure out whether Montana had lost a summer, or was instead losing something far more significant and permanent.

Fishing is, as I said, its own little world. But in the real world—the one in which we're confronting challenges to our society, our democracy, our economy, and our planet—we find ourselves asking a version of the question that consumed my friend as he considered the potential loss of one of the planet's special places. Are we living through temporary challenges? Or are we at the beginning of a downward spiral, tumbling toward irreversible catastrophe?

Then there are the questions that have less to do with the fate of the world and more to do with our individual places in it. In the face of such monumental challenges in so many different arenas, is engaging with the world and trying to improve it worth the effort, or are the odds against us too great? And if it is worthwhile to engage with the world, how should we go about it?

At a moment when so many people worry that our best days might be behind us and decline is inexorable, it is easy to understand why some might conclude that there is little point in getting involved. Others might be tempted to wish away uncertainty by seizing on comforting, if poorly founded, absolutes. Ideological rigidity leads to poor decision-making in the long term, but in the short term it can be reassuring.

I think a reasonable, considered examination of the moment

in which we live ought to lead one down a different path. The cause for concern may be greater than ever. But that also means the case for deep, thoughtful, intellectually honest engagement with the world's problems has never been stronger.

At the moment, a realistic assessment of the challenges we face is not terribly comforting. I can't recall any other point in my life in which so many different existential threats menaced us simultaneously. The planet faces climate change, which seems likely to profoundly harm humanity and, in the most extreme scenarios, could even end life on earth as we know it. Cities and countries around the world, still reeling from the effects of COVID-19, face the possibility of new variants and new pandemics. The current group of nuclear-armed states, and the prospects for additional states to join that group in the not-too-distant future, create increased threats of both nuclear conflict and of terrorists obtaining nuclear material. Democracy is under attack worldwide. All kinds of frightening risks that once seemed remote now appear to be genuine possibilities.

Nested below these existential threats is a large set of interrelated policy challenges that, while not quite existential, are hugely consequential. In the United States, that list includes public investment, health care, poverty, income inequality, racial inequality, our fiscal condition, K–12 education reform, public safety, and criminal justice reform.

These domestic concerns may be felt particularly acutely because our country has done so well for so long. Like many others, I worry that something ineffable but essential—a shared national identity and sense of what it means to be American, built around a set of common aspirations; a willingness to recognize the faults and in some cases the tragedies of our past and present; and a belief that together we can improve the lives of our people—is being lost.

This possibility would have been inconceivable for most of my life. In the post–World War II years in which I grew up, America stood in stark contrast to the Soviet Union and other Communist countries, which both repressed and impoverished their people. After the Berlin Wall fell, it was easy to imagine that the United States—both the nation and the set of principles it stood for—was destined to increase in influence, ushering in a new American century marked by ever greater prosperity and broadly shared well-being.

Over the past two decades, however, I think the conventional wisdom concerning the United States has been changing. People are far more troubled about the outlook for our economy and our society—and understandably so.

It would be a great tragedy if America as we know it were to fade away, not just for the United States but for the world. Many of the ideas that have contributed the most to human progress— strong and effective democratic government, market-based economics, fair and free elections, open debate and free expression, support for strong international institutions, and much else—have found their greatest champion in the United States. Even when America has not fully lived up to its own ideals, the world has benefited from having our country aspire to them.

Among the essential promises America stands for is that together, we can make better decisions when confronting the greatest social, economic, and national security challenges of our time. The United States has often fallen far short of delivering on that promise. But I believe it's done a better job than any great power in world history. There is little reason to assume that, if the

American experiment fades away, it will be replaced by something better or more effective. And yet as a society, we seem less and less capable of confronting large challenges together.

Still, like most questions, "Are our best days behind us?" is not a simple yes or no. Instead, this, too, is a matter of probabilities. Given the evidence and information available to us, what is the likelihood that we can overcome the most pressing challenges we face?

I do think our prospects for long-term success have become more uncertain and complicated. Partly, this is a matter of scale. The magnitude of the threats we face is noticeably larger than it was when I served in government in the 1990s.

At the same time, many of the people most responsible for setting society's course either don't seem to recognize these ever-more-dangerous threats or don't seem willing to address them with an appropriate sense of urgency.

This is a particularly serious problem in government and policy-making, but it is not limited to those arenas. Too many affluent individuals are aware of the many challenges that have impacts beyond their personal and professional circles, such as climate change or income inequality, but don't act in a way commensurate with the magnitude of the problems we face. In some cases, even though these individuals are well-positioned to make a difference, their attitude seems to be that these problems mostly affect other people, and will be solved by other people as well.

I don't think that's the case. A sense of common purpose is essential to a functioning society, but it is also, as Gus Levy might have put it, long-term selfish for those with the most to lose financially. I remember talking to a wealthy businessperson from Turkey, who told me that many leaders in the business community ignored his country's slide toward authoritarianism because they felt, essentially, that they personally would not suffer the consequences. It's an attitude that many of them came to regret—but only after it was too late.

I fear we may find ourselves in a similar situation in the United States, and perhaps in other developed democracies around the world: those who currently have the most power and influence believe their power and influence will make them largely impervious to any widespread societal breakdown. By the time they truly internalize that the dangers we face affect all of us, no matter how well off or powerful, our country might not be able to correct its course.

I worry that our sense of common purpose is being fractured in other important ways as well. On one hand, as our country diversifies, it appears that some would prefer to turn back the clock than to include more people in the American dream. Rather than come to a full reckoning with past and present failures— beginning with slavery, and persisting all the way through the economic and racial disparities that mar our country today—they would ignore our society's historic ills and exacerbate its present ones. Even more dangerous, many seem willing to abandon or even undermine democratic norms and institutions in order to achieve these goals. Such an effort is fundamentally against what our country stands for and against the interests of all of us, both socially and economically.

At the same time, I worry that others, while rightly frustrated with the pace of progress, give inadequate weight to the substantial amount of progress our country has made in closing the gap between what we say we stand for and what we actually do. When I was born, Social Security was just three years old, and about half of all workers—including those working in sectors that employed a disproportionate number of Black Americans—were not eligible to receive its benefits. There was no Medicare or Medicaid. As I mentioned earlier, I was educated in a segregated public school. I graduated from law school the year the Civil Rights Act became law.

A growing economy—and a sense that economic growth would benefit everyone, not just those at the top—is a large part of what gave people confidence about their future and contributed to a sense of national unity and pride. In these areas, too, we have made great progress during my lifetime. When I was born, the median family income was about $1,225, or about $26,000 in today's dollars. Over my life thus far, even after adjusting for inflation, that number has nearly tripled. Life expectancy has increased by more than twelve years, largely due to advances in health care and medicine. The year I went off to college, about 60 percent of American adults didn't have a high school degree. Today more than 90 percent do, and the percentage of college graduates has increased approximately fivefold.

I think that for most of my life, America's national unity was bolstered by a sense of economic unity, a belief—substantiated by evidence—that if the country as a whole became better off, so would most of its people. That is still true to some extent, and economic growth remains necessary if our people are to continue to experience a rising standard of living. But growth alone is not sufficient, and widening economic inequality has meant that more recently, the gains of America's overall economic success have been shared by too small a percentage of Americans.

It's not surprising that many people born in recent decades focus on the American experiment's many failures. But it would be equally surprising if most of us who were born in less recent decades were not acutely aware of the American experiment's many successes.

These differences of opinion and perspective ought to help us make better collective decisions. Yet today, across generations, political parties, and geographies, we struggle to embrace, even in the broadest sense, a shared understanding of what America stands for. We don't seem able to agree on, or too often even to discuss, basic questions about what it means to be an American, or how our society can be repaired or improved.

The dangers we face are too great to afford unsound choices. Yet it seems that in a wide variety of areas, the process by which those choices are made is substantially worse than it was decades ago.

In other words, while I don't think anyone is in a position to judge the probabilities with a great deal of accuracy, it feels as though the chances that we can recover what we have lost while protecting our democracy, country, and planet have diminished, perhaps substantially. Intellectually speaking, I just don't know what the path back is.

And yet, for whatever reason, I continue to believe that somehow or other we'll get there.

I recognize that, after a lifetime of trying to think probabilistically, my belief that things will somehow work out might seem like a contradiction. It is a contradiction. But it's also the way I feel.

I suspect part of that feeling stems from the way I'm wired. In some psychological sense, I need to be engaged with big problems and complex issues. I suspect I'm also wired to think that we'll find a constructive path forward on these issues.

Furthermore, I think that while it would be irrational to be overly confident about the future of our country, society, or planet, it would also be irrational to despair. "We're doomed!" is, among other things, an overconfident view.

For one thing, as I've discussed throughout this book, the United States retains enormous advantages over other countries. If we can maintain our strengths while rebuilding political functionality, we have a very promising foundation for the years and decades ahead.

I have also seen the strong correlation between sound policy decisions and positive outcomes. Just to use one example, during the early 1970s, after Lyndon Johnson's Great Society programs, poverty rates fell to record lows. When I served in government in the 1990s, I saw sound policy lift millions of people out of poverty, extend health insurance to millions of children, contribute powerfully to increasing growth and productivity, improve our longer-term fiscal trajectory, and do a great deal else to raise people's standard of living. More recently, when the child tax credit was expanded in 2021, child poverty fell dramatically—and, tragically, it rose dramatically when that expansion expired.

Unexpected developments can and do occur, and people with good intentions can make flawed decisions. But there nonetheless remains a cause-and-effect relationship between good decision-making and positive outcomes. This is critically important. While overcoming the many challenges we face won't be easy, we have the potential to materially improve our situation with respect to issues like economic growth, economic inequality, poverty, and climate change.

Younger generations seem to embrace these common goals in ways that I and many of my peers did not when we were their age. When I speak to college students or recent graduates, I am often struck by how much time they spend thinking and worrying about big-picture issues, and how—bucking a longtime characterization of young people as apathetic—they approach these issues with a keen and entirely warranted sense of urgency. When this powerful sense of shared purpose is combined with a commitment to evidence-based reasoning and a willingness to make real-world trade-offs in the service of broader goals, it can greatly improve our policy-making process, our political system, and our country.

It is also encouraging that, in many important ways, the promise of our country is open to more people than it was when I was a child. I grew up in a world where those who were not white and male, no matter their talents, work ethic, or potential, were largely excluded from many parts of American life. Today, that is much less likely to be the case.

I don't want to overstate the progress we have made in these regards. Economic inequality, poverty, racism and sexism, conscious and unconscious bias, and much else are still serious problems in our society. The prospects for children of any race born into poverty have in some important ways become worse instead of better over the last few decades.

But the world has also changed for the better in ways that would have been hard to imagine just a few decades ago.

On balance, I believe our society is significantly better off because of these ongoing changes. The more our country enables all of our people to reach their full potential, the more we will all benefit from the contributions they otherwise would not have made.

How best to do this is a question requiring discussion and debate, but the effort is a worthwhile one. If it's successful, it could meaningfully provide broad benefits to the economy, to the broader social cohesion of America, to its people, and ultimately to the world.

Giving more of our people the chance to reach their full potential could also improve our decision-making. This broader possibility—that the next era of decision-making might be better than the current one—provides room for hope. Because while the array of challenges we face is wide, whether we succumb or succeed in the twenty-first century will largely be determined by choices we make. If our choices didn't matter, it would be hard to make the case for engagement. But our choices *do* matter. That's one of the things I have seen repeatedly throughout my life and career.

And it brings me back to the big thing I learned, or at least began to grasp, in Raphael Demos' introduction to philosophy class more than sixty years ago.

Because if nothing is absolutely certain, and everything is a matter of probabilities, then there are always reasons to be engaged with the world. By grappling with the world's complexities and trying to think more effectively, we can make better decisions. Stretched over the course of decades, improving the effectiveness of one's thinking can be life changing—and can change others' lives as well.

I don't claim to know our chances of overcoming the most pressing threats we face. But I do know that if more people devote themselves in some way toward overcoming those threats—if we refuse to treat the challenges facing our world as other people's problems, and abandon the hope that other people will solve them without our deep and thoughtful involvement—it will be a tremendous boon to society.

"Increase the expected value for humanity" is unlikely to catch on as a rallying cry. But it is perhaps the most essential task in which each of us can engage. None of us can save the world. But we can each try to alter the odds in its favor.

Throughout this book, I have addressed many questions that, even when approached in a probabilistic way, have no clear answers. But in the end, there is one big question probabilistic thinking ought to clarify:

Is it worthwhile to care about the society in which one lives, engage with the problems facing that society in a serious way, and attempt to make a difference in the world beyond oneself?

The answer, it seems to me, is as close to certain as anything can get.

Acknowledgments

In some ways, this book is itself an acknowledgment, a way of expressing my gratitude for all the people, from Mrs. Collins and Raphael Demos to Gus Levy, President Clinton, and so many others, who have shaped my life, my way of thinking, or both. With that said, there are many people whose work on and support of this book made it possible, and whom I would like to recognize in these pages.

David Axelrod, Sylvia Mathews Burwell, David Dreyer, Drew Faust, Alex Levy, Kim Schoenholtz, Larry Summers, and Chris Wiegand read the entire manuscript, or substantial portions of it, sometimes more than once. They provided countless pieces of helpful feedback that shaped the final product, and they were all too happy (or at least all too willing) to engage with my questions and help me think through important sections of the text.

Delia Cohen, Kevin Downey, Bob Freeman, Steve Friedman, Michael Greenstone, Richard Haass, Michael Helfer, Bob Katz, Vikram Pandit, Chuck Prince, and Shadeed Wallace-Stepter read chapters or significant sections of chapters, providing both insight and detail. Their opinions and ideas deepened my understanding of complex issues, and their recollections sharpened my own.

ACKNOWLEDGMENTS

Joann McGrath, my executive assistant of twenty-four years, provided invaluable assistance on this book, as on all else I do.

When I began working on this project several years ago, I hoped that, along with everything else, it would be an intellectual journey— a chance to engage with new ideas, even as I shared many of the ideas I've developed over the course of nearly eighty years. I'd particularly like to thank my partners on that journey:

As a collaborator, David Litt's writing and thinking helped me organize a lifetime of ideas into chapters and paragraphs, and he helped me refine and better express my views. Meeghan Prunty, whom I've been lucky enough to work with for twenty-three years, contributed her eye for detail, her decades of policy and political experience, and her understanding of both the issues in this book and of its author. My chief of staff, Charley Landow, was the engine that drove the book forward—his abilities as an adviser and project manager are evident on every page. Jacob Weisberg, my co-writer on my first book, lent his editorial guidance, his excellent judgment, and his unmatched ability to find the right word to this new effort.

Rodgin Cohen, Steven Cook, Samuel Issacharoff, Larry Katz, Melissa Kearney, Joon Kim, Josh Kurlantzick, and Linda Robertson provided expert knowledge on specific factual questions, and Andy Young served as our fact-checker for the full manuscript. Eliza Edelstein, Chelsea Grey, Anna Lowenthal, and Daniel Yadin provided much-appreciated additional editorial assistance.

I'm also grateful to the team who brought this book from idea to reality, beginning with the legendary Bob Barnett and his colleague Emily Alden. From the start of this process, I knew exactly which editor I wanted to work with: Ann Godoff. This book was improved in countless ways by her vision, encouragement, and thoughtful criticism. Senior editor Will Heyward provided his own detailed and perceptive notes throughout the text. The entire team at Penguin—including Liz Calamari, Casey Denis, Trent Duffy, Victoria Lopez, and Danielle Plafsky—helped guide me through the publishing and publicity process and get the book into readers' hands. So did Elizabeth Shreve and her team at Shreve Williams.

While I generally believe that it is never too late to learn new things, that belief does not extend to web design, so I would also like to thank Leigh Whiting for designing www.robertrubin.com.

Most importantly, I would like to thank my family, beginning with my terrific sons, Jamie and Philip, and my equally terrific daughters-in-law, Gretchen and Lauren. I'd also like to thank my grandchildren, Eliza, Eleanor, Henry, and Millie. Being with them is and always will be an important part of my life.

Finally, I would like to thank my wife, Judy, who read this manuscript and offered many thoughtful suggestions and gentle but firm corrections. I would not be the person I am, or have lived the life I've lived, without her. We've now been married for sixty years—further proof, if it is needed, that sound decisions can have lasting positive consequences.

Robert E. Rubin

Index

INDEX

INDEX

INDEX

INDEX